Teachers as Curriculum Designers for Transcultural Communicative Competence

BLOOMSBURY GUIDEBOOKS FOR LANGUAGE TEACHERS

This series brings together books that enhance language educators' teaching practice. The books provide practical advice and applications, suitable for use in a range of contexts and for different learning styles, which are evidence-based and research-informed. The series appeals to practitioners looking to develop their skills and practice and is also suitable for use on a variety of language teacher education courses. The books feature a range of topics and themes, from critical pedagogy, to using drama, poetry or literature in the language classroom, to supporting language learners who have anxiety.

Also available in the series:
Teaching English to Young Learners, edited by Janice Bland
Critical Pedagogies for Modern Languages Education, edited by Derek Hird
A Poetry Pedagogy for Teachers, Maya Pindyck, Ruth Vinz, Diana Liu and Ashlynn Wittchow
Using Literature in English Language Education, edited by Janice Bland
Designing World Language Curriculum for Intercultural Communicative Competence, Jennifer Eddy
Performative Language Teaching in Early Education, Joe Winston
Using Theories for Second Language Teaching and Learning, Dale T. Griffee and Greta Gorsuch
Researching Language Learning Motivation, edited by Ali H. Al-Hoorie and Fruzsina Szabó
Language Learner Strategies, Michael James Grenfell and Vee Harris
Compelling Stories for English Language Learners, Janice Bland
Process Drama for Second Language Teaching and Learning, Patrice Baldwin and Alicja Galazka
Psychology-Based Activities for Supporting Anxious Language Learners, Neil Curry and Kate Maher

Forthcoming in the series:
Teaching Beginner Level English Language Learners,
Lesley Painter-Farrell and Gabriel Díaz-Maggioli
Pedagogical Translation for Language Teaching, Sarah Albrecht

Teachers as Curriculum Designers for Transcultural Communicative Competence

JENNIFER EDDY

BLOOMSBURY ACADEMIC
LONDON • NEW YORK • OXFORD • NEW DELHI • SYDNEY

BLOOMSBURY ACADEMIC

Bloomsbury Publishing Plc, 50 Bedford Square, London, WC1B 3DP, UK
Bloomsbury Publishing Inc, 1359 Broadway, New York, NY 10018, USA
Bloomsbury Publishing Ireland, 29 Earlsfort Terrace, Dublin 2, D02 AY28, Ireland

BLOOMSBURY, BLOOMSBURY ACADEMIC and the Diana logo are
trademarks of Bloomsbury Publishing Plc

First published in Great Britain 2025

Copyright © Jennifer Eddy, 2025

Jennifer Eddy has asserted her right under the Copyright, Designs and
Patents Act, 1988, to be identified as Author of this work.

For legal purposes the Acknowledgements on pp. xxv–xxvi constitute an
extension of this copyright page.

Cover design: Grace Ridge
Cover images © melita / Alamy Stock Photo and hudiemm / Getty Images

All rights reserved. No part of this publication may be: i) reproduced or transmitted in
any form, electronic or mechanical, including photocopying, recording or by means of
any information storage or retrieval system without prior permission in writing from the
publishers; or ii) used or reproduced in any way for the training, development or operation
of artificial intelligence (AI) technologies, including generative AI technologies. The rights
holders expressly reserve this publication from the text and data mining exception as per
Article 4(3) of the Digital Single Market Directive (EU) 2019/790.

Bloomsbury Publishing Plc does not have any control over, or responsibility for, any
third-party websites referred to or in this book. All internet addresses given in this
book were correct at the time of going to press. The author and publisher regret
any inconvenience caused if addresses have changed or sites have ceased
to exist, but can accept no responsibility for any such changes.

A catalogue record for this book is available from the British Library.

A catalog record for this book is available from the Library of Congress.

ISBN: HB: 978-1-3504-4673-1
       PB: 978-1-3504-4672-4
       ePDF: 978-1-3504-4674-8
       eBook: 978-1-3504-4675-5

Series: Bloomsbury Guidebooks for Language Teachers

Typeset by Integra Software Services Pvt. Ltd.
Printed and bound in Great Britain

For product safety related questions contact productsafety@bloomsbury.com.

To find out more about our authors and books visit www.bloomsbury.com
and sign up for our newsletters.

 Online resources to accompany this book are available at https://bloomsbury.pub/teachers-as-curriculum-designers. If you experience any problems, please contact Bloomsbury at: onlineresources@bloomsbury.com

To the people of Wales, you show everyday what it means for everyone to belong with identity strong.
To Steph, Dafydd, GwE administration and Global Futures, Diolch yn fawr iawn am yr anrhydedd o weithio gyda'ch athrawon.
To Steven Fawkes, who told me about ALL and LanguageWorld, thank you so much for welcoming me.
To Paul Garcia, my mentor and friend, for always believing in me, listening and giving so generously your time.
To all the teachers in this project, thank you for your creativity and dedication to this work and for your energy and expertise with your pupils. Thank you for welcoming me to your schools and communities.
Jenny

Contents

List of Figures x
List of Tables xi
List of Appendices xiii
Foreword xiv
Preface xvi
Acknowledgements xxv

1   Teacher as Designer 1
2   Designing What Matters 35
3   How Do Languages Connect Us? 71
4   How Do We Understand the World around Us and Support Others? 105
5   How Do We Express Ourselves and Engage Others? 141
6   How Do We Create and Share with Others? 179
7   Design with No End in Mind 213

Appendices 223
Glossary 240
References 243
Index 253

Figures

1.1 Intercultural Curriculum Aligns Novel Assessment Design Articulated Performance and Transfer 2

1.2 Annotated Articulated Assessment Transfer Task Template 3

1.3 Curriculum for Wales on one page, GwE 2022 3

1.4 Curriculum for Wales elements in brief CfW 2019 GwE 2022 8

1.5 Statements of What Matters planning in LLC GwE 2022 10

2.1 AATT alignment with CfW elements and planning at GwE 37

2.2 AATT Inside-Outside Spaces 45

2.3 Annotated Concept Map 68

2.4 *Liberté, égalité, fraternité* Concept Map 69

3.1 AATT Key Elements Annotated Eddy GwE 75

3.2 *Solidarité* ICANADAPT Unit Stages 1 & 2 99

3.3 *Solidarité* ICANADAPT Unit Stage 3 100

4.1 Understanding begins with Creative Transfer – I Can 109

Tables

1.1 National Curriculum and Curriculum for Wales compared 13

1.2 Assessment system contrast and alignment 14

1.3 Teacher-leader-designers from diverse school contexts 20

1.4 Key priorities for Curriculum for Wales and the AATT 24

1.5 Desired outcomes of *Ein Llais Ni* and International Languages 26

1.6 Three types of talk aligned with AATT and ICANADAPT 28

2.1 Design principles, Statements of What Matters and AATT/ICANADAPT side by side 40

2.2 Articulated Assessment Transfer Task – International *Eisteddfod* 48

2.3 Stages of Language Assessment Transfer with examples 51

2.4 Stage Three: What it is and What it is not 56

2.5 Articulated Assessment Transfer Task – *Liberté, égalité, fraternité* 63

3.1 Enduring Understandings, Essential Questions, I can/ITT and Focus Questions compared 76

3.2 Articulated Assessment Transfer Task – Ourselves and others 81

3.3 Articulated Assessment Transfer Task – Protest 89

3.4 Articulated Assessment Transfer Task – *Solidarité* 96

4.1 Seven Interpretive task types and supporting others in mediation 110

4.2 Articulated Assessment Transfer Task – *Ffair Borth* Menai Bridge Fair 114

4.3 Articulated Assessment Transfer Task – The environment 121

4.4 Articulated Assessment Transfer Task – Heroes 127

4.5 Articulated Assessment Transfer Task – Who am I? 134

5.1 Interpersonal task types and engaging others in mediation 144

5.2	Articulated Assessment Transfer Task – School uniforms	148
5.3	Articulated Assessment Transfer Task – Regional desserts	155
5.4	Articulated Assessment Transfer Task – A place in France	162
5.5	Articulated Assessment Transfer Task – *La Baguette*	170
6.1	Presentational task types and engaging others in mediation	182
6.2	Articulated Assessment Transfer Task – School life	186
6.3	Articulated Assessment Transfer Task – Extracurricular activities	192
6.4	Articulated Assessment Transfer Task – Food festivals	199
6.5	Articulated Assessment Transfer Task – *Les Maisons*	205

Appendices

Appendix A   Transcultural Mediation For Transfer 223

Appendix B   *Liberté, égalité, fraternité* 225

Appendix C   Stage One and Stage Three at a Glance 228

Appendix D   Task Types and Strategies for Mediation 229

Appendix E   Master List of Tasks 232

Appendix F   Cultural Community Authentic Texts 236

Appendix G   AATT Review Criteria 237

Appendix H   Teacher as Designer Evidence Collab 238

Foreword

*Claire Gorrara and Lucy Jenkins,
Cardiff University, UK*

It is an exciting time for education in Wales, one of change and innovation. The rollout of the new Curriculum for Wales from 2022 is gathering pace. Teachers, policymakers and learners alike are accelerating their personal and collective journeys towards understanding the needs, opportunities and challenges inherent in a radical curriculum redesign with a focus on learner-centred pedagogies.

However, change is needed, above all for language learning in the new curriculum. International languages in Wales, meaning languages other than English and Welsh, have been in decline over the last twenty years, as optional subjects in secondary schools. There has been a 28 per cent decline in entries for GCSE French, German and Spanish (the big three in Wales); GCSEs are qualifications at age sixteen for younger learners in Wales. In 2023, only 10.35 per cent of all Welsh learners sitting GCSE examinations sat a GCSE examination in French, German or Spanish. At A Level, qualifications taken typically at age eighteen; this drops even further to 3 per cent of the whole cohort sitting an A Level in French, German or Spanish. International languages, though, are not alone. Whilst Welsh is compulsory for most school-age learners at the GCSE level, it is not at A Level. In 2023, A Level uptake of Welsh dropped to 2.8 per cent, 0.2 per cent lower than the uptake of international languages at A Level. Such dispiriting statistics belie, however, a complex picture of language advocacy and innovation on the ground, which this project highlights.

This book and collaborative learning project demonstrate the importance of teacher development and empowerment at such a time of change. This impressive collection reveals the centrality of teacher and practitioner voices to these processes of change and highlights opportunities for new teaching practices to develop through such a process of implementation. A core feature is the role of 'teacher as designer', a new concept for language teaching in

Wales. This journey of change will be an iterative process. This study makes such a process visible and thereby less daunting, and more accessible for readers and practitioners. The creativity inherent in such design processes is evident and clear in the chapters and tool kit approaches showcased here which profile a range of exciting strategies and ideas. Such creativity is not only a benefit in and of itself for teachers and learners already in schools but provides inspiration and motivation for those considering entering the teaching profession in Wales. It is a time of difficulty for teacher recruitment and retention for languages in Wales, as well as for other subjects, and indeed in other countries. This volume offers new ways of co-designing language learning.

A final important contribution of this book is the transferability of its ethos and practices – not only across subjects, disciplines and school infrastructures, but also internationally. We need look no further than Scotland in the UK for national teaching contexts where curriculum design has been explicitly devolved to schools and teacher-practitioners, with mixed outcomes. We can look internationally to other nations where curriculum review and the rethinking of prescriptive national frameworks are on the agenda. The learnings from educational transformation for language learning in Wales can be adapted elsewhere, demonstrating how Welsh experiences both will be formative for this nation and offer a living laboratory for others on this global journey of discovery and change. We warmly recommend this collective endeavour to all readers and lovers of languages. The volume is a stimulus for new thinking and a place for reflection on how to engage better and more deeply with and for the next generation of global linguists.

Preface

Design for what matters when students are with us, so that they can thrive in all cultures without us.

To what extent do our curricula enable learners to reflect upon their own linguistic and cultural identities while negotiating and interacting through and among others? How can we support instructors to make using cultural community texts and resources an everyday practice? Can we encourage uptake by designing tasks valued, expected or required outside the classroom for implementation inside of it? How are the stories, practices and experiences of other people also about us? Why should all learners see themselves contributing to World Language curricula at every level and why does that matter?

These and other questions have inspired my work in language classrooms and with teachers for over thirty years. Our craft as language educators has seen many pendulum shifts over the years but we were able to stick it out and see it through. Now I am not so sure. In spite of excellent research and practice, as a profession we have faced setbacks with low enrolment, attrition, outsourced instruction, lack of uptake and teacher shortages. However, now more than ever the situation is particularly dire. Entire programmes have been eliminated from universities and primary-secondary schools are slashing language programmes even with greater demands for multilingual skills in all sectors of the workforce (ACIE, 2017; Hagger-Vaughn, 2016; Looney & Lusin, 2018). Post COVID-19, language programmes suffered again (Collen, 2023) and continue to do so. We have always advocated to become more visible. Now we must rally and reform to remain viable.

For administrators, it is often an issue of investment and returns. When speaking with them about curriculum reform and professional learning, they always cite relevance and applicability when making painful decisions about our programmes. Even in countries or states where there is a minimum language requirement, administration sees years invested in a curriculum that is not applicable, inclusive of other disciplines or relevant to the expectations of life beyond school: career, community, civic and global readiness as a productive citizen. Language exercises without these goals, focusing on grammar, vocabulary, translation and superficial treatment of basic topics and functions, confines languages as aloof, detached and unnaturally so. Unfortunately, this perception and its preservation does not lend itself to greater autonomy, motivation, uptake and the realistic expectation that one can use what they learned flexibly and securely. It does not enable that for the learner or the teacher.

With *Teacher as Curriculum Designer*, we encourage learners to solve problems and create products which reside outside the classroom and are relevant to the communities and cultures where they live and work. Intercultural Curriculum Aligns Novel Assessment Design Articulated Performance and Transfer (ICANADAPT) describes what the framework does and what the learner will do when faced with the inevitable unexpected beyond school. The Articulated Assessment Transfer Task (AATT) prepares learners to create deliverables along designated articulation points spiralled through their curriculum. Even with the earliest tasks, the learner develops mediation skills, to make languages accessible and cultural perspectives visible to others unfamiliar with them. Intercultural or transcultural communicative competence depends upon adaptation, contribution and participation with the language you own now and can use with other people, to extend and facilitate meaning within, across and among cultures. Now more than ever, that is what matters.

In 2021, during the COVID pandemic, I was completing the book, Designing World Language Curriculum (DWLC) for Intercultural Communicative Competence (Eddy, 2022b). LanguageWorld is the national conference for languages in the UK by the Association for Language Learning (ALL). They developed an entirely online conference, brilliantly conceived and executed, with an interface by KC Jones that mirrored the experience of concurrent sessions. The ALL members were such lovely people and so welcoming to me, that I was determined to attend next year in person to meet them all. In spite of ongoing challenges and restrictions, I made it to Sheffield in 2022 and presented on the AATT framework, with exemplars from the book. Ms Stephanie Ellis-Williams attended my session and spoke with me afterward. She described the new Curriculum for Wales and the Statements of What Matters. I set out to read it straight away.

I have never read a curriculum which supports languages for inter/transcultural communicative competence like the Curriculum for Wales does. It speaks about confidence and creativity as productive citizens. It wants learners to develop their identity in Wales while interacting amongst and within other cultures. The curriculum inspires learners to speak Welsh, English and at least one other international language. It encourages mediation with others, so it advocates authentic language use beyond classroom exercise. Most striking was the emphasis that Welsh belongs to everyone. Whether born there or newcomer, the Welsh language, their relationship with Wales and Welsh identity are supported in all schools. The curriculum instils *cynefin*, an ever-evolving state of belonging, and speaks to exploring diverse perspectives, identities and cultural histories to contribute, participate and respond as local, national and global citizens. I was so taken with this curriculum that I welcomed the opportunity to speak with Steph to learn more from her and the school contexts within the GwE region. This collaborative design project shifted from Steph to her core leads, then to a large group of teachers unpacking what matters in their curriculum and designing AATTs. We all met face to face, worked with Steph and Mr Dafydd Roberts. Teachers implemented the AATTs and received feedback from Steph, Dafydd and I. These teachers then had the opportunity to present for other teachers, both in Wales and at a session for LanguageWorld 2023.

In this book, you will see their designs and read their stories, their *Voices from the Field*. When faced with a new curriculum and freedom to design this way, these teachers accepted this challenge. This is not to say there were no hiccups and pitfalls; this happens with any new curriculum design endeavour. The prospect of more pupil engagement, coupled with intercultural communicative competence and transfer tasks deliverables to underpin this design, propelled these teachers to create and continue to create what you will see here. At every step, from choosing authentic cultural community texts, designing tasks at any level from this text and realizing articulation of tasks for transfer to a novel deliverable, these teachers' process was truly transformative. They modelled the exact process we want for our pupils in transcultural language learning and this is the prime takeaway:

Language curriculum design and language learning are not about retrofit, words in blanks, memorizing and delivering stage or screenplay script. It is about novelty, transfer and improvisation. By creating tasks beyond the script you are sending the powerful message of what language is, creative and novel; this is the expectation of authentic use. To remain viable and solvent in our school and university programmes, language learning cannot remain cloistered, confined and delivered as a classroom academic exercise where only one correct answer or recited sentence is accepted as evidence of learning. Those exercises are essentially selling the pupils a lie and they know it. It is not how language works. By its design, language is creative, improvised and imperfect. The tasks must be those that transfer to situations and products they witness outside of school everyday. Students need to see themselves using language in their community and beyond, for relationships and careers. The curriculum you design engages them in experiential performances for problem-solving, mediation and collaborative thinking they will need in their communities and workplaces. They need to understand language use is not about reciting a perfect script as it is about creating something new with the language you have. With the curriculum framework outlined in this book and DWLC (2022b), both teacher and learner are agents of autonomy (COE,

2001; Lamb, 2017; Little, 2012). They interact within the design to notice how cultures contribute, source meaning from texts and create new works with the language they own now.

The teachers in this book make the case that language learning for inter/transcultural communicative competence brings our unique reaction or response to anything we hear, watch, receive, read and with anyone we listen to within, across and among cultures. Anytime we engage, language springs from reflection, reform and novel response. Therefore our practice at it must come from a place of flexibility, unpredictability and creativity. Language expects that from us. For both language teacher and student, transfer, improvisation and novelty are what matter.

Designing AATTs and ICANADAPT Unit Exemplars

The sixteen exemplars in this book and on the companion website are authored by teacher leads, department heads and administrator leadership from Welsh- and English-medium schools in North Wales, large and small, serving a diverse student body. Each chapter contains their AATT exemplars with templates and tools for designing custom, bespoke curricula across at least three levels of progression or articulation, with product deliverables representative of that vertical articulation. Exemplars are in English so that all instructors may explore them and reflect on their own transcultural competence as they design across and among languages and cultures. Links to additional cultural community texts with additional resources, fillable design templates and tools are located on the companion website.

I invite you to join these sixteen dedicated professionals of International Languages, highly skilled teachers and leads from diverse schools as they share their thought process as designers with the articulated tasks and units. Their exemplars look differently at modern foreign languages (MFLs)/international language themes both typical and uncommon, but do so through a transcultural lens: iconic foods, identity, protest, solidarity, clothing, places, personal spaces, heroes, new school, well-being, leadership, festival and the environment.

Teachers as Curriculum Designers for Transcultural Communicative Competence is intended for:

- teacher training, PCGE or certification programmes for MFLs, World Language and English as an Additional Language as well as for LEAs/HUBS in-service educator professional learning/PDC at any level of instruction;

- teachers who never had curriculum design courses and now have that responsibility in their school;
- school programmes seeking an intercultural curricular framework with deliverables designed for visible language use, suitable for career and vocation within the community and beyond;
- programmes or national curricula leadership considering the shift to articulated progression, inter/transcultural communicative competence or transdisciplinary project/problem-based curriculum reform but find those efforts take a back seat to grammar, vocabulary lists, topics, functions and textbook sequencing as the initial reach for many teachers and administrators;
- post-secondary MFL faculty. Many universities have redesigned or refreshed their majors using these tools as well to increase uptake.

While listening to these teachers' voices and their reflections on their exemplars for this project, each chapter encourages you to try your hand at one more step in the design of the AATT or ICANADAPT unit from it. With the tools in this book, teachers at all levels of experience can design what matters and work collaboratively towards articulated curriculum with relevant and applicable external goals in mind, rather than confine language to artificial exercises compartmentalized by grammar point or siloed by topic and level.

This Book and Companion Website

✓ Outline the design process and implementation of bespoke curricula within an existing national framework, with teachers as designers for pupil agency and ownership.

✓ Apply transferable, inter/transcultural concepts with assessment for mediation in MFL/World Language, heritage and community language programmes, to serve as a model framework for teacher preparation and language programme development within any national or community language learning context.

✓ Describe exemplars for curriculum and assessment progression with key shifts defined from the educators' process in *Voices from the Field* and *From the Admin Desk*.

Design Features

The book unfolds the ICANADAPT/AATT design framework with Curriculum for Wales (2019) as a model alignment applicable to any school context, even within prescribed national or local curricula with textbook, vocabulary or grammar mandates.

Our chapters guide educators to meet them wherever their prior knowledge or experience may be as designers. Each exemplar unfolds the teacher's path, designing tasks to solve problems and create products responsive to the needs of the community and inclusive of both local and worldview. Pupils of all languages and acquisition contexts create deliverables across levels of progression designed for mediation and transcultural competence.

Enduring Understandings and Essential Questions

Each chapter has EUs and EQs aligned with concepts of curriculum and assessment design within the ICANADAPT/AATT framework. The first two chapters focus on the purpose of the project and the shift with teachers as designers and what matters in the curriculum. The EUs and EQs in the next four chapters examine principles for assessment task design. These provide ongoing inquiry for the educator no matter what curriculum they have in place, to reconsider and revisit during pre-service training or for self-directed professional learning goals while in-service.

Let's Consider

The start of each chapter considers curriculum or assessment matters or needed shifts in each stage of the design. Focus questions place new concepts within familiar contexts or problems language educators face every day. 'I can' statements present end of chapter outcomes from hands-on practice with steps in their curriculum and assessment design.

Put It to Practice: Collaborate to Articulate

This section poses questions or issues for teachers to discuss together in a department or with colleagues in professional learning on steps to design or reflection on AATT exemplars thus far. The questions intend to provoke other ones to move discussion forward, especially for educators who have not had a chance to work together to design articulated curriculum for vertical progression.

Teacher as Designer

This section introduces the school context and draws the reader's attention to key features in the AATT exemplar. Ms Stephanie Ellis-Williams draws our attention to evidence of progression and alignment with the Curriculum for Wales, as well as task types or strategies used for design and implementation of the tasks for mediation and intercultural competence. Her contribution helps other educators look at their own curriculum and reform questions, helping them to consider what they can do towards creative design.

Voices from the Field

Meet the teachers who designed the AATT and ICANADAPT exemplars. These educators represent diverse school contexts in North Wales, from small town, rural, to university city, large and small, and both English- and Welsh-medium schools. They speak about their own shifts while designing this way, celebrations and pitfalls, reflections on professional growth, their pupils' response to tasks, along with notable features about their exemplar. They model transformative design thinking for their pupils who will take their cue from the teacher that they can be creative too.

Articulated Assessment Transfer Task (AATT)

A set of AATT exemplars is featured in each chapter, curated for its content and concepts discussed in the Statement of What Matters (SoWM) (CfW, 2019) and communicative task features. Each AATT is presented in its entirety, even though the chapter focuses on a particular SoWM or communicative task. It is important to see how the entire AATT functions and the interdependence of all parts to see progression across levels with all stages of communicative competence intact in this assessment design.

Bridge to Design

These tasks guide educators to examine the design process of the exemplar, reveal key features and consider their role when designing their own. Each AATT exemplar has a companion *Bridge to Design*. The Bridge poses questions to ourselves and our colleagues to reveal inter/transcultural threads and facilitate their own spiral design process. Now that you have come this far, could you design a new task to follow these? Each *Bridge to Design* concludes with Participate in the Practice, to reprise practices discussed during our project and explained in the book, which both guided the designer and informed the exemplar. The *Bridge* can be used by classes, book study and PLCs to model collaborative mediation techniques and strategies for working together in a community of practice.

Teacher to Leader on Design and Implementation

After reading the AATT and reflecting on its component in the *Bridge to Design*, these are parting words of lessons learned from the designers. These are their top tips, caveats and suggestions for teachers just starting out on this design framework. A good dose of encouragement accompanies their practical advice and guidance for success.

From the Admin Desk

Ms Stephanie Ellis-Williams, International Language administrator at GwE, provides an epilogue to the AATT, pointing out its key design features and closing points to consider for optimal implementation. She gives us more to see and think about as reflective practitioners within this new design and lends her expertise as administrator involved in each step of this project.

Design for Transfer

These hands-on tasks close each chapter to complete the next design component on your ICANADAPT unit or AATT exemplar. This step-by-step plan assures that all sections of the template will be addressed.

Reflect and Revisit

Each chapter has discussion questions based on exemplars and concepts examined from that chapter or reprised from previous discussion. These questions engage teachers in professional debate on the imperative shifts suggested in the book. They are also ideal for a book study or department initiative. Each question provokes further inquiry on task design and ideas for your own curriculum reform.

Companion Website

The companion website provides teachers and teacher educators with useful ancillaries to support the AATT and ICANADAPT exemplars. Included are live links to cultural community texts, fillable blank templates, pupil work samples and other tools ideal for the methods course or for curriculum design initiatives in a school, department or LEA.

Croeso – Welcome

Welcome to our growing community of designers for transcultural communicative competence. I hope their process, exemplars and implementation inspire you to become designers of your own curriculum, even within one highly prescribed. Collaborate with your colleagues and co-create with your learners. As they understand and reflect upon their own cultural identities, let them interact and mediate with others with the language they have. For the relatively short time they are with us, show them that the products they create have value beyond school, so that they continue to participate across cultures without us. Understanding begins with creative transfer and will always continue with novelty.

Jenny

Acknowledgements

This project would not have been possible without the insight and expertise of Stephanie Ellis-Williams, who by chance attended my LanguageWorld session and understands this design process so completely. To Dafydd Roberts, thank you for sharing with me the collaborative vision of Welsh for all. I am grateful to Global Futures and GwE for their support of international language teachers in Wales. Every exemplar from this project was designed by educators and leaders from schools in North Wales. Thank you for welcoming me to your homes, schools and communities. Your dedication to this project and creativity is an inspiration to me and to anyone reading your words. It is truly an honour to work with all of you. These wonderful educators are listed here in order of appearance in the chapters:

Stephanie Ellis-Williams
Sian Bennett
Jeni Morris
Nicole Piesch
Nicola Hughes
Emma Adams
Emma Green
Jamie McAllister
Mark Cameron
Viviane Vick
Jane Byrne
Lynette Sloan
Sioned Perkins
Paul Conn
Ceri Parry
Clare Temple

To Marissa Coulehan, thank you for being my graphic designer and project assistant again. You bring your experience as a Spanish teacher and creative talent with technology to this project. You always understand the concept behind my vision for this work, right down to the last detail. I am so blessed to work with you.

ACKNOWLEDGEMENTS

Thank you to language colleagues at all levels of instruction, for all the work you do for our profession. In this book, I have made every effort to ensure accuracy, acknowledgement, attribution and inclusion; any errors or omissions are not intentional. My thanks to the researchers and practitioners who have inspired me to encourage creativity in language learning with the teacher as designer.

1

Teacher as Designer

Enduring Understandings

∞ Teacher agency, autonomy and renewal are key to any curriculum reform process.
∞ Teaching and learning happen within unique and shared social and cultural contexts.
∞ Creative design for language learning is a tool as well as a goal.

Essential Questions

Q What are the role and responsibility of the teacher as designer?
Q To what extent do teachers model themselves as active, curious and productive citizens for their pupils?
Q What does creative curriculum design for international languages look like?

I can

- Identify shifts from deliverer to designer for the teacher and consumer to creator for the learner.
- Describe the role of teacher as designer for both teacher and learner autonomy.
- Explain my steps and stages to creativity in design to someone unfamiliar or new to the process.

Let's Consider

Where are you on the journey as designer of your language curriculum? Whether this is your first time to design a curriculum or your career encounters a revision initiative, every teacher or administrator can describe moments in the process that challenge their experience. This book explores the story of language teachers who crafted milestone curricular shifts when meeting a framework to guide their process. This cohort of teacher leaders designed and implemented exemplars which align the framework Intercultural Curriculum Aligns Novel Assessment Design Articulated Performance and Transfer (ICANADAPT) (see Figure 1.1) and the Articulated Assessment Transfer Task (AATT) from *Designing World Language Curriculum for Intercultural Communicative Competence* (Eddy, 2022b) (see Figure 1.2) with the new Curriculum for Wales (CfW, 2019) (see Figure 1.3). This curriculum serves as an example of national, institutional and individual expression which engages learners across all subjects to work towards the same goals; creativity and adaptability to participate and thrive as international citizens. CfW is at once ambitious and imperative. Having reviewed many curricular documents from different nations and states, I have not seen one with tenets as inclusive of all citizens and as mindful of their needs and their role in our world as CfW.

Business leaders have defined our times as a VUCA world: Volatile, Uncertain, Complex and Ambiguous (Johansen, 2012). As educators, we

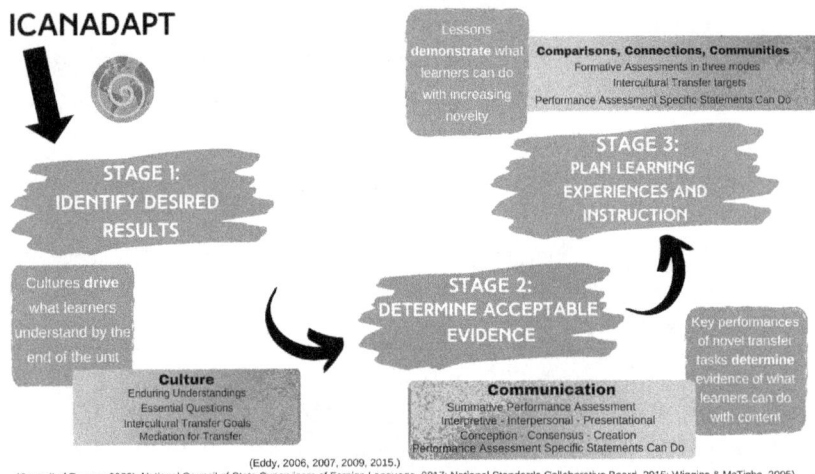

FIGURE 1.1 *Intercultural Curriculum Aligns Novel Assessment Design Articulated Performance and Transfer. Adapted from Eddy, J. (2022b)* Designing World Language Curriculum for Intercultural Communicative Competence, *with permission from Bloomsbury Academic, an imprint of Bloomsbury Publishing, Plc.*

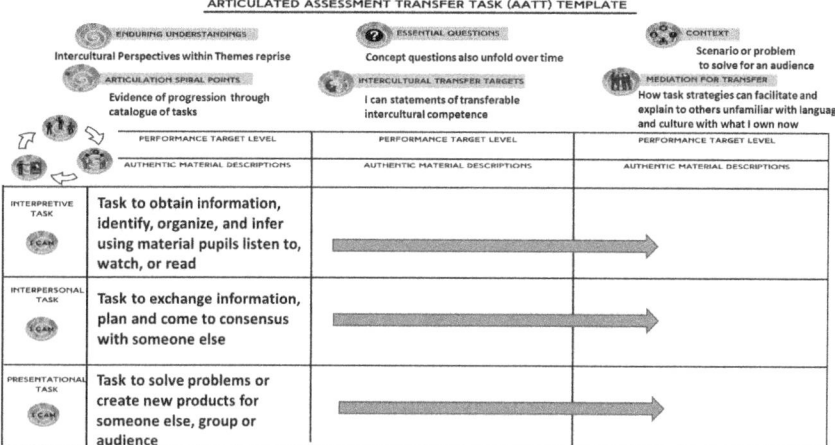

FIGURE 1.2 *Annotated Articulated Assessment Transfer Task Template. Adapted from Eddy, J. (2022b)* Designing World Language Curriculum for Intercultural Communicative Competence, *with permission from Bloomsbury Academic, an imprint of Bloomsbury Publishing, Plc.*

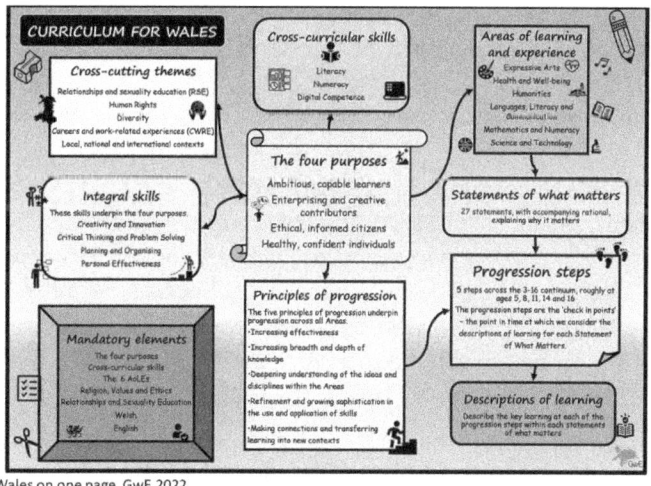

Curriculum for Wales on one page, GwE 2022

FIGURE 1.3 *Curriculum for Wales on one page, GwE 2022.*

have the power to prepare learners for the inevitable unexpected (Eddy, 2016a/b, 2017, 2022a). We must instil in our learners the ability to recognize unpredictability as a constant and manage ambiguity within various contexts. The focus of curriculum and its tasks must centre upon adaptability, flexibility, agility and creativity in response to an often-insecure and changing world. These characteristics are not just important; they are essential to managing any discipline and are the most crucial for languages because they are how we as a people participate, contribute and thrive in our own and within all cultures. Our lives are anything but predictable; they are in constant diversion, adjustment and flux from minor to major causes.

For this reason, curriculum and assessment that models and suggests certainty, stability and familiarity will not prepare young people to be confident and responsive to the unpredictable world they receive. It is inadequate for learners to echo, copy and script the consequences of artificial textbook sequentiality and subsequent teacher delivery of same. Therefore, learners must engage in tasks and create products pursued outside the classroom to develop this flexibility. They must have enough new experiences doing it early and often, that they are confident to tackle anything after they have left us, no matter how novel, complex and ambiguous the task or problem is.

> The only thing predictable about thriving with language is how unpredictable it really is. To fully understand, flourish and thrive within language and cultures, it is not through rules remembered and lines rehearsed. It is through exploration, participation, creation and reflection, via varied and novel interactions of intercultural experience along the lifespan. When intercultural concepts and practices are the framer and curricular hook, the learner is not only engaged for that time but will recognize them within their interactions long after they left your programme. You want to design for intercultural competence revealed over the course of the curriculum but, more importantly, for continued engagement without a teacher present. These concepts and perspectives unfold through key tasks, from situations, practices, products and objects one may encounter in daily life within cultures to exploring concepts that learners understand but lack all the elements of language to express. Most importantly, these tasks allow them to apply concepts, practices, knowledge and skills to new situations they will encounter, with the tools to manage and mediate communication with others.
>
> Jennifer Eddy, *Designing World Language Curriculum for Intercultural Communicative Competence*, 2022b, p. 7

For these reasons, other nations, states and communities, as well as Wales, are reflecting on not only what pupils learn, but how they acquire it and why that is important. These changes in content, pedagogy and pupil work outcomes demand revision in how teachers see themselves in our profession and respond to the call for creative curriculum design. The curricular exemplars using the AATT/ICANADAPT framework are entrepreneurial (Panthalookaran, 2021, 2022) in design and implementation because they insist on innovation and risk-taking, with tasks that explore ideas and identify critical pieces, collaborate with others, then create new products helpful to others. A design for intercultural communicative competence develops the process throughout the curriculum but, more importantly, for continued engagement without a teacher present for lifelong autonomous learning (Holec, 1988; Lamb, 2000, 2001, 2008, 2017; Lamb & Reinders, 2005; Liddicoat et al., 2003; Little, 1995, 2007, 2009b, 2012; Little et.al., 2017; Little & Kirwan, 2019). The tasks also prioritize poise and confidence over the need for perfection implicit in rote mastery exercises, allowing learners to create pieces of value with the language they own now, even for a concept they may not have all the language for just yet. Most importantly, these tasks allow them to apply concepts, practices, knowledge and skills to new situations, with the tools to manage and mediate communication with others.

Throughout these chapters, we will follow a cohort of in-service teachers and their response to these shifts in designing curricula for international or world languages. Through the AATT/ ICANADAPT framework, these teachers make the case for creativity as CfW intended, answering the important call of 'why' as Designers on 'how' rather than Deliverers of 'what'. They model their exemplars for all language teachers faced with their task of curriculum revision. Each teacher offers vital elements, lessons learned and practical suggestions to take away that will inspire and inform your journey in curriculum design. What do teachers and administrators consider when faced with new curriculum guidelines and a desire to increase motivation and uptake in languages? How do teacher leaders encourage learner autonomy and creativity through relevant, purposeful, novel pupil deliverables? How does this experience change how teachers view their profession? These questions shaped this collaborative project with the teacher as designer for intercultural communicative competence. They provide a blueprint for any revision initiative, whether open to district, state or individual interpretation or even within a highly prescribed national context.

From the Admin Desk

Wales is undergoing a huge shift in its education system, with the launch of a new curriculum in September 2022. Every new curriculum brings its share of trepidation but also anxiety and nervousness amongst teachers and administrators alike. In a system where workload and time are often difficult to balance, where the many pressures from the different stakeholders need to be constantly managed and satisfied, we are not always in the right frame of mind to contend with a brand-new curriculum.

Add to this a pandemic which zapped away not only our teachers' energy but weakened our pupils' skills and confidence and which took away two full years of preparation, launching such a revolutionary curriculum was always going to be a challenge. It was important to give the right support to our teachers. Taking time to understand the vision and purpose of this curriculum. Making teachers realize that their professional judgement and acumen were, at last, going to be not only acknowledged but needed to create a curriculum which is right for their pupils and their schools. Collaboration and professional discussions needed to take place in order to get to a common understanding of the purpose of the curriculum and the shifts we needed to make in order to realize it. As an administrator, it was my responsibility to focus on the opportunities this curriculum could offer the profession and the learners. It was important to keep a mind open and welcome different interpretations of the framework in order to give the right guidance and support to teachers. It was also my responsibility to experiment myself with different models and look further afield to see how different nations, practitioners or thinkers used education science and evidence-based practice in order to develop their own system and achieve the desired outcomes. I shared my findings and encouraged colleagues to make some time to take a step back and re-evaluate their teaching and learning. I reassured them that good practice is already taking place and is aligned with the requirements of the new curriculum.

—Stephanie Ellis-Williams, International Languages, Global Futures GwE lead.

A Discipline Faced with a New Identity, New Curriculum and Newfound Freedom

CfW is a purpose-led curriculum focused on the development of the individual. Learning is about achievement, not attainment – it is focused on the quality of the learning journey and the aspirational end goal – not on content and coverage. This high-level framework gives schools and practitioners the vision and principles of curriculum, yet plenty of questions remain: What was revised? Standards or Principles just for world languages, or a framework for the whole curriculum of which languages play a key role? Is the new framework interdisciplinary or does not assume or prescribe involvement with other content areas? What do language programmes do with new found freedom to design? What was most perplexing was to understand what this meant, in practical terms, in the classroom. What would be changing? How could we ensure that what we were going to offer next was going to be better than before?

The terminology of the curriculum needed to become familiar. For example, subjects were now Areas of Learning Experiences (AoLE). The choice of words is key and has to be assimilated by all. The learning experiences must be constantly associated with the actual teaching of the discipline area. Planning must take into consideration and ensure that the learning experiences are stimulating, effective and authentic. What does 'beautiful' look like? What should our learners 'look like' by the end of their time in secondary education? How does our input, in the area of learning or discipline, influence this? How can we make sure that our individual contributions enable the learners to build upon their existing skills, deepen their understanding and ability to learn effectively whilst developing the knowledge they need to perform well in the various disciplines they encounter?

The level of freedom given to practitioners to build a curriculum which is bespoke to their own school was not always welcome. It was too free; no examples were given and with no model to follow, it can be overwhelming and frightening. The main fear resides in not knowing if our decisions are right, not having the goal posts set out for us and realizing, a few years down the line, that our efforts do not match the actual expectations. For example, the lack of detail in terms of set summative assessments, level descriptors and external qualifications was one of the main challenges teachers had to come to terms with. When in fact, it is this very absence of summative assessments and qualification goals which helped us, as professionals, to really think hard about what our mission is and why we teach what we teach. The end goal has no end. It is not the exams, or rather, not only exams. It is much more than that.

This is nothing new, of course, but it is rather easy to forget it once in a system which is under exam result pressures and exam-driven curricula. In CfW, assessment does not drive the teaching and learning but is a tool to plan and ensure depth and quality of learning. It also encourages work, when it is relevant, within and across areas of learning (disciplines) to deepen and enhance the learning and experiences for learners. Finally, and most importantly, within its prescribed framework, CfW allows each school to tailor their curriculum to their context and their vision (see Figure 1.4).

The three most significant shifts in MFL yield a new identity and purpose:

1   Change of name: from MFLs to international languages

    The new term refers to languages other than Welsh and English which are learned at school and which can include community languages,

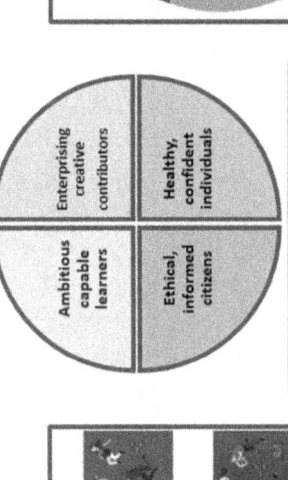
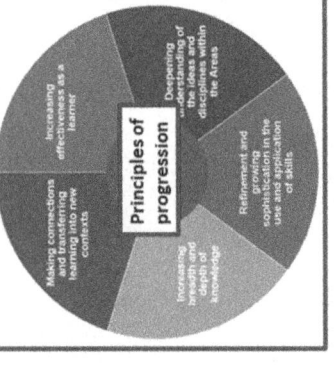

FIGURE 1.4 *Curriculum for Wales elements in brief CfW 2019 GwE 2022. CfW elements in brief, GwE 2022, CfW 2019. Adapted with permission by GwE and CfW, 2024.*

modern languages, classical languages and British Sign Language (CfW, 2019). This means that every school is now free to choose the language learning approaches that best fit their context and learners. Each school is able to teach any one additional or multiple languages in their setting in the primary to secondary sectors.

2. From September 2022, international languages are part of the Languages, Literacy and Communication Area of Learning Experience (AoLE), together with English and Welsh along one language continuum.

3. The LLC AoLE aims to make links between languages, to give a sense of identity through intercultural understanding and to raise the value of plurilingualism and mediation. CfW acknowledges the importance of the integration and respect of all languages taught and spoken at home and recognizes how these can play an important role in developing and strengthening language skills, developing a sense of identity and a better understanding of other cultures.

In this Area, languages are seen as a key to social cohesion, which can promote better local, national and global understanding. The aim is to encourage learners to engage critically with languages and literature in order to help them develop not only their own sense of identity, but also an understanding of the relationship between their own cultures and communities and those of other people. This understanding can be deepened as learners are afforded opportunities to learn multiple languages. This linguistic knowledge and these skills are needed to participate confidently and empathetically in society, which contributes to developing learners as ethical, informed citizens of Wales and the world.

CfW, 2019

The three disciplines within the Languages, Literacy and Communication Area are working together to ensure contribution from one will support another in developing the key concepts from the four Statements of What Matters (SoWMs) which are common to the whole Area. The Statement of What Matters, Languages Connect Us, is a key statement which permeates the learning in all other three Statements: understanding languages is key to understanding the world around us, expressing ourselves through languages is key to communication and literature fires imagination and inspires creativity. It highlights how learning languages enhances appreciation of the many ways in which multiculturalism connects with multilingualism and how important

Planning for International Languages in LLC
The Statements of What Matters

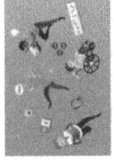

Languages connect us.
Languages connect us with people, places and communities. This Area is designed to equip learners, as citizens of a *bilingual* Wales in a *multilingual* world, with the ability to use Welsh, English and other languages in a *plurilingual* context. Meaningful language learning experiences go hand in hand with learning about one's own cultural identity

Understanding languages is key to understanding the world around us.
Languages and *literacy* are fundamental to human communication. They enable us to make sense of what is heard, read and seen, and thus to develop our understanding, empathy and our ability to respond and to *mediate* effectively.
This Area aims to provide learners with opportunities to experience

1- Languages connect us.
Learning about identity and culture through languages prepares us to be citizens of Wales and the world.

2- Understanding languages is key to understanding the world around us.
Learners who listen and read effectively are prepared to learn throughout their lives

3- Expressing ourselves through languages is key to communication.
Learners who speak and write effectively are prepared to play a full part in life and work.

4- Literature fires imagination and inspires creativity.
Experiencing literature develops new horizons and helps us become healthy and confident individuals.

knowledge and understanding and build relationships. The learning and experience supports them to develop an awareness of how they use a range of languages to express themselves for different purposes and audiences. For Welsh or English this includes both speaking and writing.

other people's experiences, beliefs and cultures is enhanced, learners can develop their ability to demonstrate empathy. This in turn can contribute to their emotional and mental well-being. In all, the literary experiences offered aim to spark learners' imagination and creativity and help to build a lifelong love of literature.

IL within LLC AoLE presentation, Ellis-Williams, GwE May- June 22

FIGURE 1.5 *Statements of What Matters planning in LLC GwE 2022. International Languages within LLC AoLE. Presentation by Ellis-Williams, GwE, 2022. Adapted with permission by GwE and CfW, 2024.*

languages are for cultural identity. Until now, multilingualism was not celebrated systematically. Despite embracing multiculturalism, practitioners did not always explore and exploit the potential of using the wide range of languages a certain class profile could have in order to enhance and deepen the learning (see Figure 1.5).

> This commitment to the social and cultural benefits of multiple language learning creates opportunities for schools to diverge from a traditional emphasis on transactional language learning towards a multilingual approach. In our article, we argue that such multilingual practices and methodologies can reinvigorate a younger learner's connection to languages by making them more dynamic and relevant to our globalised and connected world.
>
> Claire Gorrara and Lucy Jenkins, BERA Blog, May 2020

Emphasis on Empathy, Mediation and Creativity

All SoWMs return to the key concepts of building effective communication skills to demonstrate empathy and express themselves in a creative and personal manner from the increasing language they are developing.

> Given that a key aspect of effective language learning is the willingness to experiment and take risks in trying out new structures, sounds and patterns, learning and experience in this Area can empower learners to be creative and to persevere when facing challenges. Together, these skills can build learners' confidence to grasp new opportunities and to adapt to different roles which in turn can develop them as enterprising, creative contributors, ready to play a full part in life and work.
>
> CfW, 2019

The previous curriculum was the 2008 National Curriculum (National Curriculum, 2008). For MFLs, the curriculum already indicates much of what CfW is encouraging us all to do: Develop thinking skills, communications skills, ICT and number through a range of language activities and texts. Learning across the curriculum and ensuring to make links across the languages to support the development of English and Welsh. International languages also has the mission to help students compare their own culture with that of the target language communities and to develop a sense of their own identity and openness towards the world. Progression is based on language skills: oracy, reading and writing with increasing confidence and independence. Programmes of study set out what pupils should be taught; contexts and content are not prescribed.

> They develop intercultural understanding, a sense of global citizenship and learn to appreciate different cultures and communities and compare them with their own ... Learners develop their language skills in a range of interesting, relevant contexts and through a variety of enjoyable activities which support their self-confidence, independent learning and creativity and encourage positive attitudes to language learning ... listen and view material from different sources, read a range of texts and learn to cope with less familiar and more complex language
>
> National Curriculum, 2008

In designing their curriculum, schools and teachers were to ensure learners had the opportunity to develop their language skills (listening, speaking, reading, writing), language learning strategies and intercultural understanding through a wide range of activities.

Key Stage 2 (7–11) followed a non-statutory framework. Schools could decide to introduce an MFL or not in their settings.

Key Stage 3 (12–14) followed a statutory framework. Schools are required to ensure provision for additional foreign languages and pupils are entitled to study at least one MFL other than English or Welsh.

Key Stage 4 (14–16): MFL is non-statutory. Pupils opt to continue learning a language.

Assessment was clear:

7–14: Standards of pupils' performance are set out in eight-level descriptions of increasing difficulty plus one Exceptional Performance level

14–16: External qualifications are the main means of assessing attainment in the national curriculum.

Put It to Practice: Collaborate to Articulate

Table 1.1 compares five key features of the National Curriculum with the CfW, the latter of which will be uncovered in this book with the teachers' exemplars. How do these compare with your local or national curriculum? Which features of either curriculum are more familiar to you as a language teacher and learner? Which feature of CfW resonates most with you and your colleagues? What features do you want to unpack with AATT/ICANADAPT?

TABLE 1.1 National Curriculum and Curriculum for Wales compared

National Curriculum MFL 2008	Curriculum for Wales 2022
Focus on outcomes attainment Programmes of study based on oracy, reading writing, and range Teach to assess Working as separate disciplines National curriculum	Focus on the development and achievements of the individual SoWMs based on connecting languages and cultures, understanding, expressing and creating literature. Focus on progression on the learning journey. Learning, teaching and assessment as one process. Collaborating as an Area with a learner focus. Framework for local curriculum

The *Successful Futures Review* (Donaldson, 2015) explains the rationale behind this shift in thinking. In 2014, the Welsh government had acknowledged weaknesses in its assessment framework and that arrangements were confusing and no longer fit for purpose. Inspections also highlighted assessment in schools as a significant shortcoming. This was substantiated by the OECD Report in 2014 on Welsh education and the stakeholder's voice which the Review approached. Making the changes to the new CfW in MFL was therefore quite logical and welcome as many of the principles were already part of the 2008 National Curriculum. However, school systems and pressures for results as well as examination specifications at KS4 often driving the curriculum have, in many instances, constrained teachers to teach to the level descriptors or exams assessment criteria and focused on language progression mainly, leaving out the most enjoyable parts of the language learning experiences such as the cultural dimension and using the language creatively. Some teachers could not see how CfW was different to the National Curriculum and were reluctant to make changes. The phenomenon of 'the zone of innovation' (Eddy & Bustamante, 2020; Stoller, 1994, 2006, 2009) applies here and is seen within other curriculum revision initiatives, when teachers are less likely to buy in if the shift is not novel enough, but will also not change if it is perceived too estranged from current practice and therefore incompatible. Therefore, careful intention is essential with professional learning cohorts so that they see themselves in the shift, how they bring their learners into the cultural story and keep a vested interest in their language journey. That interest is in teacher as designer and learner as creator, co-collaborators for their own curriculum within and outside of school.

At the LanguageWorld conference, March 2022, Dr Jennifer Eddy led a session (Eddy, 2022a) outlining the creation of tasks which incorporate authentic texts with creative outcomes, support progression across levels and have intercultural competence in mind. These AATTs encourage pupils to think creatively and communicate with others, using language they own with immediacy. Seven guiding principles (Eddy, 2022b) inform this curriculum design framework:

- Intercultural perspectives and transdisciplinary content unfold articulated curriculum and scaffold key tasks of meaningful performance.
- Learners acquire and own language not by linear and predictable memorization of functions, structures and forms but through creative, unpredictable interaction in tasks using transdisciplinary content in texts.
- Key Performance Tasks are designed for transfer to novel contexts, situations or audiences.
- Complexity differentiates tasks, not topics, themes or texts.
- Learners are active social agents co-constructing meaning through mediation and complex tasks across languages and cultures.
- Tasks solve problems and create products relevant to college, community, work and world.
- Learners take risks to apply their repertoire flexibly but not with native-like accuracy.

Table 1.2 depicts the assessment system from the previous curriculum with the AATT and its alignment to the AATT to the new CfW, Principles of Progression and Integral Skills. (For graphics on Principles of Progression and Integral Skills, see Chapter 1 on the companion website.)

TABLE 1.2 Assessment system contrast and alignment

Assessment types in previous curriculum	Articulated Assessment Transfer Task	AATT alignment to CfW Integral skills Principles of progression
Assessment for learning in Oracy, Reading and Writing skills and language knowledge Summative assessment in skills and language knowledge Focused on grammar and language progression	Integrate cultural perspectives and intercultural competence Problem-solving tasks for creative products Focuses on answering the essential questions. Purposeful outcome:	Integrate cultural and intercultural competence: deepening understanding of the ideas and disciplines within and across the Areas Develops integral skills: critical thinking and problem-solving, creativity and innovation, planning and organizing, personal effectiveness

Assessment types in previous curriculum	Articulated Assessment Transfer Task	AATT alignment to CfW Integral skills Principles of progression
Focused on using the language more independently for personal responses or more creative tasks No real purpose to the task other than testing the language and grammar understanding and use	Towards confident, autonomous language users for a variety of contexts and audiences Novel tasks for transfer for value beyond the classroom, key deliverables for linguistic and transcultural mediation	Focuses on answering the essential questions. Purposeful outcome: Deepening understanding of the ideas and disciplines with in the Areas Develops independence and self-confidence in the use of the language: increasing depth and breadth of knowledge, making connections and transferring learning into new contexts, refinement and sophistication in the use and application of skills Creativity and innovation

From Deliverer to Designer and Consumer to Creator: Transcultural Communicative Competence

ICANADAPT and AATTs support principles within the Common European Framework of Reference (CEFR) for Languages: Learning, Teaching, Assessment (COE, 1998, 2001). This Framework informs curriculum, assessment and instruction in the context of plurilingual and pluricultural competence (CEFR Section 6.1.3, Council of Europe, 2001, pp. 133–5). The Council of Europe, NCSSFL-ACTFL Can Do Statements (NCSSFL, 2017) and ACTFL Performance Descriptors (2012) promoted the shift from a synthetic textbook progression of grammar, vocabulary and factual tidbits on culture to a curriculum which prepares adaptable, fully participating global citizens. The Standards for Foreign Language Learning (National Standards in Foreign Language Education Project, 1999/2006) stated that 'the true content of the foreign language course is not the grammar and the vocabulary of the language, but the cultures expressed through that language' (p. 43). The revised World-Readiness Standards for Learning Languages (National Standards Collaborative Board, 2015) expanded that to emphasize language application beyond the classroom. The CEFR advocates plurilingual and pluricultural competence to meet emergent and increasing requirements of citizens in day-to-day interactions. These guidelines promote the learner as an active, action-oriented 'social agent' who is ready to participate with others in society rather than feign mastery of linguistic forms and cultural facts confined within traditional classroom exercises (Byram, 1997, 2009; Byram & Wagner, 2018; Deardorff, 2006, 2008, 2009, 2011; Little & Kirwan, 2019; Piccardo, 2013; Piccardo & North, 2019; Wagner et al., 2018; Zhu et. al, 2022). Michael Byram (1997) defined Intercultural Competence (IC) as someone's 'ability to interact in their own language with the people from another country and culture'. He later defined *Intercultural Communicative Competence* (ICC) as 'the ability to interact with people from another country and culture in a foreign language' (p. 71). The Companion Volume (COE, 2020) extended this further, adding descriptors for mediation and pluricultural competence. The goal was to acknowledge different cultures and mediate communication *between* languages and cultures.

The AATT and ICANADAPT curriculum design prepares learners to participate, adapt, contribute and mediate *through, across, within and among* cultures and spaces, rather than only between them which maintains distance with the other. This is *Transcultural Communicative Competence* (TCC), which facilitates inclusive spaces to live and work without leaving behind our own cultural, ethnic, or national identities (Baker & Sangiamchit, 2019; Jurkova, 2021; Kunschak, 2021; Lewis, 2002; Slimbach, 2005; Welsch, 1999). The AATT framework encourages solving problems and creating products found in daily interactions with intentional tasks in a variety of contexts (Deardorff, 2009). Our TCC tasks ask learners to interact with identities intact for community inclusion and expanded worldview as flexible and confident global citizens. AATT design encourages a continuum of reflection, response and reprise as learners spiral big ideas (Wiggins and McTighe, 2005) to expand their perspectives and see many ways people view the world. Our curricular tasks should emphasize how and to what extent the learner clarifies, compares, explains and bridges ideas from known to new, from the unfamiliar and unaccustomed to clarified, aware, contributing and conversant. The AATT and ICANADAPT design guides teachers and learners to do just that, on a nonlinear, spiral and creative course of action with language. It prepares learners who are not only tolerant of ambiguity but also have the tools to thrive flexibly in ever-changing linguistic and cultural environments. The tools enable practitioners to consider and ensure they never miss key, non-negotiable elements in CfW or in any curriculum framework which should be part of every planning:

- Integral skills
- Principles of progression
- Inter/Transcultural competence

- Authenticity and purpose
- Links between languages and/or other areas
- Progress along the language continuum

Paolo Freire (2018) encouraged learners to be re-creators rather than merely spectators or consumers. In *Pedagogy of the Oppressed*, 'Knowledge emerges only through invention and re-invention, through the restless, impatient, continuing, hopeful inquiry human beings pursue in the world, with the world, and with each other' (71–2). All too often, we see the teacher as a deliverer of content, grammar and vocabulary to equally passive pupils. Without dedicated collaborative time and proper curriculum design tools and support, many teachers default to prescribed curricula, textbook ancillaries or reworked and adapted worksheet packets, disengaged from curriculum design entirely (Trinter & Hughes, 2021). Curriculum planning becomes a half-day task to summarize outcomes on an online mapping tool. This perpetuates pupils' practice to repeat forms and consume facts, renting temporary space to pass a test, without the investment of ownership and transfer (Wiggins and McTighe, 2005) to language useful outside of classroom exercise. Why then, would pupils care to continue language study? The decline in uptake of international languages (IL), modern foreign languages (MFL) and world languages (WL) and the shortage of teachers in many countries compels us to promote the relevance and applicability of languages (ACIE, 2017; Collen, 2023; Cruickshank et al., 2020; Garcia et al., 2019; Gorrara et al., 2020; Hagger-Vaughn, 2016; Hawkes et al., 2019; Lusin et al., 2023; Taylor & Marsden, 2014). Memorizing static facts, easily obtained via a myriad of technology applications, is not judicious use of class time. We need curricula that make learners notice and react, improvise and respond, reflect on the familiar and engage with the novel, all while solving challenges and creating products of value for their communities. These tasks allow learners to experience themselves in many languages and cultures beyond just how language resides in texts. Pupils must engage in re-invention and creativity with language, not only for the relatively brief time our learners are with us in school, but to ensure they can continue creative language use and transcultural interaction for the rest of their lives with others. Our learners must experience languages and cultures as valuable to themselves, not only within classrooms now, but with frameworks extending and enabling inquiry beyond the school building. We want learners to pursue inquiry and novelty, build relationships with all people, understand their worldview better and do so confidently, albeit without perfection, but on their own, without us. ICANADAPT/AATT is a bespoke framework that can align with any curriculum structure you may have in place. The design process tools and exemplars promote inquiry, meaning-making, critical reflection, transferable perspectives and new deliverables to prepare a confident, contributing and adaptable global citizen. The schools represented in this book run the gamut from city to rural, small to large, heritage/community language schools which are Welsh-medium, English-medium-instructed schools, well-resourced communities to less so, all with a highly diverse student body. As you follow the teachers' journey in curriculum design, you will see they all have enthusiasm for languages and cultures, honing their craft as educators and bringing their creativity and that of their pupils to the fore as they design and implement these exemplars.

Our children and young people only have a relatively short time at school. We must use that time judiciously and productively to help each one of them to grow as a capable, healthy, well-rounded individual who can thrive in the face of unknown future challenges.

Prof Donaldson, *Successful Futures*, 2015

Community Language and the Welsh Context

From the Admin Desk

Stephanie Ellis-Williams, International Languages, Global Futures GwE lead.

Wales is officially bilingual with approximately 450 schools teaching through the medium of Welsh, which is compulsory for all pupils regardless of first language up to the age of sixteen (Welsh Government, 2017). Wales is a particularly language-rich country where the Welsh language is celebrated, promoted and supported. It is mandatory for all schools to ensure that provision for the Welsh language is of high quality and ambitious. Just like for English, it is the responsibility of all areas of learning to develop the literacy and language skills for Welsh as best alongside the actual Welsh and English curriculum lessons.

In Wales, pupils are required to take an international language with Welsh and English, so that they complete their education with at least three languages. International languages have always been encouraged to make triple-literacy links with English and Welsh. By comparing and contrasting languages, our learners deepen understanding, secure learning and make faster progress in the international language as well as in English and Welsh.

So, working together with Welsh and English is not new. What CfW enables and encourages us to do more is to exploit our links with the languages within our school to share practice, action-research and identify each other's approaches which can be effective in our own areas. The CfW is now defining two types of schools in terms of the Welsh language. In Welsh-medium schools, all curriculum areas are delivered through Welsh. In English-medium settings, Welsh is learned in school and taught mainly in Welsh lessons. However, the language profile of these schools and the proficiency of the learners will be very different from one school to another and add to the challenge of providing a programme of study which will suit and help every learner to make suitable progress in Welsh.

CfW is a complex framework of high-level and overarching concepts and elements which need to be taken into consideration at every level of planning in order to realize the vision of the curriculum. In June 2022, we invited a group of heads of departments (HoDs), four from MFLs and three Welsh, to try out the AATT framework. The range of HoDs varied greatly from large departments in large schools with multiple international languages being taught to single members of staff departments in smaller schools. All HoDs lead their department in designing and delivering the curriculum they have agreed on with their team and Senior Leadership Team. All were eager to explore and develop different approaches to language teaching to inform their planning for the new CfW.

The Welsh departments also varied and reflected the very complex nature of our Welsh school settings (see Table 1.3) and often present in many districts of multilingual communities, geographic diversity and socio-economic status. The Welsh language agenda is a top priority for the Welsh government that wants to see the number of people able to enjoy speaking and using Welsh reach a million by 2050 (Welsh Government, 2017).

We immediately realized that the process of AATT creation is very flexible, aligns with the vision of CfW in many ways and can suit any school or AoLE curriculum priority and context.

Putting It Together

As for most curricular documents, within the CfW there are mandatory and statutory elements as it pertains to Languages, Literacy and Communication. This curriculum is anchored by the Four Purposes: Developing ambitious capable learners, Enterprising creative contributors, Ethical, informed citizens, and Healthy, confident individuals. There are six Areas of Learning and Experience (AoLE) of which Languages, Literacy and Communication (LLC) includes Welsh, English and IL (CfW, 2019). The key concepts within

TABLE 1.3 Teacher-leader-designers from diverse school contexts

Initial Schools June 2022	Language context and priorities	AATT for the school context: How it could help
Prestatyn High school, Denbighshire Ms Viviane Vick	11–18 French/ Spanish Large school and department Works closely with Welsh (taught as an IL) English medium East of the region, small town with deprived areas Nearer border with England	Aligning processes and methods within the LLC (school priority) Framework works well for MFLs and Welsh/ English Senior Leadership team very interested in the process and keen to introduce to all staff for professional development/ change in mindset Enables to rethink the offer in terms of contexts and tasks School wants to increase uptake at 14 + / feel this process could help raise learner motivation and love for languages
Alun School, Flintshire Mr Paul Conn	11–18 French/ German Large school and department English medium East of the region, semi-rural near border with England	Help to tweak an already forward-looking curriculum Help to re-evaluate their contexts and the questions to debate Maintain very high standards Raise aspiration and achievement of lower ability learners.
Ysgol Dyffryn Ogwen, Gwynedd Ms Emma Green	11–16 French Smaller school One member department Welsh-medium Set in rural and more Welsh-speaking area in the West of the region	Continue to raise learners' interest in language learning Develop effective and purposeful planning which can follow the school direction in terms of dealing with the 'big questions' if set by the school. Think out of the box or further in terms of contexts and cultural understanding – be more ambitious for learners Broaden the learners' awareness and understanding of the world.

Initial Schools June 2022	Language context and priorities	AATT for the school context: How it could help
Ysgol y Grango, Wrexham Ms Lynette Sloan	11–16 French Smaller school Two-member department English-medium Near border with England	Bring more cultural elements to lessons Change mindset for planning: start with the important and interesting questions Provide a curriculum which makes sense to the learners and their community-looking at local environment and using the community links
Ysgol Tryfan, Gwynedd Ms Jeni Morris	11–18 Welsh Large department Welsh-medium In town, West of the region, more Welsh-speaking area with stronger Welsh culture Many learners from English-speaking homes, no language support or reinforcement and Welsh first learner's degree of proficiency naturally varying.	Smooth transition for learners along the language learning continuum. Framework which enables all students, no matter their proficiency in the language, to be successful and achieve well whilst dealing with the same intercultural understanding as their peers. Help to tweak an already forward-looking curriculum Help to re-evaluate their contexts and the questions to debate
Ysgol Morgan Llwyd, Wrexham Ms Eurgain Hughes	11–18 Welsh Large department Welsh-Medium In town, on border with England	Raise the pride in Welsh culture, heritage and value of the language Smooth transition for learners along the language learning continuum. Framework which enables all students, no matter their proficiency in the language, to be successful and achieve well whilst dealing with the same intercultural understanding as their peers.

each area are defined by the SoWMs. For LLC, those are Languages Connect Us, Understanding languages is key to understanding the world around us, Expressing ourselves through languages is key to communication and Literature fires imagination and inspires creativity. The following five chapters unpack each Statement and its corresponding alignment within the AATT. In our schools, there is also a responsibility to contribute to religion, values, ethics, relationship and sexuality education where it is relevant and applicable across languages and cultures. Literacy, numeracy and digital competence are also mandatory and should be addressed and developed throughout the curriculum.

The first of the seven guiding principles for language curriculum design is Intercultural perspectives and transdisciplinary content unfold articulated curriculum and scaffold key tasks of meaningful transfer performance (Eddy, 2022b, p. 15). One of the most important realizations for any group of teachers as designers is to invest intentional, collaborative time together for *articulation*. For this framework, it means not only to design of transcultural curriculum, but also to demonstrate completion of your programme with a *Catalogue of Deliverables*, key performances of transfer assessments for varied disciplinary contexts as evidence of learner progress, in order to thrive as capable language users beyond school.

Vertical articulation is an area often misunderstood or overlooked in curriculum design because teachers tend to plan for the same level with horizontal articulation goals, often for years. Faculty are told to put lesson topics, outcomes, grammar and vocabulary in a grid, typically on a district-wide intake digital platform. In my experience, they work alone, even if given the release time to be together in one room. There is no revision, often adherence to textbook sequencing and prepared packets, only retrofit and not with shift in mindset to designer (Stoller, 2009; Trinter & Hughes, 2021). The input may reside on a new timeline tool, but the result is the same. They do not design curricula collaboratively and resort to speaking only about the content they teach. Teachers who may not have the opportunity to work together on curriculum design may not know what comes before and after the level they teach. When teachers are isolated or limited to only plan for the level they teach and not involved directly in curriculum design in collaboration with colleagues, schemes of work and material are often retaught or reviewed repeatedly with learners not going beyond the novice level (Byrnes, 1990, 2008, 2010; Couet et al., 2008; Lange, 1982, 1988). Grammar forms and vocabulary lists without context with classroom drill exercises disconnected from interactions, events, experiences, expectations and situations beyond school do not help learners to use the language for long-term goals (Stoller, 2006). If we want vertical articulation and progression between school buildings, key stages or levels, teachers need to design curricula between levels together, know what is happening before and after the level they teach and make progression visible, tangible and valuable, something fill-in drills with verb forms cannot fulfil. The Principles of Progression in CfW provide 'look fors' in vertical articulation: Increasing effectiveness as a learner, Deepening understanding of the ideas and disciplines within and across the Areas, Refinement and growing sophistication in the use and application of skills, Increasing breadth and depth of knowledge and Making connections and transferring learning into new contexts. Progression is further supported by Descriptions of Learning (DoL), which align with the SoWMs and how learners move through instruction 3–16. Throughout the exemplars, our teachers designed tasks which explore integral skills, including Creativity & Innovation, Critical thinking & Problem-solving, Planning & Organizing and Personal Effectiveness. These tenets serve as models for any curriculum revision plan. The initial challenge for practitioners and schools was to try and understand the framework, how the different elements fit in together and how they make sense at Area and discipline level. The ultimate challenge is to ensure we can translate this into practice at the class level, which will ensure the offer is even better than before.

Our Name Is Inclusive: International Languages

As discussed earlier, one major change in the new CfW is the use of the term 'International Languages' rather than 'Modern Foreign Languages', which has predominantly focused on the teaching of French, German and Spanish in schools. International Languages is defined as 'home and community languages, modern languages, classical languages and British Sign Language' (Welsh Government, 2019). The vision is clear: the teacher's role is to ensure our students celebrate languages and their cultures. The curriculum encourages multilingualism and plurilingualism to thrive, and learners to develop a positive curiosity about languages, learning and cultures; the intent is to ignite learners' curiosity, to provide them with a firm foundation and lifelong interest in the languages of Wales and of the world. Our role is to ensure our learners harness their bilingualism and their identity to open up to the rest of the world and thrive in the modern world by opening their horizons, keeping an open mind and developing a positive curiosity towards language learning and others.

By making connections between languages, they get to develop their linguistic skills faster but they also get to know the words and their history better, therefore making sense of the world around them. The same principles underpin the AATT model: a novice in an international language does not mean having to learn in isolated and uninteresting contexts. In addition, making the most of the learners' cultural capital (i.e. home language; different cultural community; different backgrounds and interests) and building upon it, or using it to inform and enhance the curriculum design for the language classroom is essential. This practice helps bring different communities together, fosters tolerance and gets learners to embrace differences.

The one language continuum in the new CfW erases the misconception that an international language can only or will only aim for a predetermined level. With the same language continuum as English and Welsh, the starting point of learners with previous or higher language skills is taken into account and recognized. Their progress should be made from that point onwards, avoiding any kind of plateauing or no progress at all. Similarly, learners where progress is not as fast as others, can also aim to make progress, at a pace which is appropriate to their age and ability at the time. This flexibility is also a much welcome element to the Welsh language where the actual term 'Welsh second language' has now disappeared, leaving the term 'Welsh and Welsh in English-medium settings'. In Table 1.4, priorities of CfW and those addressed by the AATT are presented side by side.

TABLE 1.4 Key priorities for Curriculum for Wales and the AATT

Key Priority for the LLC AoLE (CfW 2019, LLC introduction)	Priorities Addressed by AATT
Given that a key aspect of *effective language learning* is the willingness to *experiment and take risks* in trying out new structures, sounds and patterns, learning and experience in this Area can *empower learners to be creative and to persevere when facing challenges*. Together, these skills can build learners' confidence to grasp new opportunities and to adapt to different roles which in turn can develop them as enterprising, creative contributors, *ready to play a full part in life and work*. (CfW 2019, LLC introduction)	Presentational tasks: Productive Novel tasks: full transfer of skills and knowledge Address an audience outside the classroom: confidence, purpose and challenging Develops communication and mediation skills Develops creativity Articulation Spiral Points Mediation for Transfer

Key Priority for the LLC AoLE (CfW 2019, LLC introduction)	Priorities Addressed by AATT
Encourage learners to engage critically with languages and literature in order to help them develop not only their own sense of identity, but also an *understanding of the relationship between their own cultures and communities and those of other people.* This understanding can be deepened as learners are afforded opportunities to learn multiple languages. This linguistic knowledge and these skills are needed to *participate confidently and empathetically in society,* which contributes to developing learners as ethical, informed citizens of Wales and the world. (CfW 2019, LLC introduction)	Interpretive tasks: Receptive Develops cultural understanding Develops critical thinking Develops empathy Mediation for Transfer Interpersonal tasks: Interactive Develops critical thinking Develops collaboration and tolerance Develops language and planning skills
Ability to use Welsh, English and other languages in a *plurilingual context.* Meaningful language learning experiences go hand in hand with *learning about one's own cultural identity as well as the cultural identities of others* (LLC Statement of What matters 1, CfW 2019)	Learning experiences instructions and links to previous, and new learning Articulation Spiral Points Intercultural transfer targets Mediation for Transfer
Make sense of what is heard, read and seen, and thus to *develop our understanding, empathy and our ability to respond and to mediate effectively.* (LLC Statement of What matters 2, CfW 2019)	Interpretive tasks Mediation for Transfer
Ability to *use and adapt languages in a range of roles, genres, forms, media and styles* and in a suitable register … this also calls for the ability to *choose an appropriate language and to mediate.* (LLC Statement of What matters 3, CfW 2019)	Interpersonal and Presentational tasks Mediation for Transfer
Provide learners with *literary experiences,* appreciate a creator's craft as well as develop their own creative skills develop their ability to demonstrate empathy (LLC Statement of What matters 4, CfW 2019)	Interpretive tasks Interpersonal tasks Presentational tasks Mediation for Transfer

Ein Llais Ni-Oracy Project – 'Our Voice'

Funded by the Welsh government, *Ein Llais Ni* (2023) is a recent significant and comprehensive North Wales project to develop oracy skills for the Welsh language. It highlights many important principles, aims and desired outcomes common to the learning of any language (see Table 1.5). Through research, evidence-based practice and case studies, the project raises the importance of oracy in the school curriculum and offers strategies to promote learners' speaking and listening skills. The AATT and ICANADAPT process clearly responds and aligns to the main principles and aims.

TABLE 1.5 Desired outcomes of *Ein Llais Ni* and International Languages

Ein Llais Ni desired outcomes	IL desired outcomes which can be achieved through the AATT process and in line with research used in *Ein Llais Ni*
1. Learners enjoy speaking Welsh. 2. Practitioners foster learners' self-confidence and well-being and develop them into confident bilingual communicators who enjoy speaking Welsh. 3. Practitioners experimenting with strategies (including using digital tools) in order to promote oral skills in Welsh. 4. Developing teachers as active researchers – reflecting on contemporary research, modelling the strategies in action and evaluating the success by presenting case studies and working together with other practitioners in order to develop the pedagogy. 5. Enable teachers to plan more intentionally in order to support and develop the learners' speaking and listening skills in Welsh in the context of the CfW (taking into account the principles of progress from the AoLEs and the Literacy Framework). 6. Practitioners offer authentic experiences for the learners to use their Welsh in various situations in their everyday lives by collaborating with partners (agencies/organizations/individuals).	1. Learners enjoy speaking the IL. 2. It raises learners' self-confidence. It develops confident communicators 3. Oral skills are at the forefront of planning and progression 4. It encourages teachers to be active designers, collaborate to develop innovative and effective pedagogy. 5. It systematically reminds teachers to plan to support learners to develop speaking and listening skills, with a focus on spontaneity and autonomy. 6. The authentic contexts, the three communicative modes (Glisan et al., 2003) in the AATT and the AfL of the stage three lessons require learners to use their IL in various authentic situations and for authentic purposes and to collaborate with partners. 7. Oracy and communicative skills are explicitly taught and practised in various ways.

Ein Llais Ni desired outcomes	IL desired outcomes which can be achieved through the AATT process and in line with research used in Ein Llais Ni
7. All teachers make time to teach oracy A supportive learning environment throughout the school to develop effective speaking and listening skills. A solid progression in learning strategies and methods across the continuum. 8. Learners develop to be increasingly confident when speaking Welsh in different situations using exploratory speaking techniques and speaking techniques to present. 9. Learners imitate high-quality communication models.	8. The AATT/ICANADAPT process and planning stages enable the appropriate modelling, practice, scaffolding and support to take place before the summative assessment tasks. Learners are therefore in a safe learning environment where they are not afraid of making mistakes or not being perfect. The model can be used from day one, enabling a coherent and effective progression. Learners are encouraged to be creative to convey their messages with the language they own. 9. Learners can emulate high-quality communication models.

O Enau Plant (Thomas & Caulfield, 2022) is a quick guide for teachers on development oracy skills of children and young people. It advocates that to enable children to learn a language effectively there need to be 'opportunities for children to practice in a context where a child feels that the purpose of the task is not language specific'.

> What is needed is that children have the opportunity to experiment and practice using language for different purposes through tasks and exercises that are important to them and in a context where all children can feel comfortable
>
> Thomas & Caulfield, 2022. p. 28

> Teachers should be able to create such situations where students hold meaningful tasks that will promote their speaking proficiency.
>
> Malihah, 2010, p. 93

By basing the AATT planning around the overarching concepts and the actual context of the tasks, language learners are systematically provided with such opportunities. Richard Hull (2023) at the *Ein Llais Ni* Conference identified three types of talk: retrieval, exploratory and presentational. In Table 1.6, the alignment with the AATT/ICANADAPT process is clear again.

TABLE 1.6 Three types of talk aligned with AATT and ICANADAPT

Three types of talk (Richard Hull)	Alignment with the AATT and ICANADAPT process
Retrieval - All lessons - Questioning are part of daily classroom practice - Encourage repetition and recall of key information - To check progress and fill gaps	Learning experiences and instructions: review, spiral, new
Exploratory - Some lessons when relevant - Catalysts provided - Exchange of ideas in pairs or small groups - Teacher facilitates - Students report back	Interpretive tasks Interpersonal tasks
Presentational - Used whenever students are sharing/speaking in front of their peers - Often happens following exploratory talk - Delivering a formal/structured presentation or part of a debate to their peers or others	Presentational tasks

Successful Futures and the Teacher as Designer

Earlier we discussed *Successful Futures* (Donaldson, 2015; Evans, 2022) and their recommendations for the CfW, focused on Four Purposes and six Areas of Learning and Experience (AoLE). In order to build 'ambitious, capable learners, ready to learn throughout their lives; enterprising, creative contributors, ready to play a full part in life and work; ethical, informed citizens of Wales and the world' it leans into an articulated progression or continuum. Rather than compartmentalizing into segments, benchmarks and stages which trap topics unnaturally corralled and allocated to a level, the transfer spiral curriculum reprises the concept but does so with a novel task and greater complexity and variation. The learner goes beyond intercultural competence or between two cultures to TCC in tandem with the pieces they encounter; across, through and among cultures and disciplinary texts informed by them. This is also why themes, topics and texts should not be pigeonholed, compartmentalized and artificially limited by the year, stage, level or target range and withheld (Bruner, 1962, 1996; Eddy, 2022b; Mishan, 2005; Shrum & Glisan, 2016; Tschirner & Bärenfänger, 2012). Creativity at the start, initializing both the concept and vocabulary build, makes both early and later learning better when all concepts and texts are available. The tasks you design determine the target level and learner 'take-away' from the text. Teacher as Designer makes this possible.

Successful Futures and the AATT/ICANADAPT framework compel us to reconceive our field not as deliverers of skills and subject matter from scripts and worksheet packets but as co-creators of content with learners in order to develop creative contributors and innovative, enterprising lifelong learners. This means that our content area and any of them, for that matter, is not fodder to be collected, memorized and returned as evidence if we are truly honest about what we want. Pupils must engage in ways of thinking and reacting within cultures in tandem with teachers within novel tasks (Bruner, 1996; Coyle et al., 2021; Eddy, 2022b; Little & Kirwan, 2019). Both *Successful Futures* and AATT/ICANADAPT propel the teacher as designer and autonomous agent, with professional learning opportunities (Drew & Priestley, 2016) for all key stakeholders to work in collaborative practice. For our profession, this means as designers of articulated, spiral curricula. The teacher-designers in this book are put in the driver's seat of their own hands-on reform and revision process rather than presented with a textbook, prescriptive curriculum packets or canned webinars to consume and re-deliver. As teachers design these exemplars, they see how transcultural themes unfold, enduring ones that stand the test of time, with essential questions that we continue to probe and explore across the lifespan. They do so in collaboration with colleagues, which in and of itself is often a cultural shift in many schools. Teachers who embark upon this work often say they cannot imagine going back and returning to the way it was, declaring that it always could have been like this. The notion of professional learning as hands on design, a transformative shift (Grundy & Robison, 2004) is a departure from 'sit and get' professional development seminars or watching recorded, voiceover powerpoint slide decks with checklist concept attainment or even live webinars.

Enterprising, creative contributors must not hesitate to use language they own, however small, in new contexts inside and outside the classroom. Nor should they rely on rules, textbook sequencing, lists and finite predictability that past practice has maintained. These teachers justify this shift and make the case that curricula and tasks designed for innovation and unpredictability create active language learners for transcultural collaboration across their lifespan. Design with no end in mind. Teachers will become designers for their own and their learner's autonomy, where adaptability and agility are a necessity in our VUCA world.

Put It to Practice: Collaborate to Articulate

Our curriculum design should focus on teacher autonomy to develop learner autonomy: 'focus on what learners do which is new, so that they can continue to do it without us'. Discuss with colleagues.

Voices from the Field

The delegates believed that planning using the AATT/ICANADAPT designing tools would enable practitioners to gain a deeper understanding of the new curriculum framework. They saw how its elements fit together to make effective and practical classroom practice within the Languages, Literacy and Communication AoLE. Listen to some of their feedback on the process.

Prestatyn High School, Denbighshire, Ms Viviane Vick

It was extremely useful and finally gave us an opportunity to start planning effectively for the New Curriculum. It enabled me to start putting the vision into concrete targets/projects.

This was very enlightening and felt like a 'breath of fresh air'.

AATTs helped me think of the structure of my planning, keeping in mind every step and ensuring the ' I can' statements were relevant.

It made it clearer for me to think of transferable skills instead of topics.

The AATTs make differentiation clearer and easier to focus on.

I feel I can plan and encourage my team to plan better and more effectively for CfW.

Helps to follow a 'pattern' which ensures we are doing the vision of CfW justice.

Working with Welsh is very useful as we can exchange ideas and for MFL, it is essential we keep in mind the Welsh element of CfW.

It would be interesting to have a common approach within the LLC and it could help transition and consistency throughout the Curriculum.

Alun School, Flintshire, Mr Paul Conn

It allowed me to see how AATTs can be used to inform assessment and planning.

The idea of planning for different outcomes and planning backwards and differentiating down was an interesting concept.

I found useful to:
Collectively design the AATTs based on the International Eisteddfod. This demonstrated how a wide range of topics can be used to address assessment areas.

Using the terminology based on bloom's taxonomy to build a bank/catalogue of key question words.

I think the ideas demonstrated in the AATTs can be linked back to our progression steps.

It gives teachers a different approach to planning and designing the new CfW.

Ysgol Dyffryn Ogwen, Gwynedd, Ms Emma Green

Makes you think outside 'usual' topic areas and where you can go with them. Very useful.

It is making me consider carefully the units of work I will plan and the types of activities to include.

Ysgol y Grango, Wrexham, Ms Lynette Sloan

The AATT way of planning is straightforward and meaningful.
It seems like a simple way to plan for transference of skills

It is useful to know:
How to plan creatively whilst differentiating.
How to keep things simple and straightforward for pupils.
Planning cultural lessons isn't as difficult and over complicated as I thought.

It will allow me to create meaningful tasks that not only cover key skills and transferring of knowledge but also work within an existing SoL to bridge gaps and perhaps work with other departments to make links across the AoLEs and SoWM.

Ysgol Tryfan, Gwynedd, Ms Jeni Morris

The day really helped me as Head of Department. It gave me a new direction regarding how I'm going to plan in more detail for the new curriculum. I was able to see how such planning ensures that we are inclusive and give pupils across the range the opportunity to access the curriculum which ultimately means they succeed.

This has helped see how to:
    Design simple, suitable and purposeful planning.
    Identify opportunities to broaden pupils' horizons when planning.
    The day has made me rethink how I go about planning without a doubt. The day made me realize that it was important for the planning to be simple and clear for any practitioner reading the plans. The day also made me realize that it is possible to plan for the full range of pupils we will have in year 7.
    I have already adapted and created new plans based on the knowledge and information advice from Jenny during the day.

Ysgol Morgan Llwyd, Wrexham, Ms Eurgain Hughes

Very useful as it helped us plan for next year and think about the features of the Curriculum for Wales. Useful as it encourages us to think about designing schemes of work.

Useful to:
    Putting objectives and theories into practice
    when adapting schemes of work to meet WLS objectives
    very useful to Welsh first language teachers because this is very different from the content of the second language courses

In October 2022, North Wales secondary MFL and Welsh teachers began to design and implement their own AATTs. The tasks give an overarching context across levels, with learner outcomes differentiated according to the level of their engagement. These outcomes (performances or products) are relevant to career, community and the future. So far, GwE regional teachers have designed and implemented 20 exemplars in French, Spanish, German and Welsh.

Designing with the AATT is helpful for articulation across levels and intercultural competence because it develops breadth and depth of knowledge of various topics. Through planning the tasks in this way, differentiation is an integral part of the task and allows learners from novice to intermediate to access the lessons. It also allows creative skills to be developed at every opportunity and every level within the task.

These AATTs and curriculum design may help with the uptake of languages by inspiring further cultural curiosity. Through lessons delivered inspired by the AATT, students also see context and meaning to their work. This helps to engage their interest and make them intrigued to know more.

Ms Emma Adams, St Brigid's School, Denbighshire, Spanish

From the Admin Desk

As an administrator and support adviser, I felt the AATT model would enable teachers to make this shift and feel empowered to break away from the constraints of the system they may have been in and impede their freedom and creativity in planning. These constraints may have been self-imposed or slowly instilled by a heavy assessment, reporting, exam-driven system which tends to restrict planning and creativity.

Teachers needed to consider themselves again as active designers whose role is to research, share and collaborate to develop their practice. The AATT is a practical tool to support this mind shift with a frame which could model how teachers can experiment, change and evolve as practitioners. The process helps teachers frame the planning whilst remaining free to choose the concepts, language points and deliverables which are most suited to their vision, school context and learners.

The frame and process act as reminders of the criteria and non-negotiables to consider for excellent teaching and learning outcomes. It gives teachers the confidence they are not leaving anything out. What's more, the AATT has challenging and far-reaching intended learning outcomes which helps teachers design much more ambitious schemes of learning and helps plan a coherent and effective progression.

The spirit of the AATT process and the ICANADAPT model and the training programme we offered in 2022–2023 completely supported the idea that teachers, in order to best develop professionally, should have the opportunity to be working together, to be given time to experiment, make mistakes, trial again, evaluate and amend again. This is also the message which is conveyed to our young language learners who should be allowed to experiment, make mistakes, improve and try again. Perfection is not the aim: that perfection will never be fully reached. It is the journey towards perfection which matters, and the learning and experiences we gain from it along the way.

The AATT and ICANADAPT approaches and processes enable IL to contribute effectively and in stimulating ways to the development of these essential communication skills. CfW advocates a curriculum design that is not top-down anymore, not imposed by the government and leaders. CfW gives the driving seat to the teachers and is encouraging them to embrace such a role. The AATT enable teachers to become true designers who are free to design the curriculum they have always wanted.

—Stephanie Ellis-Williams, International Languages, Global Futures GwE Lead

Design for Transfer

With what you see thus far in this chapter and the templates, what is one element within the AATT or ICANADAPT that you want to explore first? What questions do you have about your own stage in curriculum revision? At this starting point, what is your main takeaway for how the AATT design can help you with curriculum design? How could you explain it to someone else?

Design for Transfer

How does your curriculum compare with the four SoWMs in the CfW? What are the key elements or goals of your curriculum and how might they be addressed with the AATT and the ideas expressed in this chapter?

Reflect and Revisit

1. How can language teachers encourage learner autonomy and creativity through purposeful and novel pupil deliverables?
2. How can language teachers balance the need for creativity and flexibility in curriculum design with the requirements of national or institutional guidelines?
3. What characteristics should be present in language tasks for learners to thrive in a VUCA world?
4. To what extent does our profession's mindset, perception, and purpose guide teachers as designers in the revision process?
5. How can language learners be encouraged to take ownership of their language acquisition and engage in lifelong autonomous learning?
6. What strategies can teacher leaders use to overcome resistance to change and promote innovation in language curriculum design?
7. How do teachers shift from being deliverers of content to becoming designers of innovative and relevant language curricula?

2

Designing What Matters

Enduring Understandings

- ∞ Assessments are planned backward from transcultural concepts.
- ∞ Curriculum and assessment design focuses on transfer tasks for mediation between, among, within and across cultures.
- ∞ Intercultural transferable goals unfold vertically articulated curriculum for progression.
- ∞ Mediation for Transfer strategies makes language accessible and cultural perspectives visible.

Essential Questions

- **Q** How can language and culture work together for us to mediate with others?
- **Q** Why do novelty and transfer evidence matter?
- **Q** What do articulation and progression for transfer look like?
- **Q** To what extent can I use language I own to help someone else understand?

I can

- Define what matters in developing curriculum for inter/transcultural communicative competence.

- Explain components and principles of Articulated Assessment Transfer Tasks
- Define intercultural transfer goals for my programme

Let's Consider

How do we express what matters to us as individuals, a people, a nation and a civilization? How do we bridge, clarify and connect what matters to other people? What can we show others unfamiliar with the language or unaccustomed to the culture? In the first book, we said that language is creativity by design (Eddy, 2022b). Language becomes tangible through our creativity, demonstrative in our improvisation with others or in public and shared objects, artefacts and works in every discipline. We are surrounded by these every day; they have been created throughout the lifespan of all of the world's cultures. Through our creativity, we make language accessible and cultural perspectives visible to other people all the time, whenever we interact with them. All language learners can do this too, even if that starts with just gestures, single words, images or phrases while awaiting another novel response from that person. For both teacher and pupils, it represents both autonomy in expression and confidence in creativity.

This is at the heart of the Statements of What Matters (SoWMs). When Ms Stephanie Ellis-Williams introduced me to the CfW, I was moved by the section on the SoWMs. Between these and the Principles of Progression, I had never seen anchor standards expressed quite this way. As I examined the CfW documents in detail, I discovered how the AATT/ICANADAPT framework supported these tenets and, in turn, could guide teachers. I understood why Ms Ellis-Williams was keen to dive deeper into this work and invite her teacher-leadership to the design table.

The Languages, Literacy and Communication AoLE (CfW, 2019) has four 'Statements of What Matters':

- Languages Connect Us
- Understanding languages is key to understanding the world around us
- Expressing ourselves through languages is key to communication
- Literature fires imagination and inspires creativity.

The AATT/ICANADAPT framework operationalizes these Statements by making inter/transcultural communicative competence visible through the articulated transfer tasks. When you review these Statements, what can pupils do to provide evidence of them? What kind of tasks come to mind? What might that look like in school and beyond?

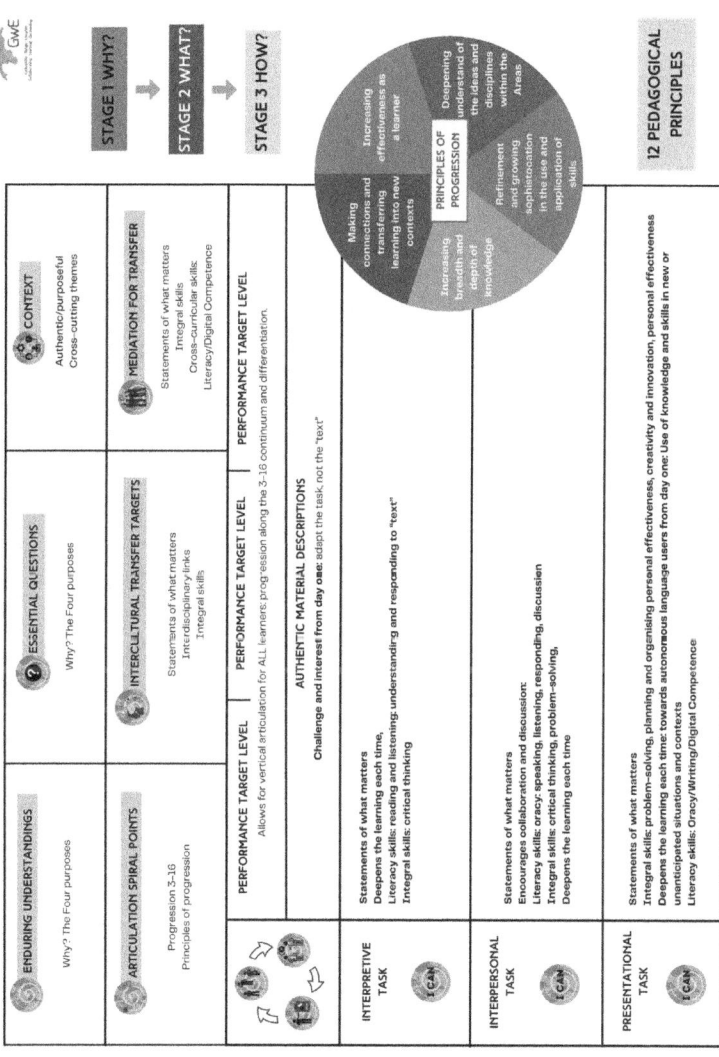

FIGURE 2.1 AATT alignment with CfW elements and planning at GwE. GwE, 2023. Adapted from Eddy, J. (2022b) *Designing World Language Curriculum for Intercultural Communicative Competence*, with permission from Bloomsbury Academic, an imprint of Bloomsbury Publishing, Plc.

Although each SoWM has distinctive goals and characteristics, they are integrated and interdependent, working in concert to promote transcultural communicative competence. Learners can participate and engage across and among other cultures while maintaining their own identities; in so many ways, they understand themselves better through tasks beyond the teacher's expectation in the classroom. In the following four chapters, we will examine AATTs selected and how they notably represented one of the SoWM. You will see that the exemplars integrate all of SoWMs while they inform and influence both intercultural and transcultural communicative competence (see Figure 2.1).

What Truly Matters: Intercultural Perspectives, Transfer and Mediation for Progression

Inter/transcultural perspectives are present in all disciplines, shaping our identity and others. These unfold articulated curriculum with scaffolded tasks of meaningful performance, as seen in the AATTs. Communicating effectively in culturally appropriate contexts is a vital skill for all individuals living and working in our communities. It requires responding to and connecting within our own and among other cultures with a diverse set of perspectives and concepts. It is essential to understand the details of language, customs and beliefs to work collaboratively in new spaces, partnerships and organizations, whether local, national or international. To facilitate the SoWMs, our curriculum design is framed with Intercultural Transferable Goals (Eddy, 2022b). These represent perspectives within a culture or cultures that intrinsically matter so much that they resurface and reprise throughout varied circumstances, venues and across disciplinary texts to experience over and over again. These transcultural perspectives are ones you want everyone leaving your programme to understand very well. They are so important that they must be reprised in vertical articulation and learner progression throughout your curriculum. They tend to be present in your day-to-day experiences over your lifespan. AATT transferable goals, such as those described in Inside and Outside spaces (Kuo-Flynn, 2022), clever resourcefulness in Axe Porridge (Kalmanson, 2022) and resilience in Capoeira (Bianconi, 2022), to name a few, speak to concepts inherent within and among cultures but made more visible, explicit and comprehensible to others via the tasks. Pupils uncover these perspectives through the tasks you design. These tasks align with the other three SoWMs. All of their tasks use *cultural community texts*, provide opportunities to explore and interact with them solo and with others and then create new works and deliverables.

> **Put It to Practice: Collaborate to Articulate**
>
> Which cultural perspectives are so essential to thrive in that community or space that it would be remiss on the part of a programme if it were omitted? What do you want the student to come away understanding very well for appropriate interaction and mediation within and among cultures? What is an Intercultural Transferable Goal for your language and culture? Consider these questions as you begin your AATT and Stage One of your ICANADAPT unit. (For AATT and ICANADAPT templates with fillable fields, see Chapter 2 on the companion website).

The previous chapter presented seven guiding principles for language curriculum design.

1 Intercultural perspectives and transdisciplinary content unfold articulated curriculum and scaffold key tasks of meaningful performance.

2 Learners acquire and own language not by linear and predictable memorization of functions, structures and forms but through creative, unpredictable interaction in tasks using transdisciplinary content in texts.

3 Key Performance tasks are designed for transfer to novel contexts, situations or audiences.

4 Complexity differentiates tasks, not topics, themes or texts.

5 Learners are active social agents co-constructing meaning through mediation and complex tasks across languages and cultures.

6 Tasks solve problems and create products relevant to college, community, work and world.

7 Learners take risks to apply their repertoire flexibly but not with native-like accuracy.

Eddy, 2022b, p. 15

These principles support all four of the SoWMs, with Languages Connect Us to underpin and nourish the others. Table 2.1 below aligns the *Statements of What Matters* side by side with the seven principles of curriculum design, the features of the AATT, ICANADAPT model (Eddy, 2022b) and three modes of communication (Adair-Hauck et al., 2006; Glisan et al., 2003; National Standards Collaborative Board, 2015; NCSSFL, 2017) to be uncovered via the exemplars in this book.

TABLE 2.1 Design principles, Statements of What Matters and AATT/ICANADAPT side by side

Design Principles of Language Curriculum Design for ICC	SoWMs within this design framework	AATT and ICANADAPT Design
Inter/transcultural perspectives and transdisciplinary content unfold articulated curriculum and scaffold key tasks of meaningful performance. Learners are active social agents co-constructing meaning through mediation and complex tasks across languages and cultures.	**Languages Connect Us** *How do languages connect us with others?* The exemplars explore cultural perspectives and practices they inform via texts from all disciplines. Enduring Understandings and Essential Questions reveal and develop the 'story' of the culture in a curriculum planned with vertical articulation, from end to beginning. Learners own more language through the culture while securing both recognition and better insight into their own. As they do so, they can connect with others unaware or unfamiliar with language and culture.	Inter/transcultural concepts inform all disciplines. They appear at all levels in tasks for any level. Learners engage in mediation strategies to bridge, exchange and clarify language across and among the cultural perspectives and the practices and products they reveal. Key performances frame curriculum, schemes of work and units. The learner is active, independent and autonomous.
Complexity differentiates tasks, not topics, themes or texts. Learners acquire and own language not by linear and predictable memorization of functions, structures and forms but through creative, unpredictable interaction in tasks using transdisciplinary content in texts.	Understanding languages is key to understanding the world around us. *How do we understand the world and support others?* The interpretive tasks are designed from authentic community texts which range from literature, film, lyrics, and prose to informational texts, paintings and posters. All texts and topics for any level; teachers design tasks for complexity and the bits to be elicited, organized and coordinated from the piece. Varied interactions with the text produce a learner that can handle unexpected questions and mediation opportunities, where memorized forms and predictable exercises cannot.	Curriculum uses authentic, cultural community texts by or from other people: to hear, view, watch and read for Interpretive-Conception receptive tasks.

Learners take risks to apply their repertoire flexibly but not with native-like accuracy.

Expressing ourselves through languages is key to communication
How do we express ourselves and engage others?
Learners involve each other in planning, choosing, and building consensus as they ask each other questions they wrote themselves and plan out the product in the next task. Poise over perfection is key and language rewards improvisation and novelty over expected routines.

Improvisation, deciding and coming to consensus with other people are key to Interpersonal-Consensus Interactive tasks and for planning the deliverable in Presentational tasks.

Key Performance tasks are designed for transfer to novel contexts, situations or audiences.
Tasks solve problems and create products relevant to college, community, work and world.

Literature fires imagination and inspires creativity.
How do we create and share with others?
Curricula inclusive of literary works across many genres move and deepen connections across cultures for both the Interpretive and Presentational tasks.
Our design framework focuses on creating products and deliverables relevant to all fields and purposes. Learners take inspiration from literary and informational texts and produce novel works to be shared with others as evidence of transfer, just as people across time have shared with them.

Learners use language to appraise, evaluate, critique and create culture, language and content. Presentational-Creation productive tasks focus on key deliverables that have value beyond the classroom, novel tasks for transfer.
Pupils solve problems and create products of value for other people.

Put It to Practice: Collaborate to Articulate

As you examined the SoWMs and the design framework principles in the above table, which details within the Statements do you want to explore next and with more depth within this framework? In your educational context, which design principles or statements are more of a challenge to you as a second language teacher or learner? Can you give any examples from your classroom demonstrating any of the features? If you follow a different curriculum framework or requirements, are any of these statements of design principles similar to yours?

From Other People, with Other People, for Other People

The AATT exemplars you will see and then design show a series of tasks in three modes of communication (Adair-Hauck et al., 2006; Glisan et al., 2003). These are intentionally designed across different articulation levels of engagement. Learners obtain information from texts, anything they can listen to, watch, receive or read, authored *by someone* or from people of that culture. Then, they share and discuss *with someone* or with others. Finally, they create an oral or written work *for someone* else or intended for a group. These deliverables demonstrate how learners can be inventive and enterprising when creating a deliverable and consider someone else's needs while doing so (Eddy, 2022b). These novel tasks facilitate *transfer*, evidence that we can solve problems and create new products within unfamiliar, unrehearsed or unanticipated situations with a different audience or recipient in mind, but with few to no teacher supports (McTighe, 2014; McTighe & Wiggins, 2004; Perkins & Salomon, 1988, 1992, 2012; Wiggins & McTighe, 2005, 2007, 2011). Transfer tasks prove learners can not only manage novelty and the unexpected that will inevitably occur in authentic situations but can create a product for that new situation, however small. Transfer is essential to show that we have learned as opposed to just manipulating duplicate or repeated items from the unit for an audience that is the same.

Transfer tasks prepare learners for *transcultural communicative competence*, to move within, across and among cultures and to handle flux and change that comes with inevitable surprises, welcome or not, big or small (Corbett, 2003). When you display novelty in task design and inquiry rather than using exercises with one correct and already-presumed answer, your pupils will follow suit and be more open to navigating small to considerable challenges creatively, precisely what is espoused in the Four Purposes, Principles of Progression and SoWM. Transfer does not occur by chance but through intentional risk-taking with languages within the cultures they are spoken or by design of tasks that simulate that unpredictability to address a new situation, need or audience. It certainly does not happen with contrived or anticipated item types from memory that do not resemble the requirements of an authentic exchange beyond school (Eddy, 2022b). Rather than promising false expectations of predictability in class, we need tasks that assess language agility so that meaning exchange and mediation can happen outside of class with what language we have. Dependable, reliable novelty in tasks now is an honest, forward-thinking means to our curriculum and assessment design goal.

Transfer tasks lead our learners to *mediation,* another fundamental tenet in the CfW. Mediation strategies facilitate meaning for others who may not understand the language and culture. Learners engage in mediation strategies to bridge, exchange, compare, reconstruct, collaborate, and clarify language between, across, within and among inter/transcultural perspectives with the practices and products they reveal. North and Piccardo (2016) explain that '[m]ediation involves the use of language in creating the space and conditions for communication and/or learning, in constructing and co-constructing new meaning, and/or in facilitating understanding by simplifying, elaborating, illustrating or otherwise adapting the original' (p. 87). Task-specific strategies are noted in *Mediation for Transfer* with each AATT. To clarify further, one can see how these align with Enduring Understandings and Essential Questions (EUs and EQs) for two popular transcultural themes for transcultural Mediation for Transfer (see Appendix A). Language learners use these strategies to help others who are unaccustomed to the culture or unfamiliar with the language, making language accessible and perspectives visible. They identify task elements and skills derived from them that extend and create meaning for someone else or between people.

We enable transfer for unanticipated opportunities that will always arise. We all have stories of creative linguistic or cultural mediation when we helped someone in another language or clarified an essential cultural point. I helped a family of tourists on the subway platform by pointing on the map and counting the number of stops on the train in Chinese to get to a New York City attraction. I admit I can only say numbers from one to ten, hello, thank you, I like, I don't like, very good, let's go and goodbye in Chinese. That is all! However, I could mediate, bridge meaning and clarify for someone else with what little Chinese I have. Share these stories with your pupils and show them that they need not be perfect to do so. Transfer tasks for mediation allow them to do more differently with the language they own. Language thrives on novelty and favours partial control of it over a predictable and complete script, no matter how flawless it is.

Mediation strategies facilitate transfer within and outside the classroom because of the value added, such as revision, reconstruction and creation of new meaning. It is not enough for pupils to have contact with authentic materials and texts and then remember events, images, sentences and vocabulary lists for verbatim recall. These all need transfer for reconstructing and revising flexibly and anew. Novel transfer tasks mirror the unfamiliar and unpredictable they will face daily, hopefully in their many travels within, across and among cultures. They provide complexity and variation not found in past practices such as fill-ins, word lists, conjugations or memorized dialogues using reflexive verbs, which no one will ask them for. Mediation for transfer conveys and facilitates another person's needs. They provide tools to make the language situation, concept or product manageable for someone else. Language engagement and practice which supports it is about access, a communication asset. We want our learners to become facile at facing and solving problems in unpredictable and dynamic transcultural spaces. Your learners can do this even at a beginner level with the language they own right now, partial language, even if it is creating a simple infographic, using images, phrases or gestures. Mediation for Transfer in this design helps learners develop empathy, tolerance of ambiguity, flexibility, improvisation and learner autonomy (Lamb, 2017; Little, 2003; Little, 2009a/b), all critical precepts in the CfW and essential for any curriculum designed for inter/transcultural communicative competence.

I Do, We Do, You Do: The Festival

When I visited the delegates in June, I modelled Gradual Release of Responsibility (Pearson & Gallagher, 1983), often described as 'I do, we do, you do'. I showed them a variety of AATT exemplars representing different languages and schools, explaining the components in the template and how these teachers designed their tasks. One of the AATTs unpacked the perspective of inside-outside spaces, *Uchi-Soto*, asking learners to create materials about Japanese inns for the Japan Day festival in Central Park, New York City (Kuo-Flynn, 2022) (see Figure 2.2). The teachers asked compelling questions about the designer's work and thought process behind this AATT. They asked about vertical articulation, the context in which everyone contributes to the Japan Day festival and the progression of deliverables at each level. They also noted that as a result of the task deliverable, how

ARTICULATED ASSESSMENT TRANSFER TASK (AATT)

INSIDE-OUTSIDE SPACES
SHIYO KUO-FLYNN

ENDURING UNDERSTANDINGS
Cultural perspectives and practices of inside-outside distinction influence the way we live.

ARTICULATION SPIRAL POINTS
Describe concept with visual supports.
Offer practical information for different needs.
Justify opinions on inside-outside space.

ESSENTIAL QUESTIONS
What does inside-outside distinction in our home space tell us about our lifestyle?
To what extent does our personal space change from one culture to another?

INTERCULTURAL TRANSFER TARGETS
I can recognize features of Japanese living spaces.
I can organize descriptions of a Japanese inn.
I can share characteristics of Japanese practices.
I can compare Japanese living spaces with those of my own culture.

CONTEXT
For this year's Japan Day at Central Park, you have been asked to volunteer at the tourism booth for educating visitors about the customs of a Japanese-style inn.

MEDIATION FOR TRANSFER
Bridge and exchange ideas and concepts of inside outside spaces.
Identify visuals, objects, and examples.
Explain features of Japanese spaces.
Compare and contrast characteristics of Japanese and Western living space.

	INTERPRETIVE TASK	**INTERPERSONAL TASK**	**PRESENTATIONAL TASK**
PERFORMANCE TARGET LEVEL	Novice High	Intermediate Mid	Advanced Low
AUTHENTIC MATERIAL DESCRIPTIONS	Webpage of Japanese inn	Inn and Hotel Finder	Article on Japanese and Western Style Inns
Task	Students watch a video on a Japanese-style inn, identify objects and form three questions about the video.	Students visit a Japanese-style inn reservation website to select three different inns from different parts of Japan. Students pose three questions and write a brief description for each inn if they selected.	Students read the online article on Japanese-style inn vs. Western-style hotel and summarize their findings by comparing and contrasting the two different types of hotel accommodation.
I CAN	I can identify and recognize the objects used inside a Japanese-style inn.	I can organize the descriptions given for each Japanese-style inn. I can write a description of each inn.	I can summarize differences and details between the Japanese-style inn and Western-style hotel and their significance.
Task	Students select one item that attracted their attention the most from the video and describe it for their peers.	Students select one inn from the website, share it with their peer and ask and answer their questions about the inns. They can discuss which inn seems more attractive to tourists with different needs.	Students exchange their summaries, decide, and agree on which summaries to include in the presentation for the tourism booth.
I CAN	I can share and talk about the item that I liked with my peer after watching a video.	I can exchange information, ask questions and discuss about the Japanese-style inn with my peers.	I can read and provide my peers with feedback for the summary related to the different types of hotel accommodation in Japan.
Task	Students design an infographic of what is inside a Japanese-style inn.	Students create a brochure that introduces the Japanese-style inn they selected for different groups of tourists.	Students prepare a video and to show at the tourism booth on Japanese-style inn vs. Western-style hotel and present advantages and disadvantages of each type of hotel accommodation.
I CAN	I can list the features and details of the inn.	I can present information related to the Japanese-style inn and explain to others in the class.	I can express opinions on hotel accommodations in Japan and support my opinions using authentic resources.

FIGURE 2.2 *AATT Inside-Outside Spaces. Eddy, J. (2022b). Designing World Language Curriculum for Intercultural Communicative Competence, reprinted with permission from Bloomsbury Academic, an imprint of Bloomsbury Publishing, Plc.*

learners could mediate and help someone else identify the physical features of the inn, explain the practice of inside-outside spaces and clarify the concept behind it (COE, 2020; National Standards Collaborative Board, 2015).

Next, before starting off to design their own, we created an AATT together as a whole group. The teachers told me about a festival, *Llangollen International Musical Eisteddfod*, the seventy-fifth anniversary in July 2022, after a two-year hiatus. The festival has competitors representing 140 countries and regions in music, dance and culture. In many language classes, even with substantial efforts to integrate culture (NCSSFL, 2017; National Standards Collaborative Board, 2015), festivals typically are treated as extras, a bit of culture when there is time and a surface treatment of facts: cultural practices and products; respectively, *what people do* and *what people make*. Our group dove deeper to explain why you could not leave their curriculum without understanding their concept of festival. We examined the transcultural perspectives behind the festival: *what people think*. To identify these intercultural transferable goals, EUs and EQs (McTighe & Wiggins, 2004; Wiggins & McTighe, 2005) are developed through the lens of cultural perspectives, cultural history and transdisciplinary content. It is important to refocus the line of inquiry from facts and very local cultural practices to perspectives that are present across disciplines and recursive throughout the lifespan. What we unpacked was quintessentially Welsh, but also one in which any culture could relate, enabling learners to reflect upon their own cultural histories and festivals.

Enduring Understandings

- ∞ Festivals celebrate cultural identities as a communal event.
- ∞ Festivals bring us together often after difficult times such as war, unrest or illness.
- ∞ Religious festivals gather families together to celebrate identity.

Essential Questions

Q What is festival? Why do we celebrate identity in a public way?

For the ICANADAPT unit design, there are three stages (see chapter 2 on the companion website). It is important to position the AATT for proper context. Teachers develop the AATT first, because it is the blueprint for the big idea themes and their vertical articulation with the summative assessments at different levels, thus it serves as the curriculum framer. EUs and EQs (McTighe & Wiggins, 2004; Wiggins & McTighe, 2005) develop our spiral curriculum with inter/transcultural perspectives. Your EUs and EQs drive *Stage One*, placing inter/transcultural competence in the drivers' seat of articulated programme design. *Stage Two* is the assessment system for that one unit. The AATT is a summative assessment system articulated for transferring of concepts and creating of products across any levels you will designate. There is one overarching *Context,* a scenario, need or situation to which all levels contribute. The Context presents a problem to solve and new products for a given audience, preferably one within the greater community or world outside school.

Context: The organizers of the International Festival want more people to come and participate.
Let's promote this year's 75th anniversary!

From there, the group developed the assessments to complete their AATTs (see Table 2.2). The AATTs present an articulated progression of three tasks for receptive, interactive and productive modalities or Interpretive, Interpersonal and Presentational (Glisan et al., 2003; National Standards Collaborative Board, 2015). These are integrated performance assessments (IPAs) (Adair-Hauck et al., 2006; NCSSFL, 2017) rather than four skills presented in unrelated, isolated exercises. The AATT (Eddy, 2006a/b; 2007a/b/c/d/e/f; 2009a/b; 2015; 2019a/b; 2022b; Eddy & Bustamante, 2020) extends and expands these features as intentional design across at least three selected levels of learner engagement and transfer for curricula and schemes of work, as either key summative or formative assessments. The AATT exemplars have been designed at more than six levels for full vertical articulated curriculum design. AATTs are intended to be implemented at the same time by multiple levels of pupils studying a given language so that they can enact the project in a cohort model, all together. This protocol enables quite a bit of camaraderie between pupils as they all know they are working on this together and contributing purposeful products, just according to their level with the language they own. Alternatively, they can be used for differentiation when multi-levels exist within one classroom. For the AATT template with fillable fields, please see Chapter 2 on the companion website.

As you can see in the above example, the variety of tasks across three levels of progression solves the problem presented in the context and creates deliverables. They are all transfer tasks and require a novel product of value beyond the classroom, ones that are relevant and applicable to different audiences. Pupils do the tasks applied to and aligned with the remaining three SoWMs. The AATT presents the tasks under one common context or

TABLE 2.2 Articulated Assessment Transfer Task – International *Eisteddfod*

Enduring Understandings ✴ Festivals celebrate cultural identities as a communal event. ✴ Festivals bring us together often after difficult times such as war, unrest or illness. ✴ Religious festivals gather families together to celebrate identity.
Essential Questions ? What is festival? ? Why do we celebrate identity in a public way?
Context The organizers of the International Festival want more people to come and participate. Let's promote this year's seventy-fifth anniversary!
Articulation Spiral Points @ Identify key components of the festival. @ Explain festival categories and instructions. @ Synthesize festival trends then and now.

Intercultural Transfer Targets	Mediation for Transfer
• I can identify clothing, colours and identity markers of participants. • I can ask and answer questions on festival choices of international participants. • I can explain and compare festival practices within my own or other cultures.	• Bridge and exchange ideas and concepts of identity and national expression. • Indicate colours, clothing, and music genres to a newcomer • Explain examples of performing arts to someone unfamiliar with the culture. • Clarify details of the festival using multimedia.

Beginner	Intermediate	Advanced
Interpretive Task Descriptions **How do we understand the world around us and support others?**		
Watch the video and read about the festival costumes, colours and cultural identities. Categorize the components of the festival.	Watch a video about the festival including food, hairstyles, clothing, arts, songs and poetry. Index the festival categories on a schedule.	Read past programs of the festival and how they have changed. Compare with festivals from other countries. Who would want to go?
I can		
I can organize elements of the festival on the chart.	I can list the different categories of the festival from a schedule.	I can summarize past events and changing trends from our festival and those of other countries.

Interpersonal Task Descriptions		
How do we express ourselves and engage others?		
In a conversation with a partner, ask questions and compare costumes, colours and clothing.	Talk with a partner and give your opinion on the food, clothing and arts.	Come to a consensus with a partner on the best features of the festival, why people attend and how traditions are maintained or have changed.
I can		
I can ask and answer questions about clothing choices of the international participants.	I can discuss my choices of festival sections and explain which category I like best and why.	I can review and distinguish the differences between past and current festivals.
Presentational Task Descriptions		
How do we create and share with others?		
1) Describe the clothing representing your identity: A modern Welsh costume for 2022. 2) Prepare a brochure about this for the festival. 3) Design the order of the parade.	1) Create a video on padlet or flipgrid on the dances and poetry. 2) Prepare guides for competitors. 3) Create your own competition category and outline the instructions for entry	1) Create a promotional video about the festival. 2) Write a story about a festival you attended or from a child's perspective. 3) Describe past performers and their experience. 4) Write a letter to the chief executive of the festival with recommendations for next year.
I can		
I can make a brochure featuring the costumes with the national identity. I can design a costume, list the colours, label the clothing and explain my choices. I can devise a schedule and put events in order.	I can produce and present multimedia content on dance and poetry competitions. I can write guides for the competition in simple sentences. I can create a category with entry instructions.	I can describe my experiences with festivals from my own and others' perspectives. I can write my opinions and recommendations on planning future events. I can compose video content for marketing and promotion.

scenario, indicating an external audience who can receive the deliverables of products, in this case, organizers of the International Festival.

1 Interpretive: How do we understand the world around us and support others?
2 Interpersonal: How do we express ourselves and engage others?
3 Presentational: How do we create and share with others?

The interpretive or receptive tasks always feature culturally authentic, community texts with intentional tasks that allow the learner to acquire and gather information from them. The texts can be anything we listen to, watch, view or read. The interpersonal or interactive task is an improvised, unscripted exchange with someone else to choose, decide and come to a consensus on information from the previous task and to plan the deliverable. Finally, the presentational, creative or productive task is the *far transfer* task, one that requires learners to use what they learned in a new way with very few to no cues or supports, to create a novel product (McTighe, 2014; McTighe & Wiggins, 2004; Wiggins & McTighe, 2005, 2007) with an audience in mind for value beyond the classroom. Each task within the AATT will be explored more deeply in the following chapters with our designers' exemplars. In Table 2.3, we see stages of language assessment transfer, with our Stage Two summative assessments at the end of far transfer. Practice with forms and structures may produce the appearance of language knowledge and have their place. However, it cannot replace or be considered adequate for meaningful interaction, novel and flexible application and cultural value. Transfer tasks rely on progressively less teacher support along a range from None, Nigh and Nearby, *Near Transfer* to entire novel Far Transfer. With transfer tasks, learners recognize similarities, predict and choose thoughtfully and respond to changeable, unpredictable demands of authentic language use when solving a problem or creating a product. These are valuable skills that grammar forms, lists and memorization cannot provide. Those give the appearance of understanding but not the reality of transfer (Eddy, 2010b, 2014a, 2016c/d, 2022b).

Transfer tasks are a better investment of time and the key to uptake and interest for pupils because they see the value of language learning as applicable to life and work; the products they create reside beyond school. Language and the transcultural competence that carries them prove far more relevant than classroom academic exercises could possibly offer. The transfer tasks also value pupil ownership of the language thus far, further convincing them that language proficiency is not only attainable but also belongs to them by virtue of the product they created, not aloof or at a distance within a textbook or residing with a teacher or expert heritage speaker.

TABLE 2.3 Stages of Language Assessment Transfer with examples

None	Nigh and Nearby	Near Transfer	Far Transfer
Drill/Decontextualized content	Familiar Task with Supports	Unfamiliar Task with Supports	Completely New Task No supports
Recall, Drill, substitution of forms. No transfer required or assessed.	Similar content and situations. Details from previous teaching examples or texts. Replication with little variation. Posing questions and indexing signals a shift to mediation transfer evidence.	Unfamiliar content and situations. Cues suggested or required approach, process, or content knowledge. Solves problems and creates products.	Unfamiliar and Novel Presented without cues. Learners use a repertoire of knowledge with new texts, novel contexts or situations. Solves problems and creates products.
Fill-in-the-blank clothing, colours, food vocabulary Dictation Verb conjugation	Ask and answer questions on festival choices of international participants. List festival categories.	Create your own competition category from the template provided. Must include listed elements.	Create a promotional video about the festival. Write a story about a festival from a child's point of view.

Adapted from Eddy, J. (2022b). *Designing World Language Curriculum for Intercultural Communicative Competence*, with permission from Bloomsbury Academic, an imprint of Bloomsbury Publishing, Plc.

After we design the tasks, we refer back to the Intercultural Transfer Goals to make sure these are present in the tasks. To operationalize it for pupils, we develop *Intercultural Transfer Targets*. These focus on perspectives, practices, transdisciplinary connections and community engagement, and are designed for utility beyond the classroom. The NCSSFL-ACTFL can-do statements (NCSSFL, 2017), inspired by the European Language Portfolio (Little, 2003, 2009a, 2011, 2012; Little & Perclová, 2001; North, 1992, 2000), provide general target-level descriptors. The CEFR Companion Volume (2020) has descriptors for mediation, building relationships and collaboration. The AATT adapts and extends these to specific areas from the tasks to address the EUs and

EQs. Transfer depends upon providing tangible evidence of the intercultural transferable goals, the perspectives that connect otherwise isolated facts, skills and experiences. We must co-create these culture-based deliverables with learners so they can experience the inter/transcultural in yet another way. The transfer tasks you will see, particularly in the presentational-creation mode, become *Articulated Spiral Points* for that concept across the levels, touchstones, if you will, within the entire curricular anthology. The collection of these milestones of evidence comprises the *Catalogue of Deliverables* by the end of your programme, which is the set of products or performances representing the transfer evidence within the programme. They are product types we see in our world or deliverables expected and created by us for audiences besides the teacher and classmates. With these tasks, pupils can demonstrate a sharper understanding of a transcultural concept by unpacking it within the context of something else or for someone else (Eddy, 2007e, 2015a, 2017, 2022b).

Put It to Practice: Collaborate to Articulate

Now that you have seen the delegates' first AATT design, let's collaborate with colleagues for additional ideas and questions to guide your design work. The Bridge to Design below is the first in this book to bring you closer to the design thinking of this group of teachers. Each AATT in this book will have an accompanying Bridge to Design with questions and ideas to consider specific to the tasks.

 *Bridge to Design*

Reflect to Reveal

1) How do the tasks help the learner to mediate for others who may be unfamiliar with the festival?

2) To what extent do you see the progression for learners? The SoWM?

3) What evidence do the Articulation Spiral Points show the teacher and the learner?

Questions for Colleagues

1) How do these tasks help to move away from a superficial treatment of one festival?

2) To what extent does this exemplar make learners feel invested and productive, even with limited language?

3) What is the most distinctive feature of the spiral points and the tasks? How do you think our delegates responded to this process? What questions do you have at this point?

Ask the Designers

1) What is one question you could ask this delegate team? What else do you want to know about this exemplar and their thinking process?

Participate in the Practice

How would you design this exemplar as it pertains to your own and the culture(s) you teach? Is this treatment the same or different from your lessons on festivals?

Adapted from Eddy, J. (2022b) *Designing World Language Curriculum for Intercultural Communicative Competence*, with permission from Bloomsbury Academic, an imprint of Bloomsbury Publishing, Plc.

From AATT to ICANADAPT Unit: Where Formative Tasks Come

Once these teachers understood the type of products and their relevance beyond the classroom, they brainstormed many ideas for the Presentational tasks and settled on several to select and choose from. Typically, when the AATT is the summative assessment, we see one or two tasks each for Interpretive, Interpersonal and Presentational. When designing AATTs with teachers, less is not more; more is more! A variety is encouraged, and they can be toggled, used to differentiate or become formative tasks depending on pupils' needs.

While we are on the subject: Formative tasks. Although learners do these first as they start and progress within a unit, teachers design them last in Stage Three (McTighe & Wiggins, 2005). After you have designed Stage Two, the final summative assessment tasks for the unit (the AATT), work backward from there for your unit and design this series of lesson-level tasks: the formative assessments for Stage Three. These have more cues and supports, so they are near transfer, as we saw in Table 2.3. They still retain the value and input of cultural perspectives to build these concepts and transfer for mediation with others' needs in mind. These tasks follow the same three-phase cycle as assessments for learning and as learning (Dann, 2014; Earl, 2003; Hattie, 2012). It is important to reiterate that teachers design the AATT Stage Two summative assessment progression first. The teacher now has the cycle of tasks at each level panel in the AATT. Next, select one to flush out thoroughly for the ICANADAPT unit. With this summative trio of tasks in place, work backward from there on formative assessments to get pupils to that outcome, that final summative assessment. Stage Three is also where you develop focus questions that can appear on the board, finite and answerable by the end of the period. Teachers reach for these first because they are more common than EQs, but they function quite differently for our curriculum design.

Although quite the opposite of traditional curriculum planning, one must design Stage Three assessments last. It is important to note that these formative tasks are not drills or are devoid of culture, but they do sustain and build transcultural communicative competence concurrently with tasks. This shift is essential because many teachers may associate these tasks with forms, vocabulary exercises and mechanical practice. Steph was indispensable in reviewing this with our group when completing their ICANADAPT units, featuring one level panel of the AATT into a unit with formative tasks (see companion website for units). It was an important lesson learned for me as well, to devote more time to Stage Three, even though this is the place where instructional design typically starts and is more familiar to teachers. These teachers did so well with the AATTs, investing a lot of time, care and intention with excellent implementation and presentation to peers. In the future, I will secure additional time to review the components of Stage Three, making sure the intercultural elements and perspectives are present throughout with knowledge and skills required for the tasks. They also must be all along the continuum of near transfer to make the summative far transfer task attainable. I am thankful to Steph for working with her teachers to complete this work and for conveying her clear understanding of this framework within their diverse educational contexts.

From the Admin Desk

What is Stage Three? A series of tasks which follow the same pattern as the AATT (three modes towards a product) but which will help the learner transition and build her or his knowledge and skills through the concept of the overarching 'theme' of the AATT/module, such as in the ICANADAPT units on education in Chinese culture (Xie, 2022); mealtimes and nutrition in French schools/canteens, and Child Labour in Mexico (Durand, 2022) and Chuseok/Thanksgiving festival in Korea (Lee, 2022).

- The AATT is the assessment of learning at the END of the unit. However, it is planned first.
- Stage Three is the series of lesson tasks that will take place before the AATT (over the course of the module or unit) to help learners develop their knowledge and apply their skills in an increasingly flexible and novel way.

Each Formative Task at Stage Three Will

- Include tasks in all three modes: interpretive, interpersonal and presentational.
- Use culturally authentic community texts and materials.
- Focus on one aspect of the overarching concept: cultural as well as linguistic knowledge will be developed here.
- Encourage learners to discuss and form opinions.
- Prompt learners to produce a response or product to respond to a new situation: ensure the intercultural competence is addressed as well as the linguistic competence.
- Provide near transfer tasks (element of novelty – beyond drilling or modelling) with supports and scaffolds – add an element of mediation and/or a specific audience.
- List briefly the vocabulary and grammar needed for this task and unit and categorize them by when they are introduced in

instruction: *Review* from the same year, *Spiral* from previous years and finally *New*, language from or for this specific unit and introduced for the first time.

These formative tasks culminate with the final AATT:

Summative assessment: Three novel tasks with an audience beyond the classroom: authentic or fictitious. Learners will use the knowledge and skills developed in the different assessment for learning (AfL) tasks at Stage Three to achieve the AATT successfully. In Table 2.4, Steph details Stage Three: What it is and what it is not for additional clarification.

There are many great examples from Jenny's work. In *Chuseok: Korean Thanksgiving* (Lee, 2022). The Context is, 'Middle or high school students will volunteer for the Chuseok Festival in New Jersey and assist in preparing for the festival with the staff. For the participants in the festival, the students will introduce various activities related to Chuseok to the participants and help them experience it.'

In this example the AATT aims to get festival attendees to learn and experience rites, food, games and traditional clothing of Chuseok. Students will create a presentation to promote the Chuseok festival.

For this, students will need to understand the different ways the Chuseok festival is celebrated, compare them to the United States or other known

TABLE 2.4 Stage Three: What it is and What it is not

Stage Three: What it is	Stage Three: What it is not
Several **formative near transfer** cycles of interpretive, interpersonal and presentational tasks. Each AfL task at Stage three **results in a product** or response with intercultural competence in mind. Each AfL task at Stage three **prepares learners to develop** different aspects of the overarching concepts and essential questions to which the AATT responds. With that in mind, each AfL uses authentic community texts to introduce the cultural aspect and get learners to **interact with intercultural** content. Each AfL task at Stage Three will **develop the skills** which will enable students to be increasingly creative and autonomous and be successful at the AATT, the summative assessment at the end of the unit.	Not the AATT Not the lesson plans Not the language acquisition drills and focused tasks. This still has its place at lesson level and in lesson plans, of course, but is not included in this document

Thanksgiving festivals and make choices of favourite or most relevant and essential activities to present.

In order to do this, through Stage Three, pupils will learn about:

- Traditional Food eaten during the festival.
- Traditional games such as Yutnori.
- Other games played during the festival.
- Extended family and ways to address each other/etiquette.
- Different ways to celebrate the festival and compare it with US Thanksgiving.

Each of these points above is an AfL task at Stage Three. Each task has an authentic material and three modes. Each task has an end product.

- Create a shopping list using the recipe that they want to use.
- Create an infographic about Yutnori rules and its origins, comparing it to a board game in the United States or their own country.
- Write descriptions with images of the game they studied in the expert group to make a group infographic.
- Create a fantasy family tree and write introductions of family members that include personal information such as name, age, birthday, place of residence, job, etc.
- Use a graphic organizer to compare and contrast Chuseok and Thanksgiving or a similar/ harvest festival of their own culture.

This will then lead to the actual AATT where students in each group will create a video or PowerPoint presentation to promote the Chuseok festival related to their booths: with the audience and intercultural transfer in mind.

In another example, Child Labour (Durand, 2022, p. 152), the Context is: 'The Pan American Development Foundation is providing a campaign to get informed about child labour. The campaign needs materials to create awareness and promote prevention of child labour that affects millions of children.' In this example the AATT aims to create awareness and promote prevention of child labour. Students will create a song video presentation that have the list of jobs, causes and effect of child labour as a way to create awareness and promote prevention of child labour. The students sing the song and share the video with the school and consider sending to an organization called 'Iniciativa: La musica contra el trabajo infantil' which promote awareness about child labour. For this, students will need to understand the causes and impact of child labour and how to prevent it.

In order to do this, through Stage Three, pupils will learn about

- Child labour jobs and conditions due to poverty.
- Reasons for child labour and rights of children in Mexico and United States.
- Prevention and enforcement of child labour.

Each of these points above is an AfL task at Stage Three. Each task has an authentic material and three modes. Each task has an end product.

- Create a brochure about the effects of child labour on children.
- Present a Venn diagram to compare and contrast the rights of children in Mexico and the United States.
- Create a video to promote child labour prevention measures.

This will then lead to the actual AATT where students will create a song video presentation that have the list of jobs, causes and effect of child labour as a way to create awareness and promote prevention of child labour.

Re-evaluating Our Practices and with AATT and ICANADAPT Design: Getting Started

The four statements that express what matters in this Area should be addressed holistically. They are interdependent, with each one supporting the development of the other three. Each statement recognizes that developing skills and knowledge in one language can support learning in all subsequent languages. Learning in 'Languages connect us' is common to all learners in all schools in Wales and applies to all languages. It also highlights how learning languages enhances appreciation of the many ways in which multiculturalism connects languages for cultural identity. Learning within this statement permeates the learning in the other three statements. Learning within the other three SoWMs are presented to reflect the pace and depth in different language learning contexts with differentiated descriptions of learning. There is no prescribed topic or text content: the key concepts of the LLC highlight what matters: language knowledge and skills developments, intercultural understanding and perspectives developments and linguistic creativity and sensitivity.

Teachers have the freedom and the responsibility to design the curriculum they feel fit to provide more purposeful, relevant, effective and exciting experiences through effective and innovative pedagogical approaches which will enable learners to fully enjoy their language learning journey in school and beyond. This freedom and responsibility are not new to teachers. However, the statements are much broader and teachers felt a little lost as to what we were supposed to 'cover' and teach. The key concepts of the statements needed to be examined very carefully to avoid the pitfalls of thinking it was the same as before but worded differently. Unpacking the key concepts and planning everything with these in mind is essential. Making sense and returning to them is what teachers will need to do for many years to ensure their curriculum responds to the vision and aims of CfW. In order to do so, it is key to give time to teachers to collaborate, experiment, review and refine the pedagogical approaches which will best suit their school, their learners, their style and which will contribute to learners realizing the four purposes of the curriculum.

In fact, the AATT/ICANADAPT framework, just like CfW, encourages us to re-evaluate our practice and ensure we constantly address the well-known essential and universal questions which are rooted in excellent teaching and learning and which lead to offering a curriculum which is purposeful, flexible and tailored to the needs of all our learners.

- Is the end game defined?
- Is knowledge building upon prior knowledge?
- Is learning linked and connected to experiences and authentic contexts?
- Does it capitalize upon the cultural capital of the learners?
- Do we build on prior learning and ensure learning is deep and secure? Less is more.
- Do practitioners and students see how their learning experiences relate to the bigger picture?
- Is the pedagogy based on evidence-based learning techniques and is it innovative enough?
- What is our responsibility as professionals?

In order to support this, as an administrator, my role is to open, facilitate and encourage professional conversations. It is not our role to suggest or impose any particular approach or to endorse or provide teachers with fully fledged and tested designs. However, I can support and guide them into developing their practice, trial models and use shared emerging practices. What is vital at this stage of our journey is to share processes rather than end products. By sharing processes, rationales and contexts behind any kind of planning, colleagues can develop their own practice further.

One of the first steps was to unpack what all of this meant for our subject within the area of learning in June 2022. Still at a high level, presentations to middle leaders were given to examine the elements and what it may mean in the classroom. A range of work done over the preceding months were shared and explained. Following this, I invited schools to engage in different projects to explore their interpretation of the framework further. The AATT process was one of them.

—Stephanie Ellis-Williams, International Languages and Global Futures GwE Lead

Any Topic, Any Level: Everyone Participates

Let us visit the other end of the spectrum, from the popular theme of festivals to the uncommon treatment of politics and leadership. Rarely seen because it is judged too complicated, Ms Ellis-Williams made a case for us earlier and cited complex AATT topics, reminding us that all topics should appear on the spiral and not be hidden until a higher level (Bower et al., 2020; Bruner, 1996; Coyle, 2007; Coyle et al., 2021). We are not expecting paragraph-length discourse yet but one can begin exploring politics, leadership and governance in order to build a vocabulary and conceptual base right at the start. There is a way to unfold concepts of leadership at the earlier levels, and Ms Ellis-Williams does just that. International *Eisteddfod* was the first AATT vision for this group and they explored festivals more deeply. *Liberté, égalité, fraternité* (See Table 2.5) is also an envisioned AATT that is now made more palatable and feasible for pupils with its portrayal of a leader, something all children should understand while discovering qualities of leadership across cultures. As pupils move forward in this articulated progression, they can reflect on the political systems they know and what participation looks like in a transnational dimension. Implementing this AATT will bring forth valuable feedback from pupils who should enjoy the inclusivity of these tasks. To that end, Ms Ellis-Williams designed high-quality transfer tasks by varying the audience for the deliverables, again making the case that participation in the process and leadership potential should be understood by everyone at any age.

Teacher as Designer – Liberté, égalité, fraternité

What you make the first time may not be the AATT but it is work in progress. This is a shift in mindset which is key to innovation, creative design and planning and which frees the practitioner from the self-imposed rule that every planning must be perfect from day one. Practitioners must embrace and accept that their AATT and planning will not be perfect from the start. Similarly, it is important they apply this to their pupils' attainment by not expecting perfection. In fact, Shirley Clarke reminds us that evidence shows that error and struggle, if addressed negatively, are a major barrier to self-efficacy (Clarke, 2023). She refers to John Hattie's conclusion that errors are to be celebrated and used as an opportunity to learn (Hattie, 2012).

Therefore, it is key for practitioners to keep improving the AATT as they deliver it. This, in turn, will develop progression and development in planning and pedagogy. Finally, it is good modelling for pupils in terms of a growth mindset to embrace challenges, persevere when facing setbacks and value effort to reach even higher levels of understanding and achievement.

—Stephanie Ellis-Williams, International Languages and Global Futures GwE Lead

Voices from the Field

For me, the AATT is also about giving the curriculum the flexibility which is sometimes difficult to achieve when schemes of learning are finalized. Being able to address some of the most current and pressing societal issues is essential to provide content which is not only interesting but relevant and vital to understanding the world around us. Our learners must be given the opportunity to delve deeper into what they hear in the news, ask questions to clarify difficult concepts or historical background, discuss with others, reflect, use their critical thinking and reasoning to develop their own opinions and positions.

In languages, we often just remain at the surface of cultural elements and are content with a straightforward transmission of the knowledge. The AATT process rightly encourages us to dig much deeper and to be much more ambitious for our learners and for ourselves, as practitioners. This is very exciting and opens the doors to a world of teaching and learning which is exciting, enriching and which should appeal much more to our learners.

Since working with the AATT and the ICANADAPT principles in mind, every news headline, debate, cultural programmes or magazines has become the source of many potential AATTs, e.g., a Quebecois song about the difference in lexis between French and the Canadian French, its origins, cultural differences, meaning and emotional reactions of the listeners or the decision to induct the stateless Second World War Resistance hero Missak Manouchian in the Pantheon Mausoleum in Paris, alongside other French heroes as tribute to all foreign fighters who fought for France, etc.

When the French president, Emmanuel Macron, announced the appointment of the very young prime minister, Gabriel Attal, I felt this would be an excellent opportunity to get our students to reflect on their role as citizens of Wales and the world. Being ethical, informed citizens, confident and enterprising contributors is part of the Four Purposes of the CfW. But do we actually give our young learners the keys to become such responsible and capable adults? Is it not our duty, as educators, to ensure that all our learners, no matter what their backgrounds, feel empowered and can actually play a role in the shaping of their future, should they choose to do so?

We currently live in a world where, even in the most stable and free countries, democracy has become very vulnerable, fundamental rights and freedom of speech are in serious danger and where the rise of populism and far-right parties is worrying.

This is the 'why' this AATT is completely pertinent today and the 'why' we should teach our pupils about the political system, the privilege to live in a country where we can have a real say, where rulers are accountable for their decisions and integrity, why and how we should preserve and protect such rights. In other words, the AATT responds to the CfW mission in dealing with the cross-curricular 'big questions'. Here, this AATT focuses on the civic rights and responsibilities whilst developing the key cultural concepts, knowledge, skills and experiences of the language and language communities.

Of course, it is important for this to be age-appropriate and appealing to the learners. In creating this AATT, it was important to keep in mind how to ensure learners related easily and willingly to this potentially very serious subject matter. The presentational tasks were designed to avoid such tedious or laborious activities.

In order to ensure learners' success in their completion of the AATT, it is crucial they develop understanding and knowledge in a range of aspects, such as the French Republic and its motto of Liberty, Equality, Brotherhood (history and current system); the president of the French Republic: Emmanuel Macron, the role of the president and that of the prime minister and the government; the prime minister: Gabriel Attal, the right to vote in France; issues which are most important for young people in France; Striking in France; Other political systems around the world.

Stage Three is planned last but will be taught first. It is planned last as you need to know what the deliverables of the AATT are in order to select the most important conceptual aspects to develop beforehand. Two teachers may develop completely different AATTs from the same context. Therefore, the content of Stage Three could also differ. Or it could be that the same teacher creates another AATT to follow up on the EUs and EQs addressed.

Here, the AATT uses three different authentic materials across the levels. It can be taught across the ages or form the differentiation within the year or class, depending on the students' levels of engagement. A follow-up AATT can also be decided by the pupils who may want to explore a particular aspect of the political system or civic rights and duties.

Stage Three plans for the most relevant intercultural elements to be developed at this stage of the learning. What our teachers and I understood later was that Stage Three was not the development and learning of the language needed to complete the AATT. Once the structure was understood, Stage Three made much more sense and allowed the space and time to develop each intercultural aspect adequately with an authentic material at its core, and the three communicative modes to structure the thinking process and skills development. The language for each AfL is selected last, just like for the AATT. The methodology to ensure the language is developed and secure remains a crucial element of the lessons but is not itemized in the Stage Three document.

—Stephanie Ellis-Williams, International Languages Lead, GwE

TABLE 2.5 Articulated Assessment Transfer Task – *Liberté, égalité, fraternité* Stephanie Ellis-Williams, GwE

Enduring Understandings
✱ Democracy enables a nation to give their citizens the right to decide who should govern their country.
✱ Democracy needs to be protected.
✱ Everyone has the right and duty to be involved in political decisions.
Essential Questions
? What is democracy?
? What is the role of government?
? What is the right to vote and is it a duty?
? Can anyone become a political leader?
? Which qualities and traits make a good leader?
? What impact can the individual play and at what level?
Context
In January 2024, the French president decided to appoint a new prime minister. Gabriel Attal, at 34, is the youngest and first openly homosexual prime minister in France. A national youth web magazine is asking young people to contribute and give their views on politics, leadership and the individual's role in shaping the future of their country.
Articulation Spiral Points
@ Create a simple poster about the personal qualities of a leader.
@ Create a presentation to persuade a young audience to vote.
@ Produce a multimedia presentation to defend and promote a political programme.

Intercultural Transfer Targets	Mediation for Transfer
<ul><li>I can identify, compare and write about some of the attributes valued and required to play a part in my community.</li><li>I can understand and explain the implications and impact of the act of voting or not on different communities.</li><li>I can identify and explain reasons behind political choices in different cultures.</li></ul>	<ul><li>Bridge and exchange attributes of political figures.</li><li>Describe leadership qualities.</li><li>Explain and clarify the rights and responsibilities of the individual in the political system of a country to someone unfamiliar with them.</li><li>Exemplify and justify the values and importance of political pledges and decisions.</li></ul>

Beginner	Intermediate	Advanced
À quoi sert le Premier ministre? video	À quoi ça sert de voter ? video C'est quoi, l'abstention ? video	C'est quoi, la politique ? text only- up to 'Savoirs' C'est quoi, la gauche et la droite en politique ? video
Interpretive Task Descriptions **How do we understand the world around us and support others?**		
Premier Ministre: Pupils watch and listen to the video and complete the organigram.	Voter: Pupils watch the video and complete a worksheet with prompt words. Abstention: Pupils watch the second video and complete the comprehension questions.	Politique: Pupils read the text and complete the worksheet with the prompts to show understanding. Gauche et Droite en France: Pupils watch the video and label the Assemblée Nationale diagram with the prompts.
I Can		
I can understand and label key concepts and facts about the role of the French prime minister and government.	I can organize the main facts about the current voting system in France and the challenges it faces. I can answer questions about the importance of voting.	I can compare, contrast and relay current political practices in France and their historical origins.

Interpersonal Task Descriptions How do we express ourselves and engage others?		
What traits are important to become an effective and fair leader/governor? Pupils discuss with their peers and come to a consensus about the most important qualities for a leader. Sort out prompt cards in order of importance.	Should the vote be given to 16 year olds? Pupils debate and compare with their pairs their views and opinions on reasons to give the vote or not to younger people.	What role can we play? What important issues should be addressed Pupils discuss and agree on the list of issues which are the most pressing to address by politicians nowadays.
I Can		
I can identify and agree with my partners on the most important personal traits required to be a political leader.	I can ask and answer questions on why young people should vote. I can listen to my peers' opinions to develop mine further.	I can come to a consensus on political choices to include in a political manifesto. I can choose relevant issues to address. I can ask and answer questions on such choices.
Presentational Task Descriptions How do we create and share with others?		
Create a simple poster to highlight the qualities and skills required to become a leader or play a part in political decisions. You may want to provide different portraits for: children, teenagers, young adults and mature adults.	Produce a short presentation to explain and encourage young people (16–24 years old) to take their right to vote as a duty.	You are a candidate for the next local election. Create a short video-clip to present and defend your manifesto and convince people to vote for you. Decide on your target audience: Young people 18–24, older people, workers, unemployed people and disabled voters.
I Can		
I can explain simply what makes a great leader and show that anyone could become one.	I can explain and justify important facts about voting rights for democracy. I can persuade people to play a more active role in political decisions in future.	I can convince others of my choices. I can explain how my choices will affect their lives for the better.

Bridge to Design

Let's get closer to Ms Ellis-Williams' design process and collaborate with colleagues for additional ideas and questions to guide your design work.

Reflect to Reveal

1) What makes leadership a key concept worthy to unfold over the length of a curriculum?
2) How does the Context in this exemplar encourage investment and ownership for pupils?
3) What can this exemplar reveal about transcultural communicative competence?

Questions for Colleagues

1) How do the presentational mode tasks facilitate Mediation for Transfer?
2) Why is it important to note the deliverables created by students along the curriculum with the Articulation Spiral Points?
3) What makes a task near or far transfer in this example? How does the context of the national youth web magazine fulfil intercultural transferable goals?

Ask the Designer

What is your question for Ms Ellis-Williams? What else do you want to know about this exemplar and her design thinking?

Participate in the Practice

Which practices guided Ms Ellis-Williams in creating her exemplar? How did she design with these in mind? Explain below for each component.

1) Articulation Spiral Points, Mediation for Transfer, Intercultural Transfer Targets
2) Transfer tasks at each level for progression
3) Inclusivity for all demographics
4) Enduring Understandings and Essential Questions worthy of curriculum and beyond school

Teacher to Leader on Design and Implementation

1 Refrain from tackling every aspect of the concept at once and within one AATT: use the Stage Three to provide the additional intercultural knowledge and other AATTs to delve deeper into the enduring understanding. Less is more. Go back to the theme and reprise.

2 Do not worry if you, as a practitioner, do not know much about the concept and/or the actual cultural details. Just like teachers constantly build their subject knowledge, we can build our cultural knowledge further and become more of an expert as we go along. Teachers are not expected to know everything initially. Plus, this discovery process enables us to select the authentic materials strategically and design the tasks which will facilitate an effective and enjoyable learning journey for our pupils. This can also create opportunities to reach out to our more expert colleagues in relevant other areas of learning and develop fruitful cross-curricular collaborations.

3 It is important to be ambitious for our pupils and not be afraid to tackle important issues with them. Our role is to make these accessible for them, no matter what, from day one.

Tools to Make It Accessible for Pupils

On the first day of the unit, pupils receive a Concept Map (see Figure 2.3), both a teacher and pupil-facing tool for elements of the unit designed by the teacher and also amended and adapted by the pupil. See Figure 2.4 for the *Liberté, égalité, fraternité* Concept Map. Pupils also receive the Unit Plan Guide, presenting EUs, EQs, the Context, I can statements and Intercultural Transfer Targets. To see the pupil-facing Unit Plan Guide for *Liberté, égalité, fraternité* see Appendix C.

See the ICANADAPT unit and ancillary materials for *Liberté, égalité, fraternité* on the companion website, Chapter 2.

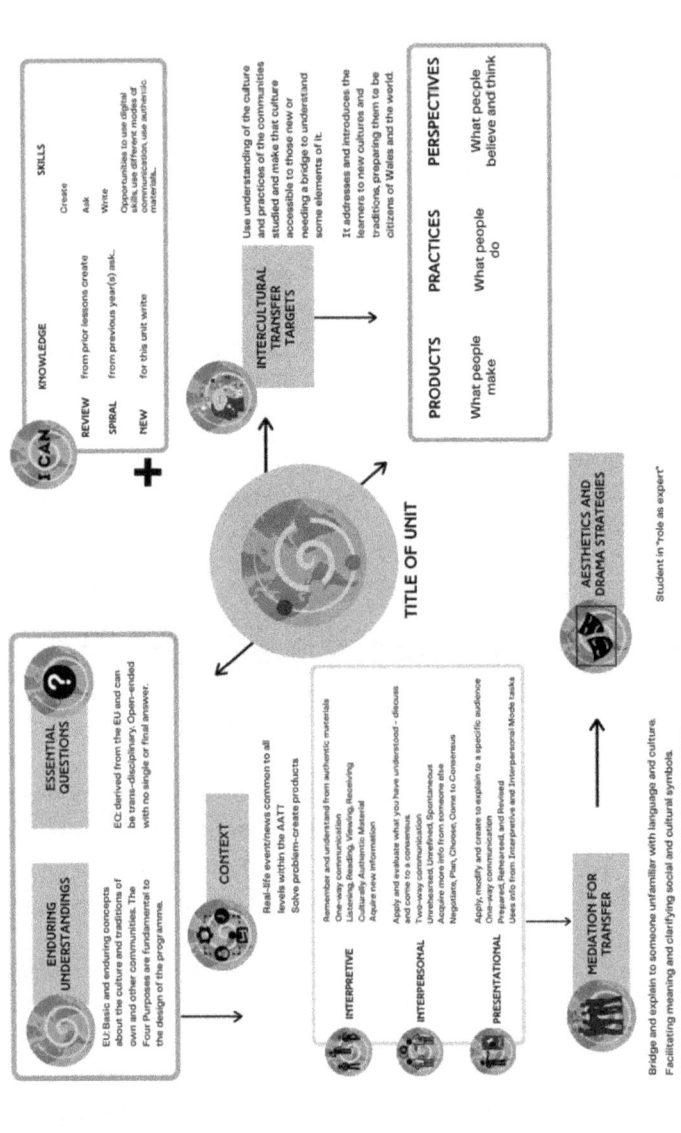

FIGURE 2.3 *Annotated Concept Map.* Adapted from Eddy, J. (2022b) Designing World Language Curriculum for Intercultural Communicative Competence, *with permission from Bloomsbury Academic, an imprint of Bloomsbury Publishing, Plc.*

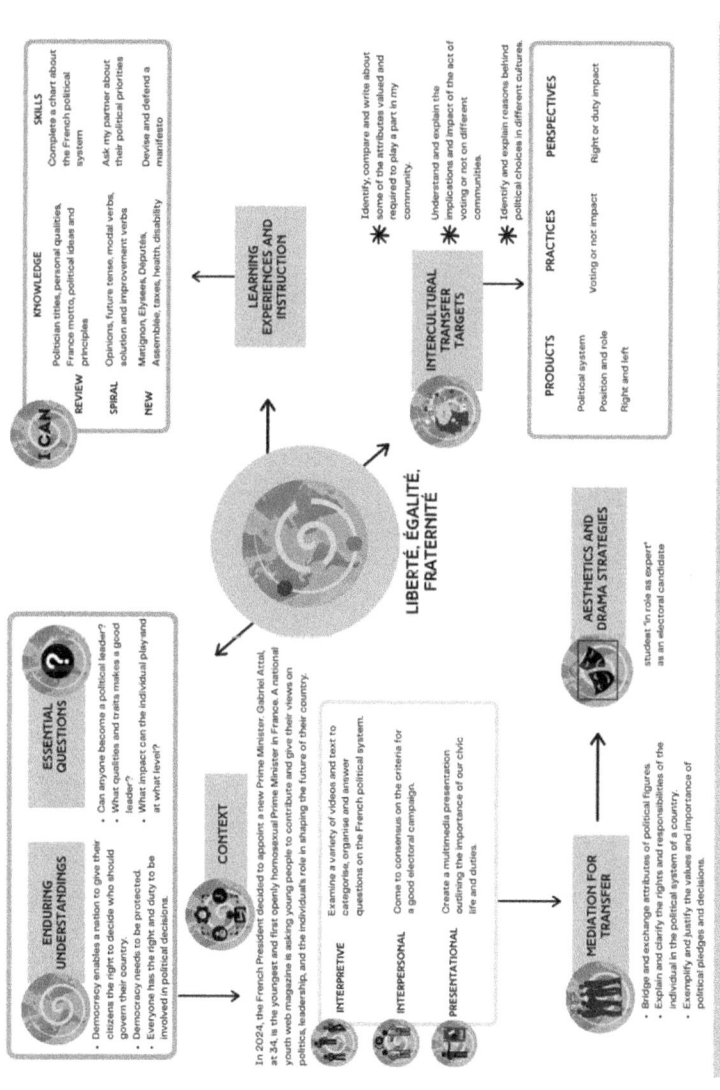

FIGURE 2.4 Liberté, égalité, fraternité Concept Map. Adapted from Eddy, J. (2022) Designing World Language Curriculum for Intercultural Communicative Competence, with permission from Bloomsbury Academic, an imprint of Bloomsbury Publishing, Plc.

Design for Transfer

With the language and culture(s) you are teaching in mind ...
Consider a concept or perspective that you envision can be unfolded throughout your curriculum.

Consider a possible task that could solve a problem or create products of value to the community or public at large. What is the Context or scenario? Who could receive these products or deliverables?

Design for Transfer

Using the Concept Map with fillable fields, begin your design and have the AATT template with fillable fields in front of you, side by side (see Chapter 2 on the companion website).

Reflect and Revisit

1. How can novel language experiences help to develop mediation, adaptability, autonomy and creativity?
2. Why do we want to design a curriculum that engages the learner over the lifespan?
3. How can the teacher as designer be a model for Mediation and ensure its role in the SoWMs?
4. Which feature of the AATT is the most compelling for you?
5. How do transfer tasks enable mediation and learner progression?
6. What evidence of mediation do you see in your tasks?
7. How does the Context set the stage for transfer and mediation of transcultural communication?

3

How Do Languages Connect Us?

Enduring Understandings

∞ All disciplines, as well as our experiences, consist of concepts, ideas and perspectives which resurface and reprise.

∞ The stories of our cultures allow learners to access, engage and make sense of the world.

∞ Our identities are present in every discipline because our cultures progress with the creativity we pursue daily for ourselves and others.

∞ Enduring Understandings and Essential Questions allow learners to reprise, reflect and respond to transcultural perspectives and issues presented in various contexts and texts.

Essential Questions

Q How do themes reprise to tell the 'stories' of the culture and what matters?

Q To what extent do our identities contribute to our sense of belonging to any culture?

Q How can we see ourselves in other cultures?

Q What does inter/transcultural mediation look like?

I can

- Determine intercultural perspectives that can reprise over a curriculum.
- Describe how inter/transcultural perspectives and experiences inform our reflection and response.
- Design Enduring Understandings and Essential Questions.
- Develop intercultural transfer targets after designing tasks.

Let's Consider

In Chapter 2, we examined 'Designing what matters' and, in this context, how SoWMs and the AATT/ICANADAPT design model guide teachers in fulfilling these principles. In the collaboratively designed AATT International *Eisteddfod,* we see how a common topic, such as festivals, shifts from local to global with its inclusive take on this tradition. Learners are asked to consider festivals and their purpose, constantly examining the 'why'. In the AATT *Liberté, égalité, fraternité,* Steph invites pupils to consider the qualities of leadership and their role in the process by contributing to a youth magazine. This AATT also provides further evidence for our discussion on transfer. We outlined the *Articulated Spiral Points, Mediation for Transfer and Intercultural Transferable Goals,* which support the SoWM. These provide evidence of learner progression featuring creative transfer deliverables, and the rationale behind how they channel and extend linguistic and cultural understanding with other people. Now more than ever, we are further connected as a society, by physical or virtual contact. We depend on communication through and across languages and cultures.

Our pupils must be able to integrate what they know and can do into contexts beyond the known and have done. They must be ready to participate among cultures with poise and confidence, and recognize and acknowledge many perspectives while still maintaining their own identities. The tasks you will see prepare the learner inside the classroom for interaction, adaptability and contribution required outside of it. What should learners revisit and reconsider throughout their curriculum? How can we set the stage for reflecting on their own perspectives, processes and practices while learning about those of others? What do learning experiences that mingle global with local look like?

Recursive Transcultural Perspectives: Reprise, Reflection and Response

In spiralled, articulated World Language/MFL curricula, we develop the best Enduring Understandings (EUs) and Essential Questions (EQs)(McTighe & Wiggins, 2004; Wiggins & McTighe, 2005) through the lens of inter/transcultural perspectives, cultural histories and transdisciplinary content (Eddy, 2006a/b, 2007a; 2022b). You want to focus on a line of inquiry, ideas and concepts so intrinsic to the discipline that it resounds and reprises across many texts. These concepts, ideas and perspectives have resonated for a long time and should matter significantly to one, many cultures, or all of them, even though the practices derived from them might differ among cultures. For example, in the next chapter we will see an AATT exemplar on the environment. One of the EUs states, 'The environment as portrayed in the media can vary across cultures.' This concept repeats in many different media, texts and works of art. One EQ is 'Who is responsible for the future of our planet?' This same concept and question are uncovered over the curriculum via different tasks. At one level, these pupils will look at recycling practices across different countries and cultures. At another level, the task is different; the EUs and EQs do not change. It is important to note that neither the EUs and EQs, nor the concepts or perspectives they came from are aligned to a level or target. These reprise over time in your curriculum, are designed to be revisited and reconsidered over again, and will reappear long after the student has left the school. The transfer tasks you design will determine the complexity and those change, unit by unit, module by module, year after year. Authentic cultural community texts yield reflection by pupils as they examine those and other cultural perspectives within their communities. The products they create and problems they resolve will move them forward, and the cycle of reprise, reflection and response continues up the spiral. This design framework uncovers and reveals languages and cultures within communities, the society and world. It enables learners to contribute their skills and creativity through novel, transferable tasks and deliverables.

The teacher leaders in our group explored issues for the culture(s) they teach, reflected on their own, and contrasted those perspectives with other languages and cultures. They discussed different languages and cultures present in their diverse school contexts and how those pupils might explore the questions and their own identities. Indeed, languages connect us. Finally, they saw how perspectives reprise and unfold in a recursive curriculum while pupils create deliverables as evidence of progression throughout the reprise. That is the objective of this chapter and the AATT exemplars you will see here.

In this framework, learners

1. Reprise inter/transcultural themes, perspectives, ideas or principles over the curriculum.
2. Reflect upon their own cultural identities by engaging with creative works across disciplines.
3. Respond through articulated transfer tasks, to contribute and offer solutions for someone else.

For each set of tasks in the AATTs, our teachers compose EUs and EQs (Wiggins & McTighe, 2005) for the inter/transcultural themes which recur, 'must-haves' over the course of their curriculum. Figure 3.1 shows the AATT template with annotations to guide you as you complete your own AATT template.

These EUs and EQs frame the concepts across and within disciplines with the perspectives and issues that inform them. These help to fuse concepts and disciplines from the cultural standpoint that informed them (Sercu, 2006; Scarino & Liddicoat, 2016) rather than the artificially separated treatment typically found in school. When first-time teachers design EUs and EQs, they often reach for familiar structures and past practices. Sometimes, teachers conflate EUs and EQs with objective statements and focus questions, respectively. EUs and EQs are recursive and often infinite; they stand the test of time and are designed to last the life of the curriculum and beyond. These are concepts and questions we may still ask ourselves about long after we have left school.

In contrast, 'I can' statements for pupils, objective statements for teachers and focus questions are finite; their expiration date is within one or two class periods or, at most, one unit of work. Focus questions are those you may offer students at the top of each class to be answered as a ticket in or out the door when class is over. To clarify Stage One and Stage Three components at a glance, see Appendix C for a side-by-side comparison of how the components function in a curriculum.

At this point, let's take a look at a taster of these key curriculum design components. These examples represent diverse transcultural themes with identity, art, colour, health, childhood, inclusion, family, cultural history, education and cuisine. As you move from left to right, we shift from curricular programme or big picture level at Stage One to task transfer takeaway at Stage Two, and then to lesson-level implementation at Stage Three. Table 3.1 below provides examples of EUs, EQs, I can, or Intercultural Transfer Targets (ITTs) and Focus Questions, representing all three stages of concept to implementation in the ICANADAPT design.

ARTICULATED ASSESSMENT TRANSFER TASK (AATT) – KEY ELEMENTS SIMPLIFIED, JENNIFER EDDY, GWE 2023

ENDURING UNDERSTANDINGS	ESSENTIAL QUESTIONS	CONTEXT
Basic and enduring concepts about the culture and traditions of our own and other communities. The Four Purposes are fundamental to the design of the programme.	Derived from the EU and can be trans-disciplinary. They are open-ended with no single or final answer: life-long questions. The task enables students to start to answer these questions.	Real-life event/audience. The context is common to all levels within the AATT. Solve problem- create products

ARTICULATION SPIRAL POINTS	INTERCULTURAL TRANSFER TARGETS	MEDIATION FOR TRANSFER
Progression/ hinging points between levels within and across progression steps. The task assesses performances across levels of engagement along the continuum with increased complexity.	Use understanding of the culture and practices of the communities studied and make that culture accessible to those new or needing a bridge to understand some elements of it. The task isn't superficial. It addresses and introduces the learners to new cultures and traditions, preparing them to be citizens of Wales and the world.	Bridge and explain to someone unfamiliar with language or unaccustomed to culture with the language you own now. Facilitate meaning and clarify social and cultural symbols conveyed with the other person in mind- novel and problem-solving.

PERFORMANCE TARGET LEVEL	PERFORMANCE TARGET LEVEL	PERFORMANCE TARGET LEVEL
eg Novice –can specify year and level-	Eg Intermediate –can specify year and level-	Eg Advanced –can specify year and level-

AUTHENTIC MATERIAL DESCRIPTIONS
Cultural Community Authentic Texts — Adapt the task to the authentic material, not the material to the task.

INTERPRETIVE TASK / I CAN	Remember and Understand elements of culture and practices from authentic materials: Identify, Index, Inquire, Interpret, Infer, Illustrate. Improve **One-Way Communication** Acquire meaning from someone else by Listening, Reading, Viewing, Receiving Cultural Community Authentic Texts I can: differentiate, match, identify, order, label, find, distinguish, arrange, elaborate, categorise, paraphrase, Infer, question, predict.
INTERPERSONAL TASK / I CAN	Apply and evaluate what you have understood- discuss and come to a consensus with partners: Ask, Answer, Arrange, Adopt, Assess, Argue, Agree **Two-Way Communication** Exchange meaning with someone else that is unrehearsed, unrefined, improvised I can: compare, contrast, select, separate, examine, investigate, discuss, conclude, appraise, judge, justify, explain, recommend, assess.
PRESENTATIONAL TASK / I CAN	Apply, modify and create to explain to a specific audience outside the classroom: Transactional, Expressive, Poetic **One-Way Communication** Create meaning for someone else that is Prepared, Rehearsed, and Revised I can: predict, demonstrate, solve, calculate, modify, choose, construct, combine, design, develop, produce, connect, invent, compose.

FIGURE 3.1 *AATT Key Elements Annotated Eddy GwE. Adapted from Eddy, J. (2022b) Designing World Language Curriculum for Intercultural Communicative Competence, with permission from Bloomsbury Academic, an imprint of Bloomsbury Publishing, Plc.*

TABLE 3.1 Enduring Understandings, Essential Questions, I can/ITT and Focus Questions compared

Stage One Enduring Understanding Curriculum or Lifespan	Stage One Essential Question Curriculum or Lifespan	Stage Two I can/ITTs Takeaway from task	Stage Three Focus Question Answered in class
Identity is both an inside and outside quest and can be about reinvention and change.	What turning points determine our path?	Create a storybook with cultural images and dialogue script.	What are five recurring images from the film *The Paper Boy?*
Texts and works of art help us construct our understanding of reality.	How can images and sounds tell a story?	Identify images, music and symbols across cultures.	Which symbols and sounds represent this work of art?
Colour has significance for all milestone events.	How does colour convey meaning? To what extent does cultural history influence the colours we see?	Choose colours for different occasions. Explain how colour meaning has changed over time.	What does orange symbolize? When do we wear red? What does green mean to you?
Words of our ancestors cure us, strengthen us and lift us up.	How do our ancestors keep teaching and caring for us?	Compare personification examples in my own and Nahua poetry. Explain foods associated with emotions in different cultures.	What are the elements of curing in Nahua culture? What is an example of personification?
Play is children's work.	What does the practice of play look like? How do children learn?	Compare play across cultures. Describe how or when a game is played.	Who plays with children? What are two examples of toys or games?

Takiwātanga: in my/his/her/our own time and space. *Ka tipu te whaihanga* – Creativity will strengthen.	What does it mean to live authentically?	Identify words and phrases from Te Reo Māori for wellness. Explain *Takiwātanga* from the Māori perspective.	What are four phrases related to autism that support creativity and inclusion?
The stereotypical nuclear family found in traditional textbooks does not represent the totality of today's family units.	How do laws, national, regional social programmes support families?	Identify examples of diversity in Germany. Select visuals across cultures to clarify family diversity.	What are three questions about different families depicted in the documentary and posters?
Cultural history inspires songwriters for all world music.	How does the history of a country shape its culture and affect its songwriters' inspiration?	Explain how historical events influence song lyrics from Haiti and my country.	Which lyrics from the song best describe the composer's view on Haiti?
Clothing defines us. From the first decision of each day to our sense of belonging or individuality.	To what extent do commonality and individuality affect our educational performance?	Organize descriptions of uniform styles. Share practices of uniforms in the UK and Germany.	What are some reasons behind the details and differences between uniforms in the UK and Germany?
Knowledge of language allows me to access different cuisines.	What local product reflects my place of interest or hobbies?	Present a menu which represents identity.	What are some foods that were more popular in the past?

Excerpts of AATTs (*Familienstrukturen in der deutschsprachigen Welt*, Garcia & McCloskey; The Paper Boy, Ilieva; *Takiwatanga*, Opai; *In Xochitl, In Cuicatl*, Sánchez) adapted from Eddy, J. (2022b) *Designing World Language Curriculum for Intercultural Communicative Competence*, with permission by Bloomsbury Academic, an imprint of Bloomsbury Publishing, Plc.

> ### Put It to Practice: Collaborate to Articulate
>
> The two AATTs you have seen thus far in the last chapter feature EUs and EQs, and you have now seen the samples above. When you consider the language(s) and cultures you teach, what inter/transcultural perspectives will recur over your curriculum? What do you want your pupils to reprise, reflect and respond to through their creative transfer tasks? Do you see potential evidence of progression in the upward and articulated spiral? How will you work together with colleagues to make it happen?

Meet Our Designers

All of the AATTs in this book show how learners unfold intercultural perspectives and the stories of our cultures with EUs and EQs as the constant throughout the curriculum. For this chapter, these three exemplars were especially selected by Ms Stephanie Ellis-Williams for their attention to inter/transcultural communicative competence, with themes that go beyond local to global and tasks that bring the learners there and back to notice their own identities. Ms Bennett extends the theme of belonging, even as a newcomer to Wales. Ms Morris explores the right to speak your own language, past to present issues and the power of protest. Ms Piesch responds to food poverty at a level accessible to beginners as she unpacks a theme all global citizens need: Solidarity.

Our Sense of Belonging

The CfW (2019) explains that the word *cynefin*, means more than just habitat. It is cultural history, community, our familiar, our belonging. This matters not only for ourselves but also for making connections with people and communities anywhere in the world. In Ourselves and Others, Ms Bennett's pupils examine language and identity to show that everyone belongs, from visiting celebrities to newcomers in a new land. How can we understand ourselves better, to connect and mediate with others here and across our world?

Teacher as Designer – Ourselves and Others

Sian Bennett is a Welsh teacher in an English setting where most pupils are from English-speaking backgrounds and with a lukewarm attitude to learning Welsh. They are not necessarily proud of their Welsh heritage. The teacher is keen to get students to reflect on what makes them who they are and why. She also wants to open the conversations around the importance of cultural heritage and the positive impact it can have on our personal development. This is particularly important in a country or region where there is a minority language which is not spoken widely in the rest of the world. Students often dismiss the value of learning the language and its culture. This AATT (see Table 3.2) enables students to understand how learning the Welsh language and culture gives them another insight in their own identity. They can reflect on what influences who they are, who other people are and what they feel.

This AATT is a good example of work which will develop understanding and knowledge of some of the key concepts from this principle around identity and sense of belonging. This task will help students achieve a better 'understanding of how languages can provide a sense of belonging to a local and global community' (SWM 1 – Progression Steps 3, CfW 2019).

Sian Bennett took advantage of the exceptional COVID pandemic context at the time of the AATT design which meant that the very famous and extremely popular TV programme *I'm a Celebrity, Get Me out of Here*, which is ordinarily filmed in Australia, was set in North Wales for two years, at very close proximity to the school. The show, which is watched widely in the UK, contributed to truly putting Wales on the map and to promote its culture and language as the presenters, who are English, made every effort to include some Welsh phrases and positive references about their three-week stay there. Not only was this a great hook to grab her students' attention but it also enabled her to use an authentic event to create her tasks. The CfW framework encourages teacher's creativity and responsive curriculum design to ensure our learners are learning within the most up to date and relevant contexts. Sian demonstrates just that. As the show is now back in Australia, Sian has managed to adapt the AATT by using a different show that fulfils similar needs.

—Stephanie Ellis-Williams, International Languages,
Global Futures GwE Lead

Voices from the Field

One of the four purposes in the Curriculum for Wales is to enable pupils to become ethical, informed citizens of Wales and the World. There are lots of important factors that contribute to making us who we are and our culture and heritage can play a significant part in our identity. Influences from celebrities can also contribute to how we behave and see the world. The authentic material will allow pupils to see celebrities valuing the Welsh language and see their journey of learning Welsh for the first time as an adult. Pupils will see the value of the Welsh language and be proud of their Welsh identity.

Other cultures should recognize similarities and differences between themselves and others. There may be a mix of cultures in the classroom, e.g. Welsh, Polish, Ukrainian, English and they should all recognize that Wales and the Welsh culture are part of all of their lives no matter where they are from or how long they have been in Wales.

This curriculum design is a very effective way of planning your teaching. You know what you want pupils to achieve when you know what the end product is. Planning backwards means you know where they need to get to and helps with knowing what they have to do to get there. This AATT has had an impact on pupil progress, as learners have taken a more active role in their own learning and, because they know what the end goal is, most learners see the value to their learning. Since completing the original assessment task, I have made some adaptations. However, learners did use language effectively to convey their own ideas and viewpoints. Learners also developed skills to communicate through speech, writing or images.

All learners have exposure to authentic material and some will gain more understanding than others but all learners will gain some knowledge or understanding of what it means to be Welsh. Learners will see that 'Languages Connect us' as we follow the celebrities on their journeys to learning the Welsh language for the first time. Novice learners will be able to present some facts about one of the celebrities in the authentic video. Learners will also begin to understand that 'Expressing Ourselves is Key to Communication' and will develop an awareness of how to use language to express themselves for different purposes and audiences.

Designing this way makes us think in more detail about what is meaningful and purposeful, thus more enjoyable for learners. Using authentic material allows learners to see the language used in a meaningful way and also allows learners to develop their knowledge of their own culture, identity and language. Learners of all abilities are able to make progress regardless of where they are on their language journey.

When learners feel that they are making progress and are able to use language in a purposeful way, pupils will be more likely to continue the journey at GCSE. With MFL and Welsh working more closely together, pupils will hopefully begin to see that skills learnt in one language can help with another. Having a positive learning experience in Welsh could have a positive effect on the uptake of other languages.

—Ms Sian Bennett, Prestatyn High School, Denbighshire, Welsh

TABLE 3.2 Articulated Assessment Transfer Task – Ourselves and others

Enduring Understandings
✽ There are various contributing factors that make us who we are.
✽ Celebrities can be influential in people's lives.
✽ Languages can provide a sense of belonging to a local and global community.

Essential Questions
? Who am I?
? What makes me, me?
? What makes people unique?
? Who is my hero?
? Can celebrities influence people's lives?
? What does it mean to be Welsh?
? Does our language play a part in our identity?

Context
I'm a Celebrity Get Me Out of Here is filming a special show back in Gwrych Castle in Wales to celebrate Welsh identity. ITV are asking viewers to send their suggestions to help decide which celebrities should appear on the show.

Articulation Spiral Points
@ Use adjectives to describe different personalities
@ Present information about a celebrity using visual support
@ Complete an oral presentation about which celebrity should appear on the show and why

Intercultural Transfer Targets	**Mediation for Transfer**
• I can compare the personalities of different celebrities.	• Bridge and exchange ideas and concepts of identity and the values of Wales.
• I can explain what makes us 'Welsh'.	
• I can explain how the sense of belonging to a community can give us pride.	• Use annotations and visuals to present a celebrity to different audiences.
• I can discuss how the Welsh language plays an important role in our sense of identity.	• Summarize information depicted in both written and oral profiles.

Beginner	Intermediate	Advanced
'Iaith ar Daith'		
**Interpretive Task Descriptions** How do we understand the world around us and support others?		
Watch various clips from 'Iaith ar Daith' and pupils tick the most suitable adjectives to describe the celebrities' personalities.	Watch various short clips from 'Iaith ar Daith' and pupils categorize some written information into a Venn diagram.	Watch various short clips from 'Iaith ar Daith' and pupils write some short sentences about the celebrities on the videos.
**I Can**		
I can identify which adjectives best describe the people in the video. I can develop my vocabulary and pronunciation through listening and reading, and use new words and phrases.	I can categorize information based on what I have heard in the video. I can develop my vocabulary and pronunciation through listening and reading, and use new words and phrases in a variety of contexts.	I can use suitable vocabulary and phrases to describe the celebrities in the video. I can develop my vocabulary and pronunciation through listening and reading, and use new words and phrases in a variety of contexts.
**Interpersonal Task Descriptions** How do we express ourselves and engage others?		
With a partner, choose one of the celebrities shown in the videos and discuss and agree what qualities make them suitable for the show.	Discuss the celebrities shown in the videos and decide which one should appear in the show. Learners pose questions to each other as though they are one of the celebrities. Learners answer the questions using the first person.	Discuss and compare the celebrities shown in the videos and decide which would be suitable to appear on the show and why. Pose questions to each other to answer about the celebrities using the third person.
**I can**		
I can talk about the celebrity I liked the most with my peers.	I can exchange information, ask and answer questions, and discuss the celebrities with my peers.	I can exchange information, ask and answer questions, and make comparisons between people. I can agree on a list of criteria which makes a celebrity a suitable candidate for the show.

Presentational Task Descriptions How do we create and share with others?		
Create an information page or fact file about a chosen Welsh celebrity.	Complete an oral presentation (as though the learner is the celebrity) to convince ITV why they should appear on the show.	Complete an oral presentation describing which celebrity should appear on the show for a particular reason, e.g. to attract younger viewers, to promote kindness, entertainment value etc.
I can		
I can use adjectives and/or short sentences to describe a Welsh celebrity.	I can use first person structures to describe a chosen celebrity. I can give reasons as to why the chosen celebrity should appear on the show.	I can describe a Welsh celebrity and use persuasive language to support my opinions. I can select and adapt the appropriate language for a range of audiences and purposes, conveying meaning effectively to the audience.

Bridge to Design

Let's go deeper into Ms Bennett's design process and collaborate with colleagues for additional ideas and reflection on this exemplar before working on your own design.

Reflect to Reveal

1) Which transcultural perspectives does Ms Bennett want pupils to understand from this exemplar?
2) What can reality TV and celebrities teach us about culture and daily life?
3) Why should identity and belonging be unpacked over a curriculum?

Questions for Colleagues

1) How does the pupil's role facilitate inquiry and creativity?
2) Is there a concept regarding identity and belonging from the culture you will teach that is essential for your curriculum?
3) How might you adapt any of these tasks for your chosen curricular theme, transfer targets and cultures?

Ask the Designer

What is your question for Ms Bennett? What else do you want to know about this exemplar and her design thinking?

Participate in the Practice

Which practices guided Ms Bennett in creating her exemplar? How did she design with these in mind? Explain below for each component.

1) Essential Questions
2) Tasks which facilitate mediation with others and compare what pupils already know with new content
3) Culturally authentic material as creative text

Teacher to Leader on Design and Implementation

1 Ensure that students have a clear idea of the end goal so they understand that there is a purpose to what they are learning.
2 Encourage students to think about their end product in all lessons running up to the assessment task so that they can use and adapt the language they see/hear in their own work.
3 Allow enough time for the interpersonal task so that pupils gain confidence with using their Welsh and have practice with an audience.

Pupils showed an interest in the work and were keen to present their work using Flipgrid. Pupils were more reluctant to present work in front of others but were confident recording themselves in a separate area or at home. Since trialling the AATT, we have made some small changes. We found that explaining what pupils would be doing for the assessment task at the beginning of the

Unit meant that pupils took the work more seriously and saw a purpose to it and therefore were more keen to learn during lessons.

Colleagues found that some pupils were taking responsibility for their own learning and many wanted to add extra details and information and chose the more ambitious task. Passive learners opted for the easier task. Having the three options of presentational tasks meant that all pupils, especially recent immigrant pupils, were able to access the work and complete an assessment task.

—Ms Sian Bennett, Prestatyn High School, Denbighshire, Welsh

From the Admin Desk

From the administrator's point of view, watching Sian embracing the process was invaluable. This process enabled her to be more ambitious for her students but also for her as a practitioner. She really questioned the barriers to learning Welsh her pupils encountered and she used the AATT principles to break these down.

Sian made the context authentic and relevant. She brought topics and learning materials from a world the students identify with and connect easily with. Students did not question why they had to learn the language. Instead, they were requesting more language and more proficiency in order to achieve the task. Their focus shifted from 'having to' to 'wanting to'. Even at a very novice level, pupils felt they were expressing important viewpoints on EQs. The language they use is therefore for a purpose and not just to learn the language. The response to the context and the actual tasks was also very encouraging. It injected an element of modernity to a Welsh curriculum which can be perceived, at times, as stale or too anchored in the past.

I believe this can be a model for any other languages as the outcome can be easily modified according to the level of engagement and level of language. Most countries have a wide range of similar TV reality programmes which are very popular amongst young people. Celebrities are now including all kinds of influencers and TikTok sensations which we can use to appeal to pupils. This AATT is a good example to show other teachers how to keep your schemes of learning relevant, stimulating and responsive.

—Stephanie Ellis-Williams, International Languages, Global Futures GwE Lead

Language Oppression-Language Justice for All

Why is protest important? How many languages have we lost? Ms Morris looks at cultural history and language oppression as pupils make the case for language survival as preservation of identity. Many cultures can relate to this theme and exemplar. Through her tasks, Ms Morris' pupils can extend these concepts among many people. They become active social agents co-constructing meaning through complex tasks and mediation across languages and cultures, the hallmark of transcultural communicative competence.

Teacher as Designer – Protest

Ms Jeni Morris teaches at Ysgol Tryfan, a secondary school in the university city of Bangor in North Wales. The school is a Welsh-medium school with the majority of the learners coming from Welsh-speaking households. However, a large proportion of the learners also come from non-Welsh-speaking backgrounds and some may be relatively new Welsh learners. The school language profile is therefore complex and programmes of study must be carefully crafted in order to support every learner achieve their potential in the language.

This AATT (see Table 3.3) is an excellent example for this principle as it uses the communicative skill of protesting to link any kind of injustice which needs to be fought. Here, Ms Morris wants to get her students to better understand the importance of fighting for the right to speak your own language and to denounce the wrong of oppression by forbidding people to speak their language. She uses history to develop a deeper understanding of the fight for the Welsh language in Wales but also current events to open pupils' minds to the power of protest, when it should happen and how.

It cleverly links the past and present to build a stronger future. It enables students to think deeply about the national issue and priorities around the Welsh language but in a way in which every individual can genuinely connect with, no matter their opinion and position on the topic. The enduring understanding and essential questions at the heart of this AATT are the common links to all communities.

The outstanding features of this AATT are the authentic resources in Welsh. They deal with older and very recent events, in a variety of digital supports which twenty-first century students relate more to. It is often quite difficult to find such materials in Welsh. The issue of racism and Black Lives Matter and the current issue of the removal of controversial statues is also dealt with within the Welsh context, which is essential to ensure students realize these are issues happening in Wales too.

As a result, students are exposed to a vast array of sources and documents which will help them make much more informed and unbiased judgements when dealing with the 'problem' set by the presentational tasks.

—Stephanie Ellis-Williams, International Languages, Global Futures GwE Lead

Voices from the Field

Cymraeg (the Welsh language) is one of the oldest living languages in Europe, if not the oldest, and her history of survival is extraordinary. The campaigns during the 1960s for official status for the Welsh language in Wales by influential individuals and Cymdeithas yr Iaith ('The Welsh Language Society') are very important events in the history of Wales and today the Senedd, in Caerdydd (Cardiff) the capital city of Cymru (Wales) is the home the Welsh Parliament, the democratically elected body that represents the interests of Wales and its people. In 2022, the introduction of Cwricwlwm i Gymru (Curriculum for Wales) and the Welsh government's campaign 'Cymraeg 2050 – Miliwn o siaradwyr' ('Cymraeg 2050 – A million Welsh speakers') are important new milestones in her historic battle for survival. Truly understanding and appreciating the background of the Welsh language's survival naturally forms a part of Welsh identity and is also woven into the tapestry that creates 'ethical, informed citizens of Wales and the world', which is one of the Four Purposes of Curriculum for Wales.

Campaigns for the survival of languages are common throughout the world and all cultures understand how one's own language forms a part of one's own identity. Expressing ourselves through language is key to communication and is also the wording of one of the Statements of What Matters for the 'Languages, Communication and Literacy' Area of Learning and Experience within Curriculum for Wales. Protest is a human right protected by Article 11 of the Human Rights Act, which is protected under international law, and protesting is also an important communicative skill.

Designing this way for Welsh within the Curriculum for Wales' Languages, Literacy and Communication Area of Learning and Experience as part of a whole school curriculum design, ensures progression in specific Welsh literacy skills. Designing this way has also created opportunities for the individual learner to understand and appreciate how their progression, in specific speaking, listening, reading and writing skills support each other holistically within their 'learning journey'.

When embarking on the 'learning journey' within the AATT, the learner understands that the presentational tasks (including the reflection on their progression in skills following this task) is the final destination in their 'learning journey' and their 'journey of progression in specific skills' within the AATT. The final presentational task will be an amalgamation of the skills developed on the learning journey throughout the AATT and when reflecting on his or her progression following the completion of this final task the learner will consider his or her progression throughout the entire journey through the interpretive, interpersonal and presentational tasks.

Within the AATT, learners will explore and analyse how the Welsh language impacts upon identity and culture and how the association between the language and culture in Wales is preparing the learner for Welsh and global citizenship ('Languages connect us' – Statements of What Matters, 'Languages, Communication and Literacy' Area of Learning and Experience). Learners read empathetically to respect and critically evaluate different people's perspectives, using them to arrive at their own considered conclusions. ('Understanding languages is key to understanding the world around us' – Statements of What Matters, 'Languages, Communication and Literacy' Area of Learning and Experience). Learners also communicate thoughts, feelings and opinions in challenging and contentious contexts showing empathy and respect. ('Expressing ourselves through languages is key to communication' – Statements of What Matters, 'Languages, Communication and Literacy' Area of Learning and Experience).

One example of how the learners showed evidence of progression aligned with the Curriculum for Wales' 'Principles of Progression' within the AATT and their individual 'learning journey', was when the learners were required to reflect on their own individual progress in specific skills, e.g. reflecting on their progression in speaking and listening skills following the 'boxing match' debate. Their reflections showed that they were moving on to more complex communication within the AATT and the learners also acquired a deeper understanding of different viewpoints and increasing command of the skills needed to interpret, evaluate, articulate and respond to differing perspectives (taken form 'Increasing breadth and depth of knowledge', which is one of the five Principles of Progression within 'Languages, Communication and Literacy Area of Learning and Experience' in Curriculum for Wales)

The AATT allows the learner to grow in confidence across every level and only when he or she is ready to 'show the work' and reflect positively on the progression made do we move forward to make even further progress. The whole AATT is a celebration of developing Welsh language literacy skills within a relevant context and it's a joy when the learner understands and appreciates the progress he or she has made.

—Ms Jeni Morris, Ysgol Tryfan, Gwynedd, Welsh

TABLE 3.3 Articulated Assessment Transfer Task – Protest

Enduring Understandings
✸ We can learn important lessons from our history to make us informed, considerate and tolerant citizens of the twenty-first century.
Essential Questions
? How does history influence us today?   ? Is it right that we interpret historical events according to twenty-first century principles?
Context
As part of their work raising young people's awareness of important world issues, the *Urdd* are keen to educate young people about the purpose and meaning of the controversial statues and portraits seen throughout Wales.
Articulation Spiral Points
@ Debating a controversial issue   @ Canvass a wide range of opinions and debate the controversiality of some statues   @ Create a short video to argue for and against the removal of statues   @ Create a podcast about the history of the statues and the arguments for and against removing them.   @ Create an interactive online article about the purpose and meaning of the statues as well as discussing the arguments for and against their removal.

Intercultural Transfer Targets	Mediation for Transfer
• I can explain the impact of historical campaigns for official status for the Welsh language in Wales on Wales and the Welsh language in our time today. • I can clarify why revisiting history is essential to a better future. • I can justify the priorities and needs of our society nowadays in terms of identity rights to defend.	• Bridge and exchange ideas and concepts related to protesting, the right to protest and how language forms a part of one's identity • Show empathy when responding to literature and understanding that others may have different views (SoWM LLC AoLE CfW) • Explain points of view regarding historical heritage in relation to ethical practices. • Share and clarify arguments for and against the demolition of controversial statues using multimedia.

Beginner	Intermediate	Advanced
Interpretive Task Descriptions **How do we understand the world around us and support others?**		
With a partner, list five facts you have learned about the history of the statues as well as five things you have learned about people's opinions about them.	With your partner, interpret the information in the reading passages and form arguments for and against removing the statues. Prioritise these arguments in order of their strength – giving reasons.	De Bono Hats – Controversial Sculptures
I Can		
I can distinguish between facts, theories and opinions.	I can distinguish between facts/evidence and bias/arguments	I can understand and explore in detail how texts may be interpreted, distinguishing between facts/evidence and bias/arguments.
Interpersonal Task Descriptions **How do we express ourselves and engage others?**		
Boxing match debate (Collaborative talk)	Boxing match debate (Collaborative talk)	Boxing match debate (Collaborative talk)
I Can		
I can explore challenging or contentious issues through a variety of authentic contexts, including sustaining a role.	I can use talk in a range of authentic contexts to explore challenging or contentious issues. I can sustain a convincing point of view, anticipating and responding to other perspectives.	I can confidently and consistently explore challenging or contentious issues through sustaining roles in formal situations, contexts and purposes.
Presentational Task Descriptions **How do we create and share with others?**		
The *Urdd* is keen to use their TikTok account in order to show the opinions of different individuals about the statues. Create a video no more than 90 seconds long for Urdd followers on TikTok, presenting three	Plan and record a poll with your partner for a new channel on *Yr Urdd's* poll www.pod.com discussing the history of the statues and the arguments for and against their demolition.	The *Urdd* is looking for young people to contribute to their monthly magazine for secondary school aged pupils. They are looking for an interactive article that educates young people about the purpose and

arguments in favour and three arguments against.		meaning of the statues as well as discussing the arguments for and against their removal.
I Can		
I can share, talk and write about my thoughts, feelings and opinions using a range of techniques to show impact.	I can share, talk and write about my thoughts, feelings and opinions showing empathy and respect.	I can select and use appropriate strategies to plan and develop my writing for a challenging range of different purposes and audiences. I can structure arguments and challenge what others say with confidence and sensitivity. (CfW SoWM)

Bridge to Design

Let's get closer to Ms Morris' design process and collaborate with colleagues for additional ideas and questions to guide your design work.

Reflect to Reveal

1) What is important for pupils to understand about protest in both national and international contexts?
2) How does Ms Morris use both old and new resources to connect with pupil's experiences today?
3) How do her pupils mediate and clarify the concept of protest and oppression for someone else?

Questions for Colleagues

1) Are there examples of protest and oppression from the culture you will teach that is essential for your curriculum? Please share it.
2) How do the tasks help learners engage in this topic as informed, confident, creative contributors?
3) How might you adapt any of these tasks for your chosen curricular theme, transfer targets and cultures?

Ask the Designer

What is your question for Ms Morris? What else do you want to know about this exemplar and her design thinking?

Participate in the Practice

Which practices guided Ms Morris in creating her exemplar? How did she design with these in mind? Explain below for each component.

1) Enduring Understanding and Essential Questions
2) Value beyond the classroom across the lifespan
3) Culturally authentic materials that connect various communities

Teacher to Leader on Design and Implementation

1 The end goal is your starting point

2 The learner's individual progression should always steer the teaching and the learning

3 The presentational task must always be authentic with a specific audience in mind

From the Admin Desk

This unit is part of a wider work programme which, in essence, develops the pupils' awareness and understanding of the impact of protest on Wales and the campaigns for official status for the Welsh language in Wales during the 1960s. By the end of the unit the pupils will understand and be able to explain what the impact of the protesting in the 1960s was on our time and our Wales today.

This is the unit that appears first in the work programme, and its aim is to ensure that the pupils understand and can explain why people protest as well as recognizing that there are two sides to every argument, and that it's important to be open minded and respect other views whatever they think.

> Although this AATT is ambitious and is aimed at advanced language students, the principles of stating the for and against of a problem can be applied to all levels. The authentic materials and the links made between the slavery trade in the Caribbeans and the local castle of Penrhyn in Bangor, North Wales can be used with very beginners with the right support. The language frames provided by the AATT can be simplified and built upon for example.
>
> Teachers could use this AATT to explore a long-life problem relating to their language communities. They could be tasked to look into AATTs which will encourage students to look at how this problem still affects the language communities, why and how to address these.
>
> Colleagues can also come up with common language progressive frameworks or sentence builders which can support students' communicative skills. This will help them to discuss and present work using the particular type of speech or form of communication, political or not, that the teachers want their pupils to develop.
>
> —Stephanie Ellis-Williams, International Languages, Global Futures GwE Lead

Food Insecurity and What We All Can Do as Acts of Kindness

In *Solidarité*, Miss Piesch carries the theme of food poverty and food insecurity from advanced to beginner. She explores social issues that all cultures face. Through song, she makes this theme accessible to all pupils, to build this concept right away, not to wait. Every level can unpack this theme with the tasks according to their level of engagement. This is the perfect example of the text and topic do not determine complexity, the task you design for it does.

Teacher as Designer – *Solidarité*

Miss Piesch is a French teacher in a very cosmopolitan school. The range of cultures and languages within the school is vast and students from all socio-economic backgrounds work alongside one another. The ethos of the languages department in this school has always been to aim high for all students and to bring authenticity to language learning. Students value languages but do not always perceive themselves as good linguists. By creating such purposeful products, students realize that their level of language at every stage is still good enough to be proficient. It helps fight the misconceptions that many students have around language learning and improve their attitude and resilience.

This AATT (see Table 3.4) is a very good example of this Principle as it aims to develop citizens of the world by addressing a global issue: food banks and food poverty. As our teachers work through their understanding of the key concepts of the Languages Connect Us statement, this AATT exemplifies how far our International Languages classrooms can take our pupils in terms of thematic and topical issues from day one. What was particularly interesting to see was how the teacher came to this AATT. Reflecting on the principles and elements of the AATT process and design, the teacher looked at her year 12/13 syllabi (for 17–18-year-old students at advanced level) and selected the Resto du Coeur part which deals with social issues and food poverty. She decided to adapt the tasks around the material so her year 7 pupils (11/12-year-old students, first-year beginners) could access it. In doing so, she reflected on the EQs to discuss and the language needed to do so, at their own level of engagement at the time.

Pupils in year 7 were exposed to serious matters which they discuss in other parts of the curriculum (R.E, History, English, Welsh etc.) but are often not given the opportunity to in languages as it is deemed too advanced. However, pupils relish such discussions and are happy to and aware that, at this point in time of their learning journey, they may be able to convey only partial responses.

In my opinion, this is an even greater benefit of such processes as language learners are constantly faced. To express feelings and opinions, language learners even at advanced levels will have to learn to simplify or find alternative ways to convey their thoughts. This can also be true in our native language as we do not always master all the necessary lexis. Therefore, this is good preparation for dealing with any unforeseen communicative situations in the future and excellent preparation for any examination they may face as well.

The particular gem of this unit is the song. Not only is it a catchy chorus but it is one of the most well-known songs in France. It has been sung by thousands of artists since its creation in 1986, and also by children more recently. Ms Piesch has managed to use the lyrics to do some language work which will support the students' own creative pieces later on whilst exposing them to a national cultural 'musical landmark' which evokes a multitude of societal questions.

First-year students are now able to explore these questions and to know about and reflect about one of the French approaches to fighting against food poverty. Most pupils will not opt to study languages at advanced levels and would never have the opportunity to delve into such essential questions in their language learning journey.

—Stephanie Ellis-Williams, International Languages,
Global Futures GwE Lead

Voices from the Field

Against the background of the cost-of-living crisis, charity work in general and food banks in particular are becoming ever more essential in both cultures. The charity and its work chosen as a point of departure is an integral part of French public life, yet is little known given our own equivalent organization. Opening up the concept to pupils at a young age that charity moves across borders and has a universal value helps pupils develop into ethical, informed citizens. The tiered concept of the AATT allows them to become ambitious learners by having the opportunity to progress at their level or even across levels by completing a more challenging assessment. The promotion of acts of kindness within their own community fosters their development into both enterprising, ethical contributors and confident individuals.

Pupils are supposed to take away the awareness that solidarity is a universal value that transcends cultures and that every gesture, however small, is important and benefits the community. The link between both cultures and the relevance of the topic becomes apparent through common points of contact, such as the existence of food banks or the organization of an annual concert for charity in both countries, which highlights the importance of public acts of solidarity filtering down into community-based initiatives in both cultures. Pupils are familiar with these acts, given the many charity events inside and outside of school, in which pupils regularly participate. This AATT is supposed to foster this awareness by letting pupils explore ways to improve their own community via material based on another culture.

I particularly enjoy the firmly culture-based approach to every AATT. With different cultures being our subjects' foundations, this concept establishes a framework which allows teachers to bring these cultures to life. But it's particularly the transfer of the topic and materials to the pupils' own world of experience which stands out to me as it highlights the link between both cultures and thus the relevance for their own pupils.

In this AATT, even a novice is able to explore and work with keywords and key phrases relevant to the topic. These can very easily be used to create a poster raising awareness amongst peers of the issues and solutions linked to the topic and hence create a valuable deliverable.

This AATT covers all four SoWMs, as it is based on connecting each other by encouraging acts of kindness (WMS 1+3) and by using our target language and culture to broaden their understanding of the world around them and the connection between us (WMS 3). Lastly, the use of video and song material as authentic resources meets WMS 4 as it ignites all subsequent work.

Designing with the AATT is particularly helpful to allow progress across levels as it inherently plans for three levels separately rather than just one main level. Rather than simply differentiating one level to meet the different requirements of a class, this concept allows a coherent approach at each level, helping pupils to succeed and produce a valued product at their level. While this helps build confidence and motivation, the topical convergence of all levels at the start also allows pupils to move up and attempt a more challenging level.

The use of authentic materials and the apparent link between the target and our own culture infinitely heightens the relevance of the topics taught and can therefore have a positive effect on pupils' motivation. Equally, the product and application-oriented approach allows teachers to assess pupils in a much more meaningful way while giving pupils a motivational purpose to the task. The AATT approach does, therefore, have the power to breathe life into MFL teaching and re-establish an approach that should naturally be used but has been supplanted by an exam-drive that seems to have removed the cultural core of our subjects.

—Ms Nicole Piesch, Ysgol Friars, Gwynedd, French

TABLE 3.4 Articulated Assessment Transfer Task – *Solidarité*

Enduring Understandings
✱ Solidarity is a universal value, defining us as caring and sentient beings.
Essential Questions
? Which attributes and actions make us caring human beings?
? Which social issues are my community facing?
? What can we do to contribute to a fairer and more caring society in general and our community in particular?
Context
Ysgol Friars is working towards being accredited as a Peace School, part of which is the promotion of various charitable causes. Against the background of the cost-of-living crisis, the school is asking you to promote Solidarity Week to help your community through acts of kindness.
Articulation Spiral Points
@ Use simple words and visuals to suggest ideas in a poster.
@ Express simple solutions in a leaflet to support people in need.
@ Create a video using persuasive language to encourage solidarity.

HOW DO LANGUAGES CONNECT US?

Intercultural Transfer Targets	Mediation for Transfer
• I can identify basic social issues. • I can identify ways that make us caring human beings. • I can prioritize actions to help my local community. • I can express ways in which to support our local community in the TL.	• Identify ideas from words, phrases and visuals (lyrics/ videos). • Explain some causes of the social issues and propose solutions. • Bridge and exchange attributes and acts of solidarity.

Beginner	Intermediate	Advanced
\multicolumn{3}{Videos and song 'La chanson des Restos'}		
\multicolumn{3}{Interpretive Task Descriptions — How do we understand the world around us and support others?}		
Pupils listen to the song *Les Enfoirés – La Chanson des Restos* (with lyrics). Pupils hold up words/ phrases related to social inequality when mentioned in the song/ shown in the video. Pupils match up an extended list of English and French vocabulary related to social inequality and categorize them into issues and solutions.	Pupils match French with English words/ phrases related to social inequality from the song. Pupils listen to the song *Les Enfoirés – La Chanson des Restos* (without lyrics). Word-snap: Pupils listen out for the terms taken from the song and hit the words when heard. Pupils categorize them into issues and solutions.	Pupils listen to the song *Les Enfoirés – La Chanson des Restos* (without lyrics). Pupils fill in gaps in the lyrics, using a list of words provided. Pupils categorize them into issues and solutions (highlighter). Pupils match English phrases to (underlined) French lyrics to increase understanding of the message.
\multicolumn{3}{I Can}		
Comparison with initiatives in GB + school I can recognize words/ phrases. I can identify common social issues.	Comparison with initiatives in GB + school I can extract specific words from spoken material	Comparison with initiatives in GB + school I can extract specific words from spoken material. I can apply reading comprehension skills to access new material.

Interpersonal Task Descriptions How do we express ourselves and engage others?		
Pupils rank the extended list of acts of solidarity based on their own priorities.	Pupils discuss an extended list of ways in which to help others. Pupils exchange ideas about ways to help people in need. Survey: Comment peut-on aider? – On peut/ Il faut … (Ext: add opinion phrases)	In small groups, pupils are each given the role of a person in need. Pupils establish the social issue and develop ways in which to support each other and find the best ways in which to tackle the respective issues. Groups are mixed. Pupils do a hot seat activity, answering questions on how best to support them (on pourrait/ il fallait …)
I Can		
I can prioritize ways to help people in need.	I can ask questions, exchange ideas and discuss acts of solidarity.	I can exchange information with a partner and listen for key details about different ways to show solidarity.
Presentational Task Descriptions **How do we create and share with others?**		
Create our school's own logo for Solidarity Day. Create a poster to be put up around the school informing pupils what they can do to help their community.	Create our school's own logo for Solidarity Day. Design a leaflet stating the issues and providing actions.	Create our school's own logo for Solidarity Day. Create a persuasive video highlighting issues in our community and promoting actions we can take to help people in need in our community (to be shown during registration/ assembly in run-up to the week etc.) Possible link: music dept > include chorus using phrases developed.
I Can		
I can display the actions we can take to help people in need in our community.	I can create a leaflet displaying issues in our community with words and visuals, stating actions we can take during Solidarity Week to help people in need in our community.	I can create a persuasive video, encouraging peers to join in with acts of kindness. I can convey ideas on how to take action, drawing on and collating my resources.

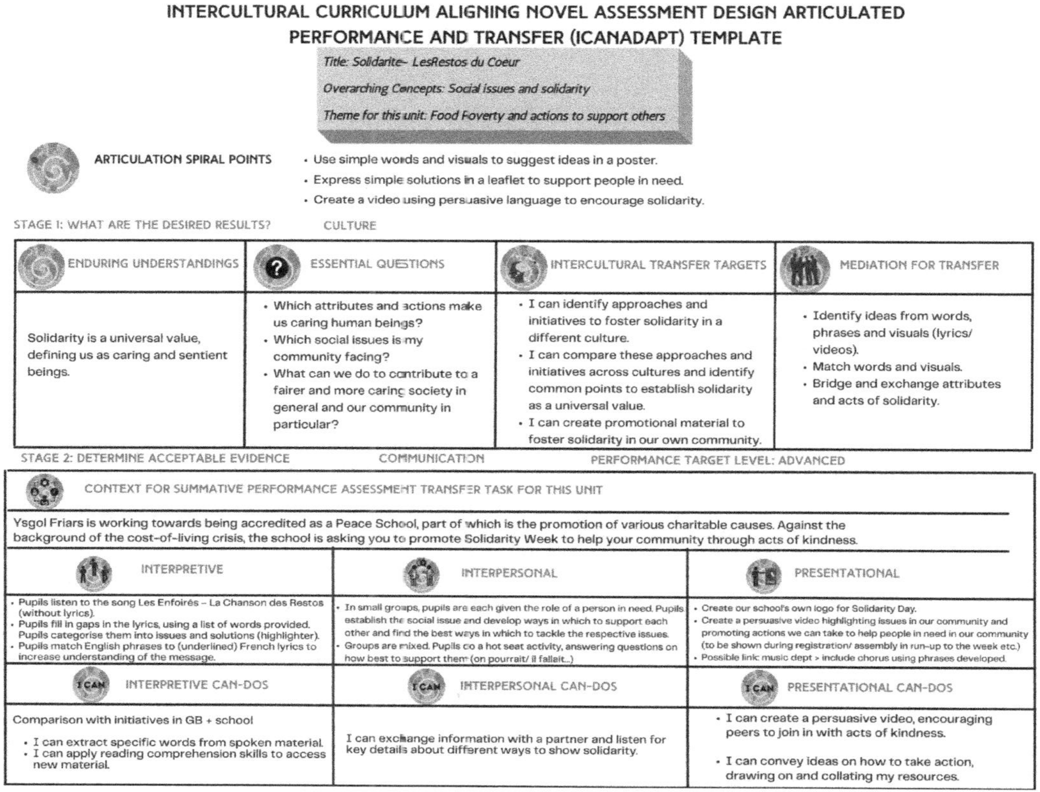

FIGURE 3.2 *Solidarité ICANADAPT Unit Stages 1 & 2. Adapted from Eddy, J. (2022) Designing World Language Curriculum for Intercultural Communicative Competence, with permission from Bloomsbury Academic, an imprint of Bloomsbury Publishing, Plc.*

STAGE 3: LEARNING EXPERIENCES AND INSTRUCTION   CONNECTIONS – COMPARISONS – COMMUNITIES

FORMATIVE ASSESSMENTS FOR LESSONS NEAR TRANSFER	MODE IN IP PR	PERFORMANCE ASSESSMENT SPECIFIC STATEMENTS I CAN...	VOCABULARY AND GRAMMAR REVIEW (R) SAME YEAR SPIRAL (S) PREVIOUS YEAR NEW (N) FOR THIS UNIT	INTERCULTURAL TRANSFER TARGETS I CAN...
Authentic material: https://vimeo.com/115154527 (Restos du coeur – 1 jour 1 actu) Pupils watch a video clip on why Les Restos du Coeur were established. Pupils answer questions on the video to ensure understanding of the cultural context.	Interpretive	• I can extract specific words from spoken material. • I can apply reading and audio-visual comprehension skills to access new material. • I can understand the cultural context in question.	R: Use of cognates (audio + visual) S: Use of basic reading strategies N: Reasons for the Restos du Coeur	• I can identify reasons for the need for the Restos du Coeur in France.
Pupils discuss their feelings/ opinions about the reasons for the Restos du Coeur. (use of Je suis/ Je me sens + adjectives of emotions) (cards to match up reasons from video + feelings :-) → il y a // Pupils can then make sentences like: Je suis triste car il y a...)	Interpersonal	• I can have a simple discussion expressing and justifying my emotions in relation to the reasons for the Restos du Coeur.	R: Basic connectives (car il y a/ parce qu'il y a) S: Opinion phrases (Je pense que/ J'aime etc.) N: Sentence starters to express emotions + Adjectives of emotion (Je [ne] suis [pas]/ Je [ne] me sens [pas] etc.)	• I can express and justify my emotions regarding the reasons for the Restos du Coeur to a partner.
Pupils create a display highlighting the reasons for the need of Les Restos du Coeur.	Presentational	• I can create a display using the reasons for the need of Les Restos du Coeur	R: Reasons for the Restos du Coeur + Basic connectives S: Structuring a sentence. N: Sentence starters to express necessity (Il faut / On a besoin des...)	• I can write about the reasons why there is a need for the Restos du Coeur in France.

Adapted with permission from Eddy, J 2017. "Unpacking the Standards for Transfer. Intercultural Competence by Design." from the Northeast Conference on the Teaching of Foreign Languages and the Editor of the NECTFL Review; (Council of Europe, 2020); National Standards Collaborative Board, 2015; Wiggins & McTighe, 2005)

Designing World Language Curriculum for Intercultural Communicative Competence, J Eddy, 2022, © Bloomsbury Academic Education

FIGURE 3.3 *Solidarité ICANADAPT Unit Stage 3. Adapted from Eddy, J. (2022) Designing World Language Curriculum for Intercultural Communicative Competence, with permission from Bloomsbury Academic, an imprint of Bloomsbury Publishing, Plc.*

It is time to dive deeper into Ms Piesch's design by examining the ICANADAPT unit. Here, she unfolds one level from the AATT and presents a set of assessments for learning (AfL) in Stage Three (see Figure 3.2 and 3.3). Notice that the inter/transcultural perspectives are present, and the near transfer tasks build towards the summative assessment in Stage Two from the AATT. Can you think of a song that could be revisited and reprised over a curriculum with tasks at different stages of complexity? What other summative products or performances could learners design based on that song? What formative tasks would you create to support learning throughout the unit for your Stage Three? Could you do this with other performing or visual arts texts as well?

Bridge to Design

Let's go deeper into Ms Piesch's design process and collaborate with colleagues before working on your own design.

Reflect to Reveal

1) How is the overarching, big idea of solidarity revealed in this song and the exemplar tasks?
2) Why is it important to reprise and revisit *Solidarité* over time in a curriculum?
3) Why does Ms Piesch want pupils to know what inspires songwriters?

Questions for Colleagues

1) Are there songs inspired from cultural history to current events that are key for your articulated and inter/transcultural curriculum? Please share them.
2) How can the issue of food poverty be unpacked across the curriculum, even at the earliest levels?
3) What would you do differently? What would you add or otherwise change?

Ask the Designer

What is your question for Ms Piesch? What else do you want to know about this exemplar and her design thinking?

Participate in the Practice

Which practices guided Ms Piesch in creating her exemplar? How did she design with these in mind? Explain below for each component.

1) Any topic, any level: The text or topic does not determine complexity, the task you design for it does.
2) Develop tasks for transfer that inspire one work of art or text to become another.
3) Song lyrics with universal, intercultural themes containing symbols, imagery, and story.

Teacher to Leader on Design and Implementation

1. Always start your AATT design process with the choice of a topical authentic resource.
2. When designing the three different levels start with the Presentational task and plan backwards.
3. Instead of trying to adapt an existing unit to an AATT, design your AATTs from scratch.

From the Admin Desk

From the administrator point of view, other language teachers can learn that every 'big question' can be dealt with in language lessons. The trick is not to let the level of language dictate your programme of study. Deciding on the issue to deal with first and breaking down how to enable the access for pupils in terms of language last is what will make language learning successful in terms of aptitude but more importantly in terms of relatedness.

Food poverty is a global issue. This AATT is easily adaptable to any other language. The authentic materials used will inform the planning. To help your teachers grow such planning mindsets, an administrator could use this AATT to get the teachers to reflect on their own end of school syllabuses and look at what could be brought down to twelve-year-olds. What part of the end of high school syllabus excites us as language teachers? What societal or literary topic or questions do we enjoy and look forward to teaching the most once our students are old enough to deal with them? What and how should be taught this at a much earlier age?

—Stephanie Ellis-Williams, International Languages, Global Futures GwE Lead

Design for Transfer

For your chosen theme, design at least two EUs and two to three EQs. These EUs and EQs are entered onto the AATT template and the ICANADAPT unit template (see companion website for templates with fillable fields, Chapter 3).

Design for Transfer

Using your EUs and EQs, design at least three ITTs. These state what the learner can do in terms of inter/transcultural competence. After you design the tasks, revisit these to revise and tighten because other targets will have emerged after all tasks are designed and in place at all levels.

 ## *Reflect and Revisit*

1. How do EUs and EQs help us uncover how people think and the content that reveals these perspectives over the span of a curriculum?
2. Do you notice inter/transcultural perspectives embedded in many disciplines that created our authentic cultural community texts? Give an example.
3. What are some must-have perspectives that even the youngest learners can understand? Do we have to have native-level proficiency to relay them to others?
4. Which Intercultural Transfer Goals resurface and recur throughout our lives in every culture?
5. Why do learners need to see these themes uncovered over their curriculum?
6. How did these teachers make the case for inter/transcultural communicative competence in their designs?
7. Are there at least three intercultural themes your learners cannot leave your programme not understanding very well that relate to the culture studied and all cultures? What do you hope will happen when the learner finishes your programme?

4

How Do We Understand the World around Us and Support Others?

Enduring Understandings

- ∞ Transdisciplinary texts with interpretive tasks enable learners to receive, react and respond to anything we watch, hear, view or read.
- ∞ Literacy-based tasks provide strategies for new language learners to support themselves and effectively mediate for others in a plurilingual context.
- ∞ The authentic cultural community text does not determine the complexity; the task designed from it does.
- ∞ The Interpretive tasks allow learners to react, then interact and enact, later creating new works with inter/transcultural intention.

Essential Questions

- Q What can we do with anything we listen to, watch or read?
- Q How do texts reflect, reveal and inform our culture(s)?
- Q To what extent are texts and images from different cultural communities also about us?
- Q Why should we ask questions?
- Q What does supporting others through mediation look like?

I can

- Determine Cultural Community Authentic Texts for my tasks.
- Describe Interpretive tasks for learner ownership of language and mediation to support others.
- Design tasks across different levels for articulation
- Develop *I can* statements specific to the task and intercultural transfer targets.

Let's Consider

In Chapter 3, we explored the question, 'How do languages connect us?' Language learning involves words and structures, but never in isolation from the cultures where languages reside and thrive. When we learn languages, we always re-discover our own cultural identities while encountering those around us. Our first contact with a culture may not always be with people speaking directly with us but with the objects or materials they created and shared. This encounter may be with art, songs, foods, pictures, objects, signs, labels or videos. This list, by no means exhaustive, represents what people make and, very often, shows what people do and always reveals what people think. These items usually produce a reaction within us, perhaps a question in our mind or a thought on how we can connect or organize their elements to make sense. These public and shared materials offer our learners all sorts of inter/transcultural contexts and opportunities to engage with them. How can we identify them? Compare them to something else? How could we support others unfamiliar with the language or culture and mediate for them with language we own now? How do these tasks help us to do that?

Own Your Reaction, Request, Response

In DWLC (Eddy, 2022b), we said Interpretive tasks (Glisan et al., 2003; National Standards in Foreign Language Education Project, 1996/2006; National Standards Collaborative Board, 2015) mirror our first encounter with anything we have to understand so that it is communication for conception. It is our first contact with the piece alone, but not in conversation with anyone else yet. These tasks are so important; they are our initial opportunity at ownership of language and culture, however small. We decide, choose and share information with someone else, and then we author our own new works for someone else. What learners do with the text now is incumbent upon any production that happens later. Thus, the learner begins at the onset of a unit to uncover recursive concepts with an transcultural mindset. Often repeated among our teacher leaders in this group was 'Own before it is shown'. That is the goal of the tasks you will see designed here.

In this framework, learners

1. Use cultural community authentic texts in a range of genres: public, shared and unchanged
2. Own new information from texts with active tasks of request, reaction and response, not passive recall
3. Identify, Index, Inquire, Infer, Illustrate, Interpret and Improve, using texts composed by other people

For each set of tasks at every level in the AATT, you will see a description of *Cultural Community Authentic Texts;* the links to the texts are found on the companion website. These texts are spoken, written, signed, created or viewed multimedia designed by people or someone from the cultural communities for the public to consume, use or experience. These texts contrast with pieces developed for language learning, prepared or edited for classrooms (Kramsch, 2006, 2013). Whether it is a food label or poem, street sign, advertisement, poster, film, news article, painting, play, podcast, infographic or novel, these are works in which intercultural perspectives reside, and all are community texts. Without even realizing it and often taking it for granted, we always see these against the backdrop of a culture or cultures by default and engage with the cultural contexts that informed them. They became accessible to everyone the moment they were made public and shared. They all evoke some response from us. It can be a simple response or a complex one. Usually, something I read or hear strikes a question in my mind about it. Perhaps it is a thought or comment. If I were in a shop and heard an item, I could probably point to it. If I read about a few apartments, I might consider what each one offered with the amenities I wanted. If I saw a poster about a music event, I might pose a question in my mind about that information, the time or date, how I can get there, who I might ask to go with me and if there are good seats left. For classroom tasks, it is the same challenge. I can react by selecting a picture or illustration that matches what I hear. I can respond with one word and eventually a paragraph. Pose a question about something I clearly see or do not see and infer.

I can group similar items, check off items I hear, or place story illustrations in order. Perhaps I can select a headline for a news article and summarize or improve upon it based on prior knowledge. In any case, with these examples, the reaction, request, or response is simple or complex. Neither the topic nor the text should be held back from the learner or postponed (Bruner, 1962, 1996). Choose texts based on how they address cultural perspectives, contributions, information or disciplinary content, not for the apparent ease or difficulty of the text itself. 'Authentic texts chosen not for level but task potential can be used at all proficiency levels' (Mishan, 2005, p. 44). It is not the text that carries complexity; the task designed from it does.

Our group used all types of texts to design tasks ranging from simple, novice responses to highly complex ones, sometimes using the same piece of authentic text for all levels. These tasks go beyond basic comprehension of facts and answering questions; those are passive tasks. Facts are easily obtained online and are not transferable evidence of learning. Neither are recall, discrete point, fill-in tasks that manipulate grammar forms (DWLC, Eddy, 2022b, p. 125). The tasks in these exemplars are interactive, whether the learner is alone or in pairs or groups. These tasks support others by facilitating mediation; they use visuals, clarify, organize, compare and elaborate. We support others even as learners by being a social agent, to organize meaning with another person or group (COE, 2020; Piccardo, 2013) if that means merely indicating meaning with an image or object. These tasks foster interaction with the original text in varied formats. They provide an incentive to produce a reaction, to derive meaning from the input we see every day outside the classroom and not pattern drills which reside only inside of it (Gee, 2012; VanPatten, 2003, 2004, 2010, 2017). In the AATTs, this mode enables learners to own language and concepts early and later again differently with more complexity as they spiral up performance target levels. Metacognitive 'I can' statements (Council of Europe, 2001; CEFR, 2020; NCSSFL, 2017) enable learner autonomy (Lamb, 2017; Little, 2003; Little et al., 2017). Our teachers derived 'I can' or Performance Assessment Specific Statements (PASS) after they designed the tasks to ensure the takeaway was specific to the task. This prevents redundant or surplus forms, functions and content not present in the task, an old habit that often recurs when 'I can' sentences are written before designing the task. For verbs to create 'I can' statements (Anderson et al., 2001; Bloom, 1956) aligned with the task stages, see Figure 4.1.

Our teachers designed tasks across seven interpretive types: *Identify, Index, Inquire, Interpret, Infer, Illustrate and Improve* (see Table 4.1 and Appendix D). The task directs the learner to notice and focus on particular elements within

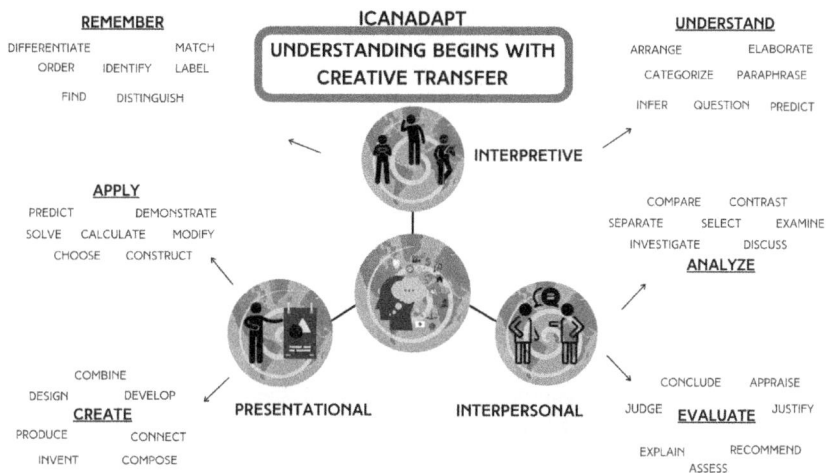

FIGURE 4.1 *Understanding begins with Creative Transfer – I Can. Adapted from Eddy, J. (2022)* Designing World Language Curriculum for Intercultural Communicative Competence, *with permission from Bloomsbury Academic, an imprint of Bloomsbury Publishing, Plc.*

the texts for a specific use. The tasks shift from literal to inferential, listing, categorizing and selecting words and images found explicitly in the text to managing implicit information hidden 'between the lines', unstated or absent entirely, requiring prior knowledge to resolve (Raphael & Au, 2005). As we progress upward on the vertical articulation spiral, learners can summarize sentences, then further ahead paragraphs, utilizing prior learning and information from previous tasks (Verhoeven & Perfetti, 2008; Vygotsky, 1978).

Forming questions is an overlooked skill within this mode and is necessary for the learner to progress to intermediate level or CEFR A2 (ACTFL, 2012; COE, 2020; NCSSFL, 2017). Whereas many comprehension tasks rely only on answering questions, the responses generally contain surface facts are isolated from culture and keep the learner passive rather than active (Lantoff & Appel, 1994). Ask yourself this: How genuine is it when it is presumed the teacher already knows the answer? Also, when we hear, watch or read anything, questions may indeed pop into our mind about it. However, we do not answer a list of them afterwards. Even though the question exchange with someone else is interpersonal, purely forming and posing questions is interpretive. It is evidence you understood the text if you can form a question, however small the bit of information is or simple it may be. When learners pose questions that shift from literal to inferential, this indicates transfer and progression. These tasks build literacy and help learners find meaning, value and significance from a piece in order to react, request and respond later on to support others through mediation. Whenever we are out and about and encounter anything we listen to, watch or read, we will notice, react to it, capture what we need, claim it and move on. In the AATTs, learners will take these bits and skills for use in the subsequent modes, sharing with someone else in the Interpersonal task and creating a new product or solving a problem in the subsequent Presentational tasks. Table 4.1 below outlines key features of each task type, a sample and the strategy the learner acquires for mediation to support someone unaware of the culture or unfamiliar with the language. For alignment of all task types with mediation strategy support, see Appendix D.

TABLE 4.1 Seven Interpretive task types and supporting others in mediation

Type	Sample Task	Strategy acquired for Mediation
Identify	Select or match image to word. Check off on a list as you listen.	Indicate unfamiliar items or actions with images, words or gestures.
Index	Categorize items on a chart. Sequence events in order.	Group similar items, places, objects for others. Retell the story.
Inquire	Develop questions from facts found in one or multiple places in text.	Bridge understanding for others by posing questions, sorting relationships and combining information.
Interpret	Listen for the gist or main idea. Compose title or headline.	Summarize and paraphrase for someone else.
Infer	Uncover not only what is directly in the text, but also what is not and only implied.	Offer examples to make language more accessible for someone else. Resolve ambiguity.
Illustrate	Reveal concrete or covert and abstract information that may be hidden in the text by drawing what is described.	Draw and illustration for someone to extract and point out explicit or tacit and implied examples. Clarify intended message for someone unaware of cultural cues, practices or products.
Improve	Form questions based on prior knowledge interpretation. Elaborate when information is not found in the text.	Elaborate to bridge and improve on text to help others using their own interpretation and collaborative background knowledge.

Put It to Practice: Collaborate to Articulate

In the five AATTs you have seen thus far, which features stand out in the Interpretive mode tasks? Do you think the tasks demonstrate that pupils can Identify, Index, Inquire, Infer, Illustrate, Interpret and Improve from the texts? As a result of doing these skills, can they support and clarify for someone else with language they own right now? Do you see evidence of progression from literal to inferential in the upward spiral? Would you add any interpretive tasks to the ones you see in the AATT?

Meet Our Designers

All of the AATTs in this book show interpretive tasks of ownership, reaction, request and response. For this chapter, these four exemplars were especially selected by Ms Stephanie Ellis-Williams for their use of cultural community authentic texts, the tasks designed from them and teacher reflections on their work. Ms Hughes unfolds changes over time for an important cultural fair, Ms Adams explores environmental solutions across cultures, the meaning of heritage, heroes and street signs merge for Ms Green's pupils and Ms McAllister's looks at identity and social media. These exemplars show how learners bring knowledge with them, develop cultural interactions and show flexibility across and within many cultural spaces.

From Past to Present, Cultural History as Advocacy

In *Ffair Borth* Menai Bridge Fair, Mrs Hughes uses a variety of texts, from a literary classic, to photos then and now, to bridge and connect yesteryear to yesterday for her pupils. Her tasks explore key literacy strategies as learners identify key features of the fair, categorize and order, and build vocabulary as they interpret, elaborate and improve upon texts. Notice the progression evident through the tasks. Most notably, these tasks facilitate mediation as pupils connect significant practices and their changes over time with present day to someone unfamiliar with Welsh cultural history. The persuasive elements at each level serve pupils well as advocates to effect change in other local, civic or national contexts, a clear indication of transfer beyond the classroom domain.

Teacher as Designer – *Ffair Borth* Menai Bridge Fair

Mrs Hughes teaches in a large secondary school on the isle of Anglesey. The school is a bilingual comprehensive school. The majority of students can speak Welsh due to them attending a Welsh-medium primary school. The level of proficiency in Welsh spans across the whole learning continuum. Differentiation is therefore key to successful outcomes and to support all learners on their learning journey.

This is a particularly good example to showcase the range of texts, images and materials which can be used to impart knowledge and develop cultural understanding. By selecting literary extracts from one of the Welsh classics, photographs across the years and twenty-first-century materials, the teacher is able to get learners to explore the context and the ethos of the Menai Bridge Fair from its origins to nowadays. In doing so, pupils get to start gathering elements of response to the essential questions around the purpose and ethos of village and town fairs. This will, later on, enable them to discuss, reflect and make critical judgements which will inform their final productive task. The annual fair, which is often taken for granted by young locals, has now become a subject worth of study and an event to value much more. Learners will also start to look at other everyday events or celebrations with a different perspective. This is instilling in learners the need and the know-how to delve deeper into what is happening around us, which will ensure they make more sense of the world they live in.

The particular gem of this AATT (see Table 4.2) is to bring an old literary classic to life and make it relevant to the twenty-first-century learners. The link between the past and the present is not forced. Learners embrace such connections as they see its relevance to the work they will need to produce.

—Stephanie Ellis-Williams, International Languages,
Global Futures GwE Lead

Voices from the Field

A New Curriculum for Wales has been an opportunity for us to revamp our learning plans and ensure that pupils' work is up-to-date and relevant. There was a presentation by Mererid Hopwood before starting to plan our New Curriculum and the important message was that we need to give 'roots and wings' to the pupils. Studying the Menai Bridge Fair gives roots as the fair is a historic and important event for the school area (Porthaethwy) but the pupils are not aware of this very often (this is the 'wings' element found by Mererid Hopwood). Designing the unit gives pupils the opportunity to learn about the importance of culture through languages and prepares learners to be citizens of Wales and the world. What is nice about the Menai Bridge Fair unit is that all pupils have access to the unit because they all have some experience of a fair.

Festivals are important in Welsh culture and therefore understanding the history and contribution of fairs helps us to appreciate Welsh culture. Fairs have appeared a lot in Welsh literature over the years so studying the Menai Bridge Fair unit gives pupils the opportunity to experience this. Planning in this way ensures that the work is relevant and interesting for pupils. Work is deliberately differentiated. Planning backwards also ensures that tasks offer enough challenge for everyone.

What has had the biggest impact on me is ensuring that there is a 'hook' at the beginning of the unit to maintain interest. Also, it is important to set a 'problem/context' that needs to be solved as part of the unit and therefore, the pupils get to solve the problem and have the opportunity to do tasks relevant to everyday life.

Another effective aspect is planning through Receiving, Sharing and Creating. Sharing the information is just as key to proving understanding as it is to creating. I've ensured that the Ein Llais Ni strategy (which promotes oracy) is in every level of Sharing. This enables pupils to practise speaking and listening as well as writing. Planning units of work following the AATT structure has maintained the interest of year 7 pupils. They have created work of high quality and enjoyed it.

—Ms Nicola Hughes, Ysgol David Hughes, Anglesey, Welsh

TABLE 4.2 Articulated Assessment Transfer Task – *Ffair Borth* Menai Bridge Fair

Enduring Understandings
✱ Learning about the importance of culture through languages prepares learners to be citizens of Wales and the world.
✱ The importance of holidays is in Welsh culture. Understanding the history and contribution of fairs helps us appreciate Welsh culture.
Essential Questions
? What is a fair?
? What is the value of education?
? Are life experiences more important than education from time to time?
? What skills cannot be learned in a classroom?
? How does understanding the history and contribution of fairs to Welsh culture help us appreciate our cultural heritage?
Context
The headmaster of the school is willing to have a meeting to listen to your opinion regarding the closing of the school on the day of the Menai Bridge fair. Prepare your arguments to persuade.
Articulation Spiral Points
@ Pamphlet advertising Menai Bridge Fair to the community.
@ Describe a day at the Fair.
@ Persuade the headmaster that the school should be closed on the day of Menai Bridge Fair

Intercultural Transfer Targets	Mediation for Transfer
• I can appreciate how fairs have changed over the years.	• Pupils can describe the Menai Bridge fair to someone unfamiliar with the culture.
• I can appreciate the history of the Menai Bridge Fair.	• Pupils can explain the importance of the fair and how it's changed over the years.
• I can appreciate the importance of Menai Bridge Fair for the area	

Beginner	Intermediate	Advanced
Video clips, story cards, blog from Hull Fair		
Interpretive Task Descriptions How do we understand the world around us and support others?		
Watch a video clip (up to 1 minute 20 seconds) Look at a picture of Fair and label it with Welsh terms.	Strategy What's the Story – *Ein Llais Ni* Story cards – put the cards in order Read the story of Elen and Alun and rearrange the cards Read The Fair Poem.	Watch the blog below from Hull Fair. Draw a table for and against closing the school on the day of the fair.

HOW DO WE UNDERSTAND THE WORLD?

	I Can	
I can use Welsh terms to describe the Fair.	I can listen to a story and remember key facts.	I can explain how fairs have changed over the years. I can describe the importance of the Menai Bridge Fair to the local area.

Interpersonal Task Descriptions How do we express ourselves and engage others?		
Using the picture as a trigger, fill in the 5 senses table at the fair with partners. Word for Word Strategy – *Ein Llais Ni* Using your senses table, choose a few senses. Describe the word with partners without using the key word (playing a game like Charades).	Create 5 Similes and 2 Metaphors to describe the fair Strategy I am the expert – *Ein Llais Ni* Writing a Menai Bridge Fair *Ffair Borth* poem (each group to get one sense and create a verse based on the sense).	Silent Compiler Strategy – *Ein Llais Ni* Using your table of pros and cons, it is necessary to discuss closing the school on the day of the fair. One of you will be in favour and the other against. There will be a third person listening attentively and summarizing the argument for the rest of the class.

	I Can	
I can use my 5 senses to describe the Fair.	I can create interesting similes and metaphors to describe.	I can find points for and against a certain subject (closing YDH on the fair day).

Presentational Task Descriptions How do we create and share with others?		
Show a picture of the current Menai Bridge Fair advertisement. Porthaethwy Community Council has contacted the school asking for help to advertise the day of the fair. Draw up a pamphlet presenting information about the Menai Bridge Fair.	The school principal has never been to the fair. Describe a day at the fair so that it gets a flavour of the day.	The YDH School Council pupils have asked you to present an argument to the headmaster that the school should be closed on the day of the fair. Your task will be to persuade the headmaster in an official meeting. Prepare a speech with your arguments.

		OR YDH School Council pupils have asked you and one other pupil to present an argument to the headmaster that the school should be closed on the day of the fair. Work with a partner to prepare your arguments.
	I Can	
I can recognize and use the characteristics of a persuasive poster. I can write persuasively to design an advertisement.	I can recognize the characteristics of descriptive writing.	I can weigh up arguments and come to a conclusion. I can implement the characteristics of verbal persuasion.

Bridge to Design

Let's go deeper into Ms Hughes' design process and collaborate with colleagues for additional ideas and reflection on this exemplar before working on your own design.

Reflect to Reveal

1) What do fairs teach us about culture and daily life?
2) How does Ms Hughes connect the history of the Menai Bridge Fair to the pupil's experiences today?
3) How can the interpretive tasks help someone extend the cultural story to someone else?

Questions for Colleagues

1) To what extent can older texts reveal perspectives and practices for contemporary audiences?
2) Do you have an example of a festival or celebration from your own culture that has changed over time?
3) How does this exemplar go beyond the typical treatment of celebrations? Which components give pupils a vested interest?

Ask the Designer

What is your question for Ms Hughes? What else do you want to know about this exemplar and her design thinking?

Participate in the Practice

Which practices guided Ms Hughes in creating her exemplar? How did she design with these in mind? Explain below for each component.

1) The context that solves a problem or creates a product for a given audience.
2) Tasks which facilitate mediation with others and clarify from known to new content.
3) Pupil reflection informed by background knowledge and cultural response to interpretive tasks.

Teacher to Leader on Design and Implementation

1. Create an effective and controversial 'hook' to maintain pupils' interest and catch their attention immediately, e.g. Ysgol David Hughes must be closed on the day of Menai Bridge Fair so that everyone can visit the fair.
2. Ensure that *Ein Llais Ni* oral tasks are planned in the Creation section so that pupils have the opportunity to practise speaking and listening skills regularly.
3. Create relevant tasks that give pupils the opportunity to solve some kind of problem. For example, change the task 'Write a description of Menai Bridge Fair' to 'The headmaster of the school has never been to Menai Bridge Fair. Write a description of the fair so he can get a taste of the day'.

The pupils have responded very well to the AATT lessons. They see purpose in the task and it is relevant to their lives. All pupils have experience of the Fair and they feel strongly about closing the school on the day of the Fair! Having a task that requires persuading the principal has also appealed as they enjoy seeing the principal play a role in her Welsh lessons. Since implementing the model, I have changed my way of thinking when creating and setting tasks for pupils. I ensure that the task answers a problem that is relevant to everyday life, this ensures that the pupils see value in the task and increase their effort when undertaking the task. Several members of the Welsh Department are working on creating units of work based on the model since I attended Jenny's training. The method of receiving information, sharing information and creating a task that is relevant to everyday life is now rooted in our plans. Creating a hook or question at the beginning of a unit of work has also received a lot of attention from us to ensure that it immediately engages the learners' interest.

—Ms Nicola Hughes, Ysgol David Hughes, Anglesey

From the Admin Desk

Other language teachers could learn that revisiting older materials which may have relevance to contemporary issues may be one way to develop the essential knowledge pupils need to have to be able to make sense of the world around them. In a time where literacy and in particular reading skills are in decline, it is our role to design tasks which will raise literacy levels.

Therefore, language teachers should embrace and make good use of the wealth of literary work at their disposal to spark learners' interest and develop their understanding of the community that they study and in turn that they live in.

Connecting the past to the present in this way will also enable any language teachers to drill and secure grammatical knowledge and skills whilst ensuring such language work is carried out in a meaningful context and for a real purpose.

—Stephanie Ellis-Williams, International Languages, Global Futures GwE Lead

The Environment Belongs to Everyone

Ms Adams works at all points of vertical articulation in her school and this AATT exemplar demonstrates that dedication to it and her learners' success. By using readily available and recognizable images of recycling bins, pupils are prompted to react, question and categorize, comparing efforts across countries and cultures. From literature to multimedia, the texts provide the potential for any level of task (Mishan, 2005) and novelty for solving problems and creating products. The environment is often held back until higher levels in many curricula because it is presented within an artificial textbook sequence. Our youngest pupils all share an affinity for nature. Learners may be novices but it does not mean they cannot or should not experience content that is conceptually familiar, start investing early in their language repertoire and manage what they own at the time. These tasks make a complicated subject like the environment more accessible while uncovering its transcultural significance and the learner's role as responsible global citizen.

Teacher as Designer – Environment

St Brigid's school is a 3 to 19 school, a unique set up which allows for a smooth transition between learning stages. The Spanish teacher oversees the whole range of learning and can therefore plan programmes across the ages. The AATT process is therefore particularly useful as it supports the five principles of progression consistently along the continuum. Pupils respond very positively to such planning and progress is very much enhanced by it.

This AATT (see Table 4.3) is a good example of this principle as it develops an understanding of the problems and solutions of the environment in other communities. The interpretive tasks enable students to get an insight into ways other communities address some of the issues regarding the environment. Learners can compare, contrast and relate to these other cultures, whilst reflecting on their own position regarding these problems.

The environment continues to be a very hot topic which students from a very young age feel passionate about. Using authentic materials such as photographs of recycling bins in various communities is an accessible and interesting way to deal with the essential questions of the AATT. The work is age appropriate whilst remaining relevant and serious. Learners develop their intercultural understanding whilst learning and revisiting key language points and vocabulary. The teacher consciously designs planning to build upon the specific environment vocabulary and phrases with the appropriate exercises to secure the learning. However, the pupils are directed to focus on the questions set rather than the language work, which raises interest and motivation. Pupils naturally engage with the language work as it is the means to express their opinions and convictions on the topic and enable them to solve the problem set.

Mrs Adams selects and uses materials which are authentic but accessible. Photographs and infographics are on point. It is the task set which develops pupils' understanding from awareness to deeper understanding of the issues raised with recycling. Students are asked to make educated guesses, encouraging them to think critically from the start. This hooks their interest and actively engages their learning. The interpretive stage is not a passive transmission of information on the environment. It is an opportunity for intercultural knowledge and competence as well as language learning strategies and development.

—Stephanie Ellis-Williams, International Languages, Global Futures GwE Lead

Voices from the Field

As part of the new curriculum, the four purposes include enabling students to become ethical, informed citizens of Wales and the world. In terms of the Presentational tasks, these will allow students to come up with creative solutions to relevant world issues. It doesn't matter which language you will be delivering your AATT through – conversations involving the environment are essential for every young person in any country as it is their future this pressing issue will affect.

They should understand that our treatment of the planets resources has a different effect in different cultures and different countries. We may not experience drought in Wales and other countries may not have the same positive attitude towards recycling. They can connect with the theme by reflecting on their own cultures, attitudes and actions.

We have enjoyed approaching planning in a different way and working backwards from an agreed deliverable objective or task. We feel we are certainly maximizing our use of authentic materials and realistic, relatable tasks to encourage learners' enthusiasm and it feels good to step away from using textbook models.

The environment is traditionally regarded as a difficult area to teach and for pupils to unpack especially at GCSE due to the nature of very topic specific vocabulary. Our aim is to make it more approachable and even enjoyable at KS3 level. Our AATT can be set across three different year groups or even covered with just one year group. It would be up to the individual teacher to decide how much they might want to explore, for example, learning about recycling could coincide with the teaching of colours and basic grammar patterns involving modal expressions or infinitive verbs. Even on the simplest level, the environment is still a more traditionally difficult topic to teach. However, the aim of the new curriculum is to produce ambitious capable learners and covering this topic matter in KS3, could certainly be regarded as ambitious. Our AATT also allows our learners to be enterprising and creative contributors, sharing their ideas and solutions to very real-world problems.

This AATT enables:

1) Understanding connections between languages and cultures.
2) Making progress in their grammar and punctuation and applying these to a variety of tasks.
3) Firing creativity and imagination.

The AATT develops breadth and depth of knowledge of various topics. Through planning the tasks in this way, differentiation is an integral part of the task and allows learners from novice to intermediate to access the lessons. It also allows creative skills to be developed at every opportunity and every level within the task.

The AATT inspires further cultural curiosity. Through lessons delivered inspired by the AATT, students also see context and meaning to their work. This helps to engage their interest and make them intrigued to know more.

—Ms Emma Adams, St. Brigid's School, Denbighshire, Spanish

TABLE 4.3 Articulated Assessment Transfer Task – The environment

Enduring Understandings
* Our lifestyle and the lifestyle of others is endangering the future of the planet.
* The environment as portrayed in the media can vary across cultures.
* Attitudes towards the environment depend on many factors such as our own experiences and culture.
Essential Questions
? Who is responsible for the future of our planet?
? Do attitudes towards the environment vary from culture to culture?
Context
The theme for the National Environmental Awareness Week is #onlyoneearth. Students have been invited to prepare materials for this international conference, which celebrates our wonderful world and promotes environmental responsibility.
Articulation Spiral Points
@ Describe concepts with visual support.
@ Offer practical solutions/information for a variety of environmental issues.
@ Justify opinions on environmental issues.

Intercultural Transfer Targets	Mediation for Transfer
<ul><li>I can recognize differences in recycling campaigns in different cultures.</li><li>I can show how poetry across different cultures reflects the importance of water for life and the consequences of droughts and floods.</li><li>I can compare the effects of global management of energy resources within different cultures.</li></ul>	<ul><li>Bridge and exchange ideas/concepts of how to protect the environment.</li><li>Identify visuals/objects/examples.</li><li>Use inference skills to glean information about environmental topics.</li><li>Compare/contrast global approaches to protecting the environment.</li><li>Collaborate to discuss similarities and differences in views and perspectives.</li><li>Formulate questions and give feedback to make these concepts more accessible.</li></ul>

Beginner	Intermediate	Advanced
Interpretive Task Descriptions **How do we understand the world around us and support others?**		
Students compare a variety of visual aids (images of global bins/ recycling containers/ waste management) Students categorize and fill in audio tasks and tables about materials which can be recycled across a variety of countries. Students provide a spoken or written response to how these images make them feel. Students compose three questions about the materials.	Students read and respond to texts(poems/idioms/ articles) Students create a Wordwall/mindmap to highlight the importance of water to the planet. Students watch videos from different areas worldwide Students devise questions to ask peers as how they have been affected by floods or drought.	Students view videos which outline what type of 'green energies' are being developed in target countries/areas. They take notes and summarize information on green energies.
I Can		
I can recognize the object of discussion after using the stimuli. I can categorise materials for proper recycling. I can write questions about the objects for recycling.	I can organize the text from wordwalls, mindmaps, and videos to write some points and questions on the importance and effects of/lack of water.	I can summarize the problems and possible solutions regarding energy use.

Interpersonal Task Descriptions		
How do we express ourselves and engage others?		
Group discussion in response to stimuli: why do we recycle? Is it important to recycle? Stimuli to include info graphs. Students ask three questions based on their discussions.	Students explain important events from a cultural and worldwide perspective such as droughts and floods. Students ask peers their questions as to how they have been affected by these phenomena. Students share personal experiences of floods with peers and in groups.	Students create a diamond ranking activity where they evaluate the merits of eco-energy production options.
I Can		
I can share and talk about the importance of recycling after watching a video.	I can exchange data and information about floods and droughts with peers.	I can discuss/compare the merits of and accept/reject solutions.
Presentational Task Descriptions		
How do we create and share with others?		
Students create a collage/model from recycled products to present their findings. They provide commentary using a puppet made from recycled material (animating a previously inanimate object). They use Voki/flipgrid and present the process.	Students produce a brochure/guide stating the issues/problems and solutions regarding droughts/floods for a select number of areas worldwide.	Students create a news report set in 2052. They report on how the earth is now more sustainable. They illustrate where good practice has happened and where we can still improve.
I Can		
I can list the features and discuss the process of recycling.	I can present information on the importance of water and its effect on the planet to others in class.	I can voice and relay opinions on energy and its effect through an interview or discussion process using gleaned resources from stimuli.

Bridge to Design

Let's go deeper into Ms Adams' design process and collaborate with colleagues for additional ideas and reflection on this exemplar before working on your own design.

Reflect to Reveal

1) How do the authentic materials make the language accessible and the perspectives visible?
2) How does Ms Adams help her pupils unfold this complicated topic over the curriculum?
3) In what ways do the interpretive tasks help learners to mediate for someone else?

Questions for Colleagues

1) Is there one great piece of authentic text that you use for a variety of interpretive tasks?
2) Does your choice of authentic/cultural community materials determine the direction of your tasks? The new products pupils create and share?
3) How do interpretive tasks prepare pupils for planning and consensus with other people?

Ask the Designer

What is your question for Ms Adams? What else do you want to know about this exemplar and her design thinking?

Participate in the Practice

Which practices guided Ms Adams in creating her exemplar? How did she design with these in mind? Explain below for each component.

1) Authentic community texts we see every day.
2) Visual thinking for symbolic competence.
3) Solving a problem in the context with products across all levels.

Teacher to Leader on Design

1. Don't worry about how small your idea is! Our ideas grew simply by looking at different waste receptacles and an entire project was formed. The simpler the idea the better.

2. Find your authentic resources early on! There is no sense in planning the entire project and then scrambling to find authentic resources which may be few and far between.

3. Let your learners inspire their learning! You may have planned for the project to go one direction but be open to suggestions and let the learners inspire further questions and ideas. As we found, this helped us form more EQs for the next time we approached the same AATT. Be open to the ideas you yourselves will inspire in the students and encourage them.

From the Admin Desk

As an administrator, this AATT can be used to show how selecting the right authentic material is key to the success of the AATT. Very often, this is what comes first. It is from the authentic material that the AATT will be created. This could be a headline and news article, or a photograph, current event which can be explored.

Many teachers have commented on the importance of selecting the material carefully and first. It is often too problematic and time-consuming to do this after planning the AATT. It can also feel like we shoe-horn some material to fit the planning and it does not work as well.

Finally, this AATT is a good example of how to address big questions and societal questions, just like the AATT mentioned in Chapter 3 which deals with Solidarity.

—Stephanie Ellis-Williams, International Languages, Global Futures GwE Lead

Photographs as Living Memory Texts of Our Communities

Ms Green shows us how holiday photos and street names in our travels reflect upon the heroes in our time. Using photos as living memory texts with other multimedia, learners uncover qualities of a hero and how those may have changed. Our exemplar here shows differentiation just within year 7. These pupils can pose questions, categorize and elaborate while making the case for the heroes we honour in naming our streets.

Teacher as Designer – Heroes

Dyffryn Ogwen is a small rural secondary school in a mountainous valley of North Wales. It is a Welsh-medium school. The community around the school can feel a little insular at times and learners can feel shy and lack confidence when out of the school confines. Opening them to a world far away from their valley enables them to understand and reflect on other people's values, perspectives and rationales.

This AATT (see Table 4.4) is a good example for the Principle as many layers of the EU is covered by a very simple but effective authentic material: the French street name signs. Not only do learners learn about the very specific way to name streets in France but it opens a door into the cultural and historical heritage of that country. In turn, it encourages pupils to reflect on their own heritage and how significant national and regional figures are or are not, should or should not be publicly and proudly remembered.

This can also show how different countries value their own heroes and how this could influence contemporaries to act heroically or positively for society.

The language used for this AATT remains basic and at beginner levels. Yet, it is used much more imaginatively and for much-deeper messages than it would traditionally be introduced for: i.e. describe who I am, describe my family ....

A particular gem for this unit is the use of the 'holiday' photographs. All language teachers have, over their various holidays in one of the target language countries, taken pictures of street signs or other major landmarks. Once back in class, when these are used, they are often shown for practice or to illustrate and drill vocabulary. Here, these are used to develop much more culturally and start conversations around EQs which pupils will ask themselves beyond their time in school.

—Stephanie Ellis-Williams, International Languages, Global Futures GwE Lead

Voices from the Field

Streets are named after celebrated people in France. Students will look at how heroes are celebrated and discuss the qualities of a hero in order to help them develop into ethically informed citizens who have secure values.

Everyone has a hero or someone they admire; the students will question what makes this person a hero. Students can consider how they would celebrate a hero in their own community.

It ensures that cultural perspective is an integral part of the learning. The EU and questions fit in very well with CfW. Students are building upon prior knowledge to develop their language skills as well as developing their empathy and values.

The framework of the AATT allows natural progression of skills through the different activities.

Pupils have shown evidence of the Principles of Progression by developing their range of sentence structures whilst describing other people. They are using what they have read and listened to develop their language. They have developed strategies to deal with unfamiliar challenging vocabulary.

It ensures that cultural perspective is an integral part of the learning. The EU and questions help ensure that the four purposes of CfW are covered. The format of the AATT ensures differentiation across the levels of ability.

I'm hopeful that the increased cultural understanding will encourage students to be eager to discover more about the wider world.

—Ms Emma Green, Dyffryn Ogwen, French

TABLE 4.4 Articulated Assessment Transfer Task – Heroes

Enduring Understandings
✷ The definition of a hero has changed over time and different cultures celebrate heroes in different ways.
Essential Questions
? What is a hero? How do different countries celebrate their heroes?
? How do we recognize and honour our heroes?

Context

The local council wants to name a street after a celebrated person as they do in France and is looking for suggestions.

Articulation Spiral Points

@ Describe other people.
@ Identify the qualities of a hero.
@ Create a presentation of a hero.

Intercultural Transfer Targets	Mediation for Transfer
• I can describe other people. • I can identify the qualities of a hero.	• Provide justification for choices – why a person deserves to be celebrated. • Explain which qualities are important. • Bridge and extend ideas – justify my choice of hero, match qualities to a visual.

Year 7 Novice	Year 7 Novice +	Year 7 Novice ++
Video – C'est quoi un héros? Text – 10 qualités d'un super-héros		
Interpretive Task Descriptions **How do we understand the world around us and support others?**		
Watch the video and identify qualities of a hero. Form questions about a hero.	Watch the video and put statements in order from the video.	Watch video and identify how the role of a hero has changed.
I Can		
I can identify the main points from a video. I can draft questions on characteristics of a hero.	I can sequence events in the correct order.	I can listen for details and make notes on changes.
Interpersonal Task Descriptions **How do we express ourselves and engage others?**		
With a partner, ask questions about the qualities and label images of the qualities of a hero.	With a partner, ask questions and match descriptions of the qualities of a hero with the definition.	With a partner, pyramid rank the qualities in order of importance and justify choices.
I Can		
I can ask and answer questions using words to describe heroes.	I can ask and answer questions on the qualities of a hero. I can choose the qualities of a hero and explain them with a partner.	I can consider and come to consensus on the importance of different qualities of a hero.

HOW DO WE UNDERSTAND THE WORLD?

Presentational Task Descriptions How do we create and share with others?		
Adapt a model description to describe your hero.	Write a description of your hero with their qualities.	Create a presentation to nominate a hero of your choice to the local council.
I Can		
I can use simple sentences to describe my hero.	I can use new language I have learnt to create a description.	I can justify my opinions and present to others.

Bridge to Design

Let's go deeper into the design process and collaborate with colleagues for additional ideas and reflection on this exemplar before working on your own design.

Reflect to Reveal

1) Why is it important to reprise and revisit the qualities of a hero over time in a curriculum?
2) How do different disciplines define a hero?
3) To what extent do heroes preserve the historical memory of a culture?

Questions for Colleagues

1) How are the heroes created and remembered in the culture (s) you teach?
2) Upon which authentic texts do stories of heroes reside?
3) How does the concept of the hero change for us over time?

Ask the Designer

What is your question for Ms Green? What else do you want to know about this exemplar and her design thinking?

Participate in the Practice

Which practices guided Ms Green in creating her exemplar? How did she design with these in mind? Explain below for each component.

1) Photographs as living memory community texts of heroes for interpretive tasks.
2) Use of public images for both input and creative product or output.
3) Heroes across disciplines and areas of learning.

Teacher to Leader on Design

1. Start from a cultural perspective, what cultural aspect of the country would you like the students to understand.
2. Do not be put off by challenging authentic materials, the tasks can still be at an accessible level for beginners.
3. Don't be afraid to experiment with new types of tasks, even if they aren't successful the first time!

From the Admin Desk

A similar AATT could be designed around names of schools, leisure centres or music and art establishments to look into celebrating outstanding achievements in a specific domain. This could be a segue for colleagues to start planning across areas of learning with colleagues from different subject areas.

Language teachers can be tasked to look again at what visuals, objects and practices they feel are characteristics of the target language country or region or community and which are essential for their students to come across during the course of their language journey. Teachers can then decide on the language they could develop for it, moving away from the more traditional topics whilst covering the language blocks which best fit the learner progression.

—Stephanie Ellis-Williams, International Languages, Global Futures GwE Lead

Infographics Hold Layers of Cultural Identity: My Name to My Family, Nation, World

Miss McAllister examines the cultural history of names with her pupils as they explore identity and how names have changed over time. The key outcomes of these tasks to identify, index, interpret and improve authentic resources are how well they prepare learners for the subsequent production tasks. This teacher demonstrates how learners can mediate for others to define their own identity within pluricultural contexts.

Teacher as Designer – Who Am I?

Ysgol Aberconwy is a large secondary school set in the heart of the very touristic Conwy area. The pupils are from a range of socio-economic backgrounds and English is the first language for the vast majority of pupils. There is a range of cultures in school from European countries and more recently, from Ukraine with an increase in the number of refugees finding shelter in the region.

This AATT (see Table 4.5) is a good example of this principle in that it demonstrates the evolution of names and how it clearly also highlights the increasingly multicultural nature of an individual's identity. When exploring the idea of names as representing who we are, Miss McAllister was herself quite surprised by the range of names currently most common in Germany. Delving into this aspect did not only enable children to understand that names evolve as people travel and mix much more commonly due to various factors, but it also enabled the teacher to avoid reinforcing the misconception that the typical German names were still the traditional names from thirty years ago when she was herself a student.

The authentic material infographic is a particular treasure, found as the teacher revised her AATT and featured in Stage Three formative tasks. This is a good example of how far such an infographic can take your teaching and learning. Multiple layers of intercultural elements can be drawn from a simple and yet effective authentic document.

—Stephanie Ellis-Williams, International Languages, Global Futures GwE Lead

Voices from the Field

Our names are a crucial part of our identity. They carry deep personal, cultural, familial and historical connections and give us a sense of who we are. It is important to understand the value of a name in another culture because it is their most significant connection to their identity. This concept of identity supports its learners to become ethical, informed citizens of Wales and the world as it develops their knowledge about their culture and that of the language they are learning.

Creating and designing this way have really helped enrich my understanding of the CfW framework so much that culture is now the driving force behind my planning. It has challenged me to think about how we can make language learning more real, more authentic and more relevant to our learners. My planning of assessment tasks now focuses on learners creating something for an audience beyond the classroom.

Planning and designing this way have definitely been processes which aren't fully embedded yet but my mindset is definitely shifting in the right direction. When I plan future AATTs as the CfW rolls out, I will ensure that I identify my authentic material before designing and revising tasks. The difficulty I had with my first AATT was that I designed the tasks first and then couldn't find the authentic material to fit my content which was so frustrating and time-consuming. That experience helped shift my mindset in curriculum design, and if there is one thing I have learned through this whole process is that if we are to create an engaging and inspiring curriculum for our learners to ensure they develop towards the four purposes, then we cannot design it just so it fits our current resources. It needs to be revamped, not just re-hashed.

I like designing backwards. Knowing and having the end goal at the forefront of lesson planning give more focus on the more important aspects of the language and concepts I want to teach. I particularly like the intercultural transfer targets and mediation for transfer. They really made me think hard about how the 'I can' statements relate to the culture and how learners can transfer what they have learnt outside of the classroom. Beforehand, my focus has been on what topic, language and grammar we are going to teach without making the link to culture. It was more of an add-on to suit the topic if relevant, i.e., Easter, Christmas, food & drink etc.

The AATT I designed focuses on novice learners as we introduced the language to our classes for the first time. We had previously done a project in September/October exploring multilingualism to challenge negative attitudes to languages and language learning in our school context, therefore didn't start teaching our international languages until November 2022. In this AATT, I framed the series of assessments around identity so learners would not just be able to introduce themselves with the basic name, age, birthday, brothers and sisters as they had in the past, but to consider and challenge the concept of identity. This aligns with 'Languages Connect Us' as we learn about our cultural identity as well as the cultural identity of others. They should understand what makes us similar and what makes us different. If there is a mix of cultures in your classroom, e.g., Welsh, Ukrainian, Polish, Argentinian, Northern Irish, they should understand who they are and where they are at that moment. This can of course be built upon in subsequent projects and AATTs. This also aligns with 'Expressing Ourselves Is Key to Communication' in that it supports learners to develop an awareness of how they use language to express themselves for different purposes and audiences.

Although I had to alter my 'authentic materials' for next year, pupils did show evidence of the Principles of Progression with these tasks. In one pupil's example:

- **Increasing effectiveness as a learner**: language for physical description and blog have been found independently.
- **Increasing breadth and depth of knowledge**: developing an understanding of linguistic concepts that support the skills to communicate effectively through writing and images.
- **Deepening understanding of the ideas and disciplines within and across the Areas**: engaging in ideas and communicative purposes and development of language awareness.
- **Refinement and growing sophistication in the use and application of skills**: adapt and manipulate language to communicate effectively to a range of different audiences.
- **Making new connections and transferring language into new contexts**: transfer of existing knowledge and skills into new context.

Designing using this model doesn't put a glass ceiling on learning. It really makes you think harder about curriculum design. It feels more meaningful and purposeful. It has significantly shifted my way of thinking in a positive way in terms of what it is I want our learners to be able to do with the language we teach them. The cultural concepts developed are deeper and more stimulating than in traditional topics because they are relevant and authentic. Tasks are designed to enable learners of all abilities to develop knowledge of culture and language in order to communicate successfully, regardless of where they are on their language learning continuum. And although this way of designing is not completely embedded yet, I am excited to see how our bespoke curriculum develops by using it.

I think by integrating more culture into curriculum design, it allows us to create more engaging projects of work which hopefully will make our lessons more meaningful, and create more motivated language learners who will want to continue their language learning journeys into GCSE and beyond. Learners become more autonomous linguists from day one, they are challenged to be creative and express deeper ideas which they relate to. The impact of the AATT on our learners is still very much in its infancy, however, the immediate difference for me that I see is that our learners are being more creative with the language and saying what they want to say, regardless of linguistic ability.

—Ms Jamie McAllister, Ysgol Aberconwy, Conwy, French and German

TABLE 4.5 Articulated Assessment Transfer Task – Who am I?

Enduring Understandings
✱ Everybody has their own identity.
Essential Questions
? What is in a name?
? To what extent does nationality influence identity?
? Does my family define me?
? What is online identity?
Context
Ysgol Aberconwy is setting up a new social media platform called 'YAC' and is encouraging young people to join in order to connect with learners in partner schools in Europe.
Articulation Spiral Points
@ Present personal identity with visual supports.
@ Create a poem describing personal identity.
@ Create an online profile using a blog or video for school social media platforms.

Intercultural Transfer Targets	**Mediation for Transfer**
• I can compare what makes up German or French identity with my own culture. • I can explain my own identity to those unfamiliar with it.	• Bridge and exchange ideas and concepts of identity. • Use annotations and visuals to present myself to different audiences. • Summarize information depicted in both written and oral profiles.

HOW DO WE UNDERSTAND THE WORLD?

Beginner	Intermediate	Advanced
Videos: Linguists watch a video of people on the street being interviewed in the international language.		
Interpretive Task Descriptions **How do we understand the world around us and support others?**		
Linguists classify information after watching.	Linguists circle the correct word or phrase from the video.	Linguists fill in a table with the information they understand.
I Can		
I can select basic information from what I read and watch and put it into a table.	I can identify and recognize basic details with support.	I can infer, interpret and summarize information.
Interpersonal Task Descriptions **How do we express ourselves and engage others?**		
Linguists diamond rank profiles and come to a consensus who they would be friends with on 'YAC'. I can organize profiles according to preference after reading them.	Linguists select one profile that attracted their attention the most and describe it to their peers. I can talk about the profile I liked with my peers after watching a selection of profiles and justify my opinion.	Linguists put profiles into order of preference, share it with their peers, and ask and answer their questions about the profiles. I can exchange information, ask questions and discuss other people's profiles with my peers.
I Can		
Presentational Task Descriptions **How do we create and share with others?**		
Linguists create a poster of themselves for the partner school about what represents their identity to be best matched with a peer.	Linguists create an acrostic poem using their name that best describes their identity to be best matched with a peer e.g. Welsh identity, LGBTQIA+ identity, food, personal interests.	Linguists create a blog or multimedia profile to be best matched with a peer at the partner school.
I Can		
I can present some simple information about who I am in words and images.	I can present details about myself in phrases and full sentences in written form.	I can present details about myself in full sentences in written form. I can use connectives to extend sentences.

Bridge to Design

Let's go deeper into Ms McAllister's design process and collaborate with colleagues for additional ideas and reflection on this exemplar before working on your own design.

Reflect to Reveal

1) What do names over time tell us about our culture and history?
2) How do authentic texts prepare learners for the products they create?
3) In what ways do the tasks encourage learner autonomy?

Questions for Colleagues

1) Are you familiar with texts, films or songs from the culture you teach which are essential for exploring identity? Please share them.
2) How does the pupils' design of the social media site help them engage in mediation?
3) What cultural perspectives does Ms McAllister want pupils to take away from this exemplar?

Ask the Designer

What is your question for Ms McAllister? What else do you want to know about this exemplar and her design thinking?

Participate in the Practice

Which practices guided Ms McAllister in creating her exemplar? How did she design with these in mind? Explain below for each component.

1) Relevance and creativity wherever pupils are on the curriculum.
2) ReVision is required, not merely re-hashing.
3) Intercultural targets take the lead on authentic texts rather than language outcomes of past practices.

Teacher to Leader on Design

1. Find your material first before considering what you are going to assess (I wasted a lot of time). This could be a song, a video, a piece of artwork, information on a website, anything that is directly linked to the international language and its culture.

2. Dip in and out of Jenny's book to help you if you get stuck. I found (still find) it really useful to help me structure, for example, intercultural targets, mediation for transfer, but I also use it to get ideas for different types of tasks that learners can do for an audience beyond the classroom.

3. Your AATT doesn't have to be and won't be perfect the first time. Once you do the assessment tasks with your classes, there will be things you will want to do differently next time. Just annotate it with your ideas and update for next year.

From the Admin Desk

The process the teacher went through could be a great help to any administrator in supporting colleagues. Miss McAllister struggled initially to find the right kind of authentic material. As she explains clearly in her Voices from the Field, she fell into the trap of planning an AATT to suit her devised outcomes in terms of language rather than planning the AATT around the intercultural aspects the authentic material could lead to.

However, the AATT does not have to be perfect from the outset. It can evolve as teacher understanding deepens. This can also be a good model for pupils as they see their teacher adapt their practice.

For language teachers, who often place a great importance on being perfect and ensuring their lessons are just so, it is important to remain flexible and adjust as times move on and as practices change. Making mistakes is part of the learning process. Learning never ends.

—Stephanie Ellis-Williams, International Languages, Global Futures GwE Lead

Design for Transfer

For your chosen theme, select Cultural Community Authentic Texts, including images, videos, infographics, photos or objects. These are all texts. For a list of texts, see Appendix F.

Design for Transfer

With your selected texts and concept, design at least one listening, one viewing and one reading Interpretive or receptive task across **three levels of learner engagement**. Try to incorporate the seven types: Identify, Index, Inquire, Interpret, Infer, Illustrate and Improve. Use the fillable template on the companion website, see Chapter 1. For a master list of task types, see Appendices D and E.

Design for Transfer

Now that you have designed an interpretive task at each level, compose the I can statement for each. Keep in mind the function, skill, purpose, content and audience.

Design for Transfer

Check your tasks carefully. As a result of this task, could the learner bridge communication with someone unfamiliar with the language or culture? How does doing this task enable the learner to make language accessible and cultural perspectives visible for someone else? Find this evidence of Mediation for Transfer in your interpretive tasks.

Reflect and Revisit

1. How do Interpretive tasks help learners with mediation?
2. With the exemplars in the book so far, explain at least three types of Interpretive tasks.
3. Why should we make adjustments on the 'ask' of the task and not the text itself?
4. How do these tasks support literacy within all texts?
5. Why should our learners know how to pose questions?
6. How did these teachers make the case for transcultural communicative competence in their designs?
7. How can one great piece of authentic material be used for task design across all levels? What message does that convey to the learner?

5

How Do We Express Ourselves and Engage Others?

Enduring Understandings

- ∞ Interpersonal tasks engage the learner to react, express views and negotiate intercultural meaning with someone or other people.
- ∞ Improvisation prepares learners for the inevitable unexpected, adaptability and mediation within various roles and registers.
- ∞ We plan, get more information, decide and come to consensus for different purposes and audiences.
- ∞ We own language not by reciting forms posing as communication skills; we acquire language when we do new things with it.
- ∞ Our improv tasks enable learners to react to what others say, not how well they say it and to solve problems in social situations.

Essential Questions

- Q Why do unpredictability and improvisation matter?
- Q What does engaging others through mediation look like?
- Q What am I asking for?

I can

- Determine how to express information from input to improv for my tasks.
- Describe Interpersonal tasks for consensus and mediation to engage others.
- Design tasks across different levels for articulation.
- Develop *I can* statements specific to the task and intercultural transfer targets.

Let's Consider

In Chapter 4, we examined the question, 'How do we understand the world around us and support others?' Whenever you are faced with anything you listen to, watch, receive or read, you take some information away from it in words, phrases, images and thoughts. You may have questions about it. For the time being, that information is just for you. The moment we want to engage someone else, that information is now social and shared. We interact with others not knowing what we will get back in return. The unpredictable favours adaptability and, therefore, improvisation. How do we engage someone else when we might not have all the language? Do we really need to be perfect? We just encountered new information for the first time and made some sense of it. How can we expand meaning for ourselves in collaboration with others?

Interaction from Input to Improv

Interpersonal (Glisan et al., 2003; National Standards in Foreign Language Education Project, 1996/2006; National Standards Collaborative Board, 2015) tasks are interactive, unrefined and unrehearsed, involving negotiation and exchanging information, opinions and decisions with someone or a group of people. This ability does not happen by practising inert forms or memorization masking as knowledge or skill; instead, acquisition, ownership and authorship happen while you are doing something new with what language you have (VanPatten & Rothman, 2015). As I said in DWLC, 'drills give the appearance of understanding, but not the reality of transfer' (Eddy, 2022b, p. 81). The best tasks value novelty, improvisation and risk-taking because – understatement of the millennia – not all communication exchanges are predictable in the language realm; most actually are unanticipated. For that reason, the exchange must be a new, unscripted reaction to input from a partner or group of people. Improvisation values the unforeseeable and teaches us to respond to the unexpected, which is what we are faced with most of the time. Every improv task is an opportunity for transfer, novel and unfamiliar, giving us the chance to make language more accessible to someone else. These tasks enable flexibility, autonomy (Little, 2020; Little et al., 2017; Little & Kirwan, 2019) and tolerance of ambiguity which predictable exercises and memorized forms can never provide. The purpose of these tasks is to prepare learners to share, plan, decide, choose, question and reach a consensus for mediation with diverse audiences in real time. Agency right from the beginning is the goal of the tasks you will see in this chapter by our designers.

In this framework, learners

1 Use the information from previous texts.
2 Interact with others in an improvised and unrehearsed exchange for clarity and more information.
3 Ask, Answer, Arrange, Adopt, Assess, Argue and Agree with other people.

We have said that 'the learner owns language not by predictable exercises with forms and memorization of dialogues but through creative, unpredictable interaction in tasks' (Eddy, 2022b, p. 15). This happens with content in texts for Interpretive tasks and now with others for Interpersonal tasks. When you stop and think about it, every interaction is a co-created, improvisational experience between friends, family, work colleagues or people you speak with for the first time. It is always a reaction in real time, to our thoughts, what we hear, watch, receive or read and also to question and respond to what other people say to us. For this reason, our tasks in the classroom need to prepare learners for what always happens outside of it. Memorized scripts are misplaced and inappropriate here; they seek perfection by design, set learners up for circumstances which rarely if ever occur, and do not prepare them for what does. The fact is we do not use scripts when talking with people. Our exchanges are co-created when we listen intently to what is offered, then we react and respond, however haltingly or blemished. Truly improvisational tasks reward the imperfect because the unanticipated is the rule of the day; perfection is not required or expected. What is foreseeable is reaction, invention, adjustment, flexibility, collaboration and negotiation: this is how communication happens and moves us forward. The tasks you will see from our designers challenge the risk-averse intentionally and progressively, preparing confident, resourceful and creative learners ready to engage in mediation with the language they have. Table 5.1 below outlines each Interpersonal task type in the AATTs and the strategies they enable for mediation with others.

TABLE 5.1 Interpersonal task types and engaging others in mediation

Type	Sample Task	Strategy acquired for Mediation
Ask and Answer	Ask questions composed in the Interpretive task; ask and answer questions based on items and information from previous tasks: lists, charts, images. Ask and answer questions in any conversation.	Relating new information to previous knowledge. Using gestures, images and objects while asking and answering. Breaking down complicated information. Identifying questions and giving feedback.
Arrange	Plan with someone else, schedule or organize in steps.	Simplifying, clarifying, or organizing with someone unfamiliar with culture or language content
Adopt	Choose or decide on items or ideas.	Link to previous knowledge. Distinguish, sort or separate information or concepts for someone.
Assess	Judge, appraise or give opinion or express feelings on an issue or concept.	Facilitate communication in pluricultural space. Describe emotions and clarify facts. OK/not OK, like/dislike, positive/negative. Change style, register or words depending on the audience.
Argue	Debate, discuss or dispute an issue.	Understand different points of view. Assist and ease sensitive situations or relay difficult information.
Agree	Negotiate and come to consensus with someone else.	Accept alternative ideas and methods. Manage interaction and collaboration.

> **Put It to Practice: Collaborate to Articulate**
>
> In the nine AATTs you have seen thus far, which features stand out in the Interpersonal tasks? Do you think the tasks demonstrate that pupils can ask, answer, arrange, adopt, assess, argue and agree? Could they engage, facilitate, simplify or clarify information or concepts with someone else? Do you see evidence of progression from concrete planning and decision-making to solving problems on the upward spiral? Would you add any interpersonal tasks to the ones you see in the AATT?

Meet Our Designers

All of the AATTs in this book show how learners plan, decide, choose and come to consensus through tasks of improvisation and engagement across three levels of progression. For this chapter, these four exemplars were especially selected by Ms Stephanie Ellis-Williams for their use of improvisational strategies, extension of meaning from prior tasks and teacher reflections on their work. Mr Cameron explores school uniform culture through pupil choice and opinion, Ms Vick uses data and collaboration tasks to elevate regional food and national identity, Dr Byrne's pupils come to consensus and distinguish travel plans for various audiences, and Ms Sloan dives into argument and decision with a differentiated year 8 class on iconic foods. These teachers show how their pupils progressively question, reflect and mediate with others, incorporating previous knowledge with lessons learned in novel challenges. These tasks help shape transcultural learners and guide them to manage their world with flexibility and autonomy.

Different Views and Decisions on Dress

In school uniforms, Mr Cameron explores German school culture and encourages Welsh pupils to reflect on their points of view to make informed decisions on what to wear. They describe features of uniforms, compare and contrast the UK and Germany for those unfamiliar with school uniform culture, share opinions, and plan the presentational deliverable during these improvisational tasks.

Teacher as Designer – School Uniforms

Ysgol Emrys ap Iwan is a large secondary school where Welsh is taught within an English setting. Pupils come from different socio-economic backgrounds with a high percentage from deprived areas.

This AATT (see Table 5.2) is a good example of this principle because it enables students to exchange opinions in a frame which allows some control whilst allowing more spontaneous speech. Pupils feel confident and supported but are also encouraged and able to decide the level of language and depth of questioning they wish to do. The differentiation within each task per and across the levels enables this. Learners have to make decisions in the choice of uniform and the rationale behind wearing a uniform in school. Pupils can rely on what they have learned about the uniform culture in Germany to compare and contrast with their own experiences. In doing so, they are compelled to understand and reflect on the reasons for their choice in order to explain it to their partner and in order to inform their selection later on in the Presentational task. Similarly, learners need to listen to their partner and understand their choice and reasons for them. This opens the door to new points of view and is helpful to develop ideas when planning the work to present to a particular audience.

This AATT allows an easy path across the levels. Pupils can build their language skills in confidence and learn to speak more spontaneously and in more depth as the levels increase. This can be done within the same group or at a later stage in their development. As our learners understand that making mistakes and expressing simple messages are expected at this stage, they will embrace taking more risks and aspiring to higher levels. This can radically change the way we structure our lessons and class time with groups of levels and/or groups of transition to the next level relevant to pupils' response and development.

—Stephanie Ellis-Williams, International Languages,
Global Futures GwE Lead

Voices from the Field

This concept sits within the school life topic (key GCSE topic too). The cultural aspect allows learners to delve deeper into the pros and cons of school uniforms and the different viewpoints available. This leads to more cultural awareness and understanding of others. This concept works two ways, allowing Welsh students the opportunity to study German perspectives on school uniform, whilst simultaneously providing German students with a Welsh take on school uniform practices.

This process allows the teacher to approach a commonly taught topic from a different, often overlooked, angle. The concept promotes independence and creativity of thought, whilst also being intrinsically challenging in nature.

A novice learner can contribute in meaningful ways at the bronze level of the package, namely describing and comparing different uniform practices and giving and justifying opinions on both. Novice learners can also produce infographics to showcase their findings. This AATT aligns with the SoWM (CfW, 2019) in the following ways:

Languages connect us – Meaningful language learning experiences go hand in hand with learning about one's own cultural identity as well as the cultural identities of others.

Understanding languages is key to understanding the world around us – This area aims to provide learners with opportunities to experience languages, as well as images, in a range of forms and genres. The rich and varied nature of these experiences can improve learners' ability to become creative and enterprising in their use of a range of languages in a plurilingual context.

Learners showed progression through the creative outcomes at the end of each of the three lessons.

Bronze
Produce labelled notes and images on traditional school uniforms in the UK to inform infographic design. Using Canva or an equivalent, produce an infographic that showcases all traditional UK school uniform pieces.

Silver
Find key info on different uniform practices and compare them to our uniform.

Write a short description of each uniform type – correct use of adjectival endings.

Make a costing of different uniform types and provide opinions and justify.

School uniform – give opinions and justify.

Gold
Understand a complex article on pros and cons of uniform – stepped approach using gist, dictionary skills and targeted translation.

Plan your video presentation slide by slide with a partner – highlight what information will be on each slide (narration over the top). Produce a Canva video to showcase their findings.

> I believe these tasks and curriculum design lead to capable, ambitious and problem-solving learners, the exact type of skillset studying a foreign language requires. The AATT approach fits perfectly with the aims and objectives of the new CfW and the ultimate requirement of skills to succeed in examinations. The focus on culture is often overlooked and is equal in importance to why someone chooses to study a new language.
>
> —Mr Mark Cameron, Ysgol Emrys ap Iwan, Conwy, German

TABLE 5.2 Articulated Assessment Transfer Task – School uniforms

Enduring Understandings   ✱ Clothing defines us. From the first decision of each day to our sense of belonging or individuality.
Essential Questions   ? How does clothing define us?   ? To what extent does commonality and individuality affect our educational performance?
Context   The school has asked the student body to consider the suitability of traditional school uniforms in the twenty-first century.
Articulation Spiral Points   @ Describe concept with visual supports.   @ Offer information on clothing for different needs.   @ Justify opinions on uniform and identity.

Intercultural Transfer Targets	Mediation for Transfer
• I can recognize the two different uniform styles. • I can organize descriptions of uniform styles. • I can share ideas/practices of uniforms in the UK and Germany. • I can compare UK and German attitudes to uniforms.	• Bridge and exchange ideas on different approaches to school uniforms. • Identify visuals, objects and examples. • Explain features of UK and German school uniforms to those unfamiliar with the traditions. • Compare and contrast characteristics of UK and German approaches to school uniforms.

HOW DO WE EXPRESS OURSELVES?

Novice Bronze Medal	Intermediate Silver Medal	Advanced Gold Medal
School website on uniforms and articles on German and UK school uniforms.		
Interpretive Task Descriptions **How do we understand the world around us and support others?**		
Students study websites of different UK schools and categorize school uniforms with vocabulary in the target language.	Students visit two websites from regions in Germany that have introduced a form of school uniform. Students pose three questions and write a brief description of each area's uniform. Learners research the average cost of each type of school clothing (UK full school uniform vs German) and consider how this affects different groups of people with different needs/backgrounds.	Students read the article on UK vs German school uniform practices and summarize their findings by comparing and contrasting the two different practices.
I Can		
I can identify and recognize items of school uniform.	I organize the descriptions of each uniform style. I can write a description of each style.	I can summarize differences and details between the German and UK practices of school uniforms and reasons behind them.
Interpersonal Task Descriptions **How do we express ourselves and engage others?**		
Students select items from the website and describe them to their peers.	Students select one uniform style, share it with their peers, and ask and answer questions about the uniforms. They can discuss which style seems more attractive to learners with different needs (religion, male/female styles, budget).	Students exchange their summaries, decide and agree on which summaries to include in the presentation.

I Can		
I can share and talk about the items I like from the websites with a peer.	I can exchange information, ask questions and discuss the different uniform styles with my peers.	I can read and provide my peers with feedback for the summary related to the two different approaches.
Presentational Task Descriptions **How do we create and share with others?**		
Students design an infographic on UK style school uniforms for German students.	Students create a brochure that introduces the two different uniform styles for different types of students.	Students prepare a video to show about UK vs German school uniform practices and present the advantages and disadvantages of each type of school clothing.
I Can		
I can list the features and items of a UK school uniform for German students.	I can present information related to the German style of uniform and explain to others in the class.	I can express opinions on German school uniform approaches and views and support my opinions using authentic resources.

Bridge to Design

Let's go deeper into the design process and collaborate with colleagues for additional ideas and reflection on this exemplar before working on your own design.

Reflect to Reveal

1) Why is it important for pupils to work with this concept of individual expression early, even at the novice level?

2) Why should all new language speakers be able to identify and mediate this concept with examples for someone else, even just with the language they have?

3) How do pupils show evidence of progression on this concept of individuality? What are they able to do?

Questions for Colleagues

1) How do these interpersonal tasks prepare the presentational deliverables?

2) How might you adapt any of these tasks for your chosen curricular theme, transfer targets and cultures?

3) What other types of products or deliverables could pupils create as a result of their negotiation in the Interpretive mode?

Ask the Designer

What is your question for Mr Cameron? What else do you want to know about this exemplar and his design thinking?

Participate in the Practice

Which practices guided Mr Cameron in creating his exemplar? How did he design with these in mind? Explain below for each component.

1) Learners organize, plan and come to consensus for cognitive as well as social purposes.

2) Connecting socio-cultural perspectives between personal/cultural/community assets pupils bring and those of the culture(s).

3) Tasks which facilitate mediation with others and compare what pupils already know with new content.

Teacher to Leader on Design and Implementation

1 Make an account on Canva, invite learners to join your class and familiarize yourself with the website's functions.

2 Teach learners how to adapt infographics, templates and video production.

3 Task without context for later use on comparing uniform costs: ask learners to plan their wardrobe for one week of non-uniform and provide a total cost.

> **From the Admin Desk**
>
> This AATT can be useful to other language teachers at the start of the process and whose pupils need to build more confidence in using oracy skills more independently. It gently moves from the more traditional language speaking activity to a more authentic and purposeful exchange in order to draw genuine information.
>
> The language support within the interpersonal tasks can be a frame to replicate in other AATT and slowly removed as pupils get more and more familiar with it. The interpersonal skills are further reaching than the traditional language drill and confined conversation model which usually takes place in language lessons.
>
> Colleagues can reflect on the expectations we have of our own pupils and whether these expectations are understood by our pupils. Do they understand that this stage is not about fluency but one of the many steps towards it?
>
> —Stephanie Ellis-Williams, International Languages, Global Futures GwE Lead

Promote a Dessert; Promote an Identity to the World

Ms Vick drives beyond the typical superficial take on regional desserts by exploring practices and perspectives with her pupils. With this AATT, they demonstrated transcultural competence on their own desserts and those from other cultures. They can make a compelling argument for particular desserts as well as discuss and compare them for someone unaccustomed to the traditions and cultural histories supporting them.

Teacher as Designer – Regional Desserts

Prestatyn High School is a very large secondary school where Welsh is taught within an English setting. International Languages are well perceived and uptake at option level after the age of fourteen is generally healthy. However, as in many schools in Wales, this is only thanks to a very active and hard-working team of teachers who design their programmes to ensure students build self-confidence in their ability to learn languages and truly value the importance of learning other languages.

This is a good example of this Principle in that it ties in the information and knowledge learnt in the previous stage but also in the Stage Three part of the module in order to feed the conversations. The Interpersonal task itself is simple in its instructions but learners now have a much wider range of elements to come to their consensus. They can decide, independently, what speaks more to them and what would speak more to another audience. The criteria to be on the UNESCO list can be their own now but their decision-making relies on the understanding of what makes such a list and why there is one. In other words, the learning outcomes of such a task are multilayered and carefully designed by the teacher, whilst keeping the actual pupil-facing task clear and accessible. Learners can reflect later on the different skills and knowledge they have developed whilst doing this task. Their engagement is genuine and voluntary because the task is important to them. They are motivated by a purposeful and authentic activity whose focus is not language specific only.

The AATT (see Table 5.3) is a great example of a turnaround point in the teacher's cultural practices and perspectives. In designing but especially in delivering this very first AATT, the teacher realized the array of other intercultural elements she needed to include in her Stage Three in order to enable successful presentational outcomes, namely what is UNESCO and what is the heritage list of UNESCO, what makes a dessert specific to a region, what are French and Welsh desserts and how can we qualify them in terms of regional specialty, what represents the identity of a certain food: the ingredients, the recipe, the know-how, the eating of it? These questions had never been addressed in this teachers' teaching before. This is what elevated her practice to new levels and clearly appealed to her pupils.

—Stephanie Ellis-Williams, International Languages,
Global Futures GwE Lead

Voices from the Field

As part of the new curriculum, the four purposes include enabling students to become ethical, informed citizens of Wales and the world as well as being ambitious, capable learners. To learn a language, it is essential to familiarize yourself with the culture. The culture element of this task enabled the learners to reflect and discover a variety of different customs from around the world. The Presentational tasks allow students to become creative and adventurous. They are not restricted to a very 'narrow' format and can be ambitious. This encourages discussions and independence.

They should see that we are open to discovering a variety of traditions and respect them. It allows learners to reflect on their own customs and traditions. This is focused on French desserts and how it influences them, but it promotes discussion on Welsh desserts and their importance.

It is very enjoyable to plan and design in this way as we have a clear focus on the end goal. Traditionally we have taught topics required for the curriculum, and maybe slightly losing sight of the 'bigger picture' and of what the learners will take away with them long term, further than the end assignment. They take away some deeper understanding of culture and how languages connect us around the world. The use of authentic materials and practical tasks are very engaging. The learners take ownership of their learning. Having a clear end task or project means that they see a purpose in the language and information they are learning as they will need it for their project which they are very enthusiastic about. This way of planning allows each school to have a tailor-made curriculum adapted to the needs of their learners.

This AATT caters for novice learners allowing more advanced learners to choose a more challenging end task, requiring them to collect and learn more language. The enduring understanding is clear and learners watch/study the same authentic materials but have to complete adapted tasks to show their understanding. This context and presentational task allow students to be enterprising and creative contributors. They can become more informed, ethical citizens (Fair Trade), also ambitious capable learners as it is a very ambitious task to convince UNESCO that their dessert should be part of the World Heritage list.

My pupils demonstrated evidence of the Principles of Progression with the AATT tasks by:

- Increasing effectiveness as a learner.
- Increasing breadth and depth of knowledge: developing an understanding of linguistic concepts that support the skills to communicate effectively through writing and images.
- Deepening understanding of the ideas and disciplines within and across the Areas: engaging in ideas and communicative purposes and development of language awareness.
- Making new connections and transferring language into new contexts: transfer of existing knowledge and skills into new context.
- Understanding connections between languages and cultures.

- Making progress in their grammar and punctuation and applying these to a variety of different contexts.
- Firing creativity and imagination through use of authentic materials.

This way of designing means that we don't limit the learning to a specific topic. We integrate a wider range of activities and concepts we might not necessarily have allowed ourselves to include in the past as we would worry it would not fit. This has made me rethink the way I teach and approach new languages. I am able to pass on more enthusiasm and show how purposeful their language learning is. Learners from all abilities can access authentic materials and feel more confident in communicating in the other language. The more confident learners are able to access more challenging content as before they would have (I would have) been limited to the topic at hand. This is only the beginning, and I would refine or approach some aspects differently, but this has revived my enthusiasm for teaching the languages I love. I can pass on the cultural knowledge I have so far but also discover new habits and customs with the learners as our world is changing so fast.

The learners are more engaged in the tasks they are creating, and they take ownership of their learning. Their projects can sometimes be quite visual to the rest of the school and tease the curiosity of others. The more culture we integrate in our curriculum, the more engaged the learners are becoming. It allows them to compare it with their own culture. They become more motivated to learn the language as they want to learn more about traditions, what people from the other cultures do and say. This way of teaching encourages multilingualism and promotes intercultural exchanges.

—Ms Viviane Vick, Prestatyn High School, Denbighshire, French

TABLE 5.3 Articulated Assessment Transfer Task – Regional desserts

Enduring Understandings   ✱ Food represents cultural identity and brings people together.   ✱ Traditions are changing with more global desserts but it is essential to conserve the cultural identity of a region or country.
Essential Questions   ? To what extent does our culture influence our diet?   ? How can desserts be our ambassadors around the world?
Context   The baguette has been recognized by UNESCO as part of the World Heritage. UNESCO is now looking for a dessert to include in the famous list. You have been given the task to find the perfect dessert to represent France and convince UNESCO of your choice.

Articulation Spiral Points
@ Explain the characteristics of a dessert to represent a region.
@ Use persuasive language to promote your dessert.
@ Justify opinions on the most suitable dessert to promote the region.
@ Present evidence with infographics or video.

Intercultural Transfer Targets	Mediation for Transfer
• I can compare and discuss the values, beliefs and perspectives that regional products convey and how they contribute to creating and shaping national identities. • I can understand cultural appropriation across different cultures.	• Bridge and exchange ideas about desserts from specific regions. • Identify and clarify traits or regional desserts. • Collaborate to explain features of a good dessert to represent your region around the world.

Beginner	Intermediate	Advanced
Videos on regional desserts		
Interpretive Task Descriptions **How do we understand the world around us and support others?**		
Students watch a variety of videos/websites about desserts from different regions and make notes of ingredients and recipes seen in the video. Tick off key words when you hear them. Match the key words with the English.	Students watch a variety of videos and visit websites about desserts from different regions. Make a list of words that you recognize or hear in the video. Translate the key words into English. Decide which dessert would deserve to be on the list.	Students watch a variety of promotional videos and visit websites and look at brochures about desserts from different regions. Make notes about what you see/hear on the video. Write some short sentences using their notes. Fill in a table/chart with the information obtained from the stimulus.
I Can		
I can identify and recognize different areas of France with their typical dessert	I can organize information about the different desserts I have read about.	I can summarize differences and details between different types of desserts and their suitability.

Interpersonal Task Descriptions		
How do we express ourselves and engage others?		
Students select one dessert that attracted their attention the most from the websites and brochures and describe it to their peers.	Students select one dessert from a website/selection of brochures, share it with their peers, ask and answer their questions about the desserts. Discuss which dessert seems more attractive to be on the list.	Discuss and compare desserts with a partner/group and decide on the best dessert to include in your video.
I Can		
I can share and talk about the dessert that I liked with my peers after reading information on a website.	I can exchange information, ask questions and discuss features of a dessert with my peers.	I can collect information and provide my peers with feedback for the summary related to different types of desserts.
Presentational Task Descriptions		
How do we create and share with others?		
Create a poster to advertise the best facts and features of the dessert of your choice.	Write a letter to UNESCO to persuade them to choose your dessert to be the next item on the UNESCO list.	Create a promotional video to show why UNESCO should choose your dessert to add to the list.
I Can		
I can list the features and details of the best dessert.	I can present information related to desserts and explain to others in the class.	I can use persuasive language to support my opinions using authentic resources. I can use DCF to enhance my presentation.

Bridge to Design

Let's go deeper into Ms Vick's design process and collaborate with colleagues for additional ideas and reflection on this exemplar before working on your own design.

Reflect to Reveal

1) How do we elevate a common topic like food for a better spiral and meaningful reprise?

2) Can you explain cuisine in the collective identity to someone else? Do you have an example from your own culture?

3) How does transfer come into play here through the tasks? Why does the 'audience' matter?

Questions for Colleagues

1) Is there a concept regarding the cuisine from the culture(s) you will teach that is essential to reprise and spiral in your curriculum? Please share it.

2) How can you turnaround a tired topic into a more relevant and applicable transfer beyond the classroom?

3) What is the value of using the same texts but changing the task?

Ask the Designer

What is your question for Ms Vick? What else do you want to know about this exemplar and her design thinking?

Participate in the Practice

Which practices guided Ms Vick in creating her exemplar? How did she design with these in mind? Explain below for each component.

1) Tasks with complexity and variation, creating new meaning, creating new products.
2) Same text, different task, different deliverable.
3) Active learners and ownership engages others for uptake and mediation.

Teacher to Leader on Design and Implementation

1 Ensure the students have a clear idea of the end goal so they see the purpose of what they are learning.

2 Emphasize to students that they can be ambitious, they don't have to put a limit on the language they are learning and that they are capable of communicating more than they would have done in previous learning formats.

3) Encourage the students to embrace the question as a whole and to share with people at home. It will lead them to take what they are studying beyond the classroom.

Students were notably more engaged as they felt a better connection with the culture being studied, recognizing the relevance of their learning. This connection allowed them to compare and relate the new knowledge to their own cultural backgrounds, enriching their understanding.

My planning approach has changed quite a lot, prioritizing cultural exploration and liberating students from rigid grammar constraints, fostering more enthusiasm for my subject, which I hope has inspired my students as well. It has helped us find a way to ensure efficient planning, and it has also helped us understand better how to fulfil the expectations of Curriculum for Wales.

—Ms Viviane Vick, Prestatyn High School, Denbighshire

From the Admin Desk

Other language teachers can use this AATT to re-evaluate one of their existing modules in order to inject more depth in terms of the cultural transfers and enduring understanding. Here, the traditional pancake recipe module has been transformed: from a maybe rather superficial and rapid overview of the tradition of Chandeleur / Shrove Tuesday in France to a much more exploratory module on the legacy of a particular food. This can span across lots of cultural elements: the actual recipe, its origin, ingredients, method, know-how, practice, evolution in time and spread across regions, countries and continents. This in turn will enable students to reflect on their own food heritage and its impact on the individual and society on a wider scale.

Every language will have their own particular specialty or cultural landmark which is worthy of study, be it recognized by the UNESCO heritage list or not. It is therefore easy to adapt such a model to any other language communities. Colleagues can be encouraged to review their own modules and select the most pertinent areas where such easy turnarounds can be made in the first place.

—Stephanie Ellis-Williams, International Languages, Global Futures GwE Lead

Lifestyle, Heritage and a Holiday by the Sea

Dr Byrne's pupils research Cannes and use film as authentic material to decide, plan materials and come to consensus on destination plans for different groups, an excellent transfer task. These interpersonal tasks effectively plan the deliverables in the Presentational task. Now that they have convinced themselves on this lifestyle destination, they can persuade others as well.

Teacher as Designer – A Place in France

Ysgol Uwchradd Tywyn is a small secondary school situated in a very rural area deep in the Welsh Gwynedd community. The teacher in the school is aware of the potential insularity of the region – the school is on the outskirts of the educational authority which governs it and is in an area recognized to be one of the most poverty-stricken – and is keen to continue to develop stronger cultural understanding and knowledge in her pupils. This is not only to widen their horizons but also to instil interest and a sense of purpose to her lessons. Pupils respond very well to such stimuli and thrive when given the opportunity. The teacher is keen to develop this aspect of her practice further and feels AATTs are the way forward.

This AATT is a good example for this Principle as it encourages students to use not only the language they know, but to ask and answer on elements they don't know yet. Plus, they need to agree what is important to look at when visiting a famous place. This places the student in a new position: that of a tour operator who needs to select the essentials of a place. This in turn, will naturally get students to reflect on what are the essentials: What makes a place famous or worthy of interest? Is this different for different people? At a later stage, they could even ask the same questions about places which are not famous and seemingly less important. Are all places worth visiting if the narrative is of interest? How can this relate to art, heritage and communities?

The 'What could I find out' question in the interpretive mode is a powerful one as students' conversations achieve the intended linguistic and conceptual objectives.

—Stephanie Ellis-Williams, International Languages,
Global Futures GwE Lead

Voices from the Field

This AATT (see Table 5.4) researches awareness of a lifestyle on the French Riviera and particularly France's contribution to the world of cinema. Students often say they won't be going to France and I wanted to introduce them to the wider, beautiful, cultural world. Different things could be highlighted in a similar project in a different place.

Four Purposes – developing informed citizens, expressing ourselves through languages, creativity and languages connect us.

Climate and location affect what happens in an area. We are a community by the sea, too, but warmer, not necessarily glamorous, clothes are more important here. Our study considering what happens in another part of the world brings important dimensions and aspects to our lives – film, farming, art, cuisine.

Four purposes – understanding the world around us; informing citizens.

I like the sense of reality drawn into my teaching. I want students to see what can be loved and appreciated about the wider world and I enjoy building the ambition to see things for themselves and the curiosity to learn the language that will access that. For example, we talked about a perfume company – definitely associated with the things that can be enjoyed in the world of glamour but this also allowed us to talk about ethical issues such as use of the things that can be grown in the south of France and cost of brand names.

Four purposes – understanding the world around us; expressing ourselves.

Novice learners were urged to consider what they could gain from visuals, subtitles and cognates as they watched a video. We then looked at some useful expressions they already had and considered how they could use that to convey a message. We compared some of the lengthy texts they were tempted to put through Google Translate and then unpacked what they could actually say without doing that. Students were surprised to see what they were able to do for themselves.

This enabled pupils to become ambitious and self-aware learners. They became aware of more aspects of how communication works.

Students were making connections between their knowledge and their ambition – identifying potential gaps in knowledge. This taught them about how their teacher could help them and also how to collaborate with others and conduct independent research. We had the opportunity to talk about sensible use of online translation. Students have definitely learnt about a place in France – many want to visit now. They've made links with a Mr Bean film they've seen and this allowed us to talk about Tati and M Hulot.

Students have told me how much they are enjoying this sense of purpose – in terms of generating interest it is much better than just looking at language alone.

Working with the AATT has allowed me to open links with the countries whose languages we are studying. Students from a rather small town are able to see what else is out there and there is a sense of excitement about that. The increased interest level means that fear of making grammar mistakes has fallen far behind the joy of being able to talk about something the students have discovered. As a teacher, I feel that I am able to show much more of something that inspires me. I love languages because of what I can see and do as a result of knowing them. Now my students are doing the same.

The regular refrains we meet as language teachers are 'What's the point' or 'I don't understand x'. With this approach to learning, there is something for everyone to relate to. Seeing how they feel about other things in the world allows students to learn more about themselves but also to recognize what good and interesting things exist in other cultures. This surely builds better relationships with others and shows that there is more than their own way to live.

Recognition of the interrelationship between language and culture must also bring home the importance of the Welsh language as part of identity. The great question to consider for a lifetime is 'What words and expressions have arisen amongst the people who live in a particular place to allow them to discuss the things they do and encounter'? How wonderful to start working on that now!

—Dr Jane Byrne, Ysgol Uwchradd Tywyn, Gwynedd, French

TABLE 5.4 Articulated Assessment Transfer Task – A place in France

Enduring Understandings
✻ The French Riviera attracts and has attracted a glamorous lifestyle, cinema and artists.
Essential Questions
? What do we mean by 'style' and 'lifestyle'?
? Why do so many people head for the south of France?
? Why did many impressionist painters like to paint in the south of France?
Context
You have been asked to help someone plan a trip to a place in France – in this case, Cannes – by making recommendations about what would be interesting places to visit.

HOW DO WE EXPRESS OURSELVES?

Articulation Spiral Points
@ Research, present and make recommendations for a place to visit in the south of France.
@ Give opinions in writing.
@ Present details about places to visit.

Intercultural Transfer Targets	Mediation for Transfer
• I can identify links between the cinema and France. • I can recognize names from the fashion and beauty world associated with France. • I can name dishes which come from the south of France	• Ability to explain the lifestyles on the French Riviera. What makes it possible? • Ability to give one's opinion on cultural themes such as fashion and cinema. • Recognize and explain to others what is valued in this lifestyle – what prizes are awarded for films.

Entry	Intermediate	Advanced
Photos and videos of Cannes		
Interpretive Task Descriptions **How do we understand the world around us and support others?**		
Pupils look at the presentation on Cannes and listen to the simple narrative about Cannes and what it is like. Pupils complete the worksheet to note and answer questions about what they have understood and learnt. Pupils will be asked to complete the 'what could I find out' in English. In preparation for the next stage of research work.	Pupils look at the presentation on Cannes and answer simple questions to elicit descriptions of the slides in order to show where Cannes is and what kind of town it is. Students complete the worksheet to record their understanding and reflections. Pupils watch a video on Cannes and recognize important words and phrases relating to the topic.	Pupils look at the presentation on Cannes and describe the slides in order to show where Cannes is and introduce aspects of the town. Students complete the worksheet to record their understanding and reflections. Pupils watch a video on Cannes and relay and paraphrase what they have heard and understood.
I Can		
I can understand and summarize information. I can use what I have learnt to further my research work.	I can infer and relay information from narrative visuals.	I can understand and relay a wide range of information on Cannes. I can start to identify other potential places to explore in my research.

	**Interpersonal Task Descriptions** How do we express ourselves and engage others?
Students discuss with a partner what they have learnt about Cannes, what else they could learn about it and agree on what should be on their list of recommendations.	Students discuss and agree with a partner the criteria needed to attract visitors to a place and find examples of such places to include in a list.	Students discuss and agree with a partner what a place can bring to different groups of people when on holiday there. Students share examples from previous research or knowledge of such places.
	**I Can**
I can discuss and agree on what to recommend in Cannes.	I can exchange ideas about tourism. I can discuss and agree on what will attract tourists to a place.	I can share and compare my opinions. I can use my research to further sustain my choices. I can discuss what makes a place interesting.
	**Presentational Task Descriptions** How do we create and share with others?
Produce a simple infographic or brochure presenting Cannes and its attractions.	Produce a holiday brochure about Cannes giving details about its attractions and making recommendations to visitors on cultural, historical, leisure and gastronomical aspects.	Produce a short video presentation – either as an interview or a presentation presenting Cannes and its attractions for different groups of people: families, young people, people with special needs or disabilities.
	**I Can**
I can express simply what makes this destination attractive to visitors and make recommendations.	I can understand what is in a place and explain what people do there and why a place is of interest.	I can give opinions about what is there and make recommendations for things to see for different groups.

# Bridge to Design

Let's go deeper into Dr Byrne's design process and collaborate with colleagues for additional ideas and reflection on this exemplar before working on your own design.

Reflect to Reveal

1) How do novelty and improvisation play a role in this exemplar?
2) In what ways does 'What could I know' prepare pupils for the interpersonal conversations?
3) To what extent can authentic texts help transition from Interpretive to Interpersonal tasks?

Questions for Colleagues

1) Why is it important for pupils to decide and come to consensus for Interpersonal tasks?
2) How do the tasks Dr Byrne designed help pupils with mediation for transfer?
3) How can we shift from conventional lessons on tourism to a better spiral and meaningful reprise, as seen in this exemplar?

Ask the Designer

What is your question for Dr Byrne? What else do you want to know about this exemplar and her design thinking?

Participate in the Practice

Which practices guided Dr Byrne in creating her exemplar? How did she design with these in mind? Explain below for each component.

1) Context and tasks with pupils 'in role' as experts on Cannes.
2) Active ownership of language and problem-solving.
3) Tasks with complexity and variation, creating products for different audiences.

Teacher to Leader on Design and Implementation

1. Your primary route to success is by transferring your passion for your subject to your students. Most will not have travelled – I have found that most do not know where other countries are. This means that you have an opportunity to open up a whole world to them.

2. Most pupils have not ever considered how communication works. They need to realize that in your lessons there will be a lot of non-voiced clues to topics in hand. I played an audio of a weather forecast from Cannes to pupils to see whether they could gain any information and then I played them the audio and video together. They were astonished and very satisfied to realize what they could now figure it out.

3. We are all motivated by enjoyment and not by failure. I have learned that when I stop worrying about my students having perfect grammar all the time and just enjoy our conversations, they enjoy them, too and then become the ones wanting to get things right.

Pupils loved the lessons – they were talking about the topic as they were packing up and leaving and several came up to me and said it was fun. I like that we now have some cultural things to refer to when we are doing other topics. Parents have mentioned that their children have talked about the topic at home.

—Dr Jane Byrne, Ysgol Uwchradd Tywyn, Gwynedd

From the Admin Desk

Although based solely on the town of Cannes, Dr Byrne makes great use of her authentic materials in the interpretive mode to feed into the interpersonal tasks. Other languages teachers could look into ways of exploring authentic materials further in their proactive planning. These materials are often real treasures. For pupils to access the material, teachers spend a lot of time to design and prepare the necessary tasks and support. What is more, students often feel frustrated for not having exploited and understood the whole text, video or song etc., which actually piqued their interest and inspired them to think and express themselves about issues which are relevant to them. A single ten-minute activity is not enough to unlock its potential.

Colleagues could look at questions students could ask or explore to delve further into what has been exposed in the interpretive. This series of questions could be a good reference to students as they could be asked for any topic they wish to address. This can be a frame to develop oracy and thinking skills. The language knowledge is provided and reinforced at every occurrence, embedding both knowledge and skills.

—Stephanie Ellis-Williams, International Languages, Global Futures GwE Lead

Iconic Foods from Two Cultures or Even More

Ms Sloan's year 8 differentiates these tasks all by themselves and uses the interpersonal tasks to prepare the final deliverables, which iconic foods to feature for Welsh Week. In these improvisational tasks, pupils identify, choose and come to consensus on which foods to include. Which food is so essential that it is the embodiment of your cultural heritage and can never be omitted?

Teacher as Designer – *La Baguette*

Ysgol Y Grango is a medium-sized secondary school in a rural area of Wrexham County, near the English border. Welsh is taught within an English setting. The languages department is very dynamic and always aims to keep their learning schemes up to date and engaging for pupils. Uptake at option levels is generally good thanks to the energy and hard work of the language teachers.

This is a good example for this Principle as the Interpersonal task in each level clearly directs students to go beyond descriptions and transmission. The activity is clearly framed but the content and end-product will be informed by the arguments and decisions made by the learners themselves. The task clearly solves a problem, explaining what makes a product traditional and/ or regional, and lets each group the freedom to take it in the direction they decide. Their consensus is their response at this stage and there is no right or wrong as long as they agree.

The nature of the conversation is therefore very much improvised even if clear language patterns and support can be provided to allow these conversations to take place in the target language.

The particular gem of this AATT (see Table 5.5) for this principle is the prompt card provided to learners (Interpersonal speaking cards novice +). The language used is simple enough to be easily understood and learned and yet it is relevant and specific for this particular task. In selecting such prompts, the teacher shows the impact of backward planning on progression and success. With these prompts, pupils are able to carry out the task with the intended learning outcomes in mind and the tools to achieve them.

—Stephanie Ellis-Williams, International Languages, Global Futures GwE Lead

Voices from the Field

The concept of food playing a pivotal role in the daily lives of French nationals is not a new or alien concept among other nations. We centre most of our day around meal taking and this concept is easily transferable to our own culture. We also share in our meal taking practices around the world, and *La Baguette* is far reaching and therefore relatable to my target audience (Year 8 French studying food and drink). Designing this way helps implement culture perspectives and intercultural transfer into my lessons and these AATTs fit perfectly with the Four Purposes of the CfW, and on most occasions hitting all four at once. For example, the AATT that I have chosen to showcase matches at least one bullet point from each purpose;

'Ambitious capable learners who: set themselves high standards and seek and enjoy challenges (they have an option to choose beginner, intermediate or advanced and in most cases, pupils will choose above their capabilities as they enjoy challenges).

Enterprising, creative contributors who: connect and apply their knowledge and skills to create ideas and products.

Healthy, confident individuals who: have the confidence to perform.

Ethical, informed citizens who: find, evaluate and use evidence in forming views.'

I hope other cultures understand that food is not only a necessity but it plays a much bigger role in our heritage; our upbringing, our daily lives, what we pass on to generations. By UNESCO recognizing that foods should have heritage status and in my example, putting *La Baguette* on this pedestal, it opens up the debate for other cultural food identities to be recognized and protected also.

The first time I met with Professor Jenny Eddy and was introduced to the AATTs, I came away full of excitement and enthusiasm, and if I felt that way, all I could imagine is how my pupils would feel. I had a buzz that language was purposeful (and I already know that as an adult and a language teacher!) and there was more than just learning the language, there was a 'bigger picture'. I want my pupils to feel the way I feel when I visit other countries, not just France (their language opportunities in the school I teach in). I feel brave, nervous, curious, adventurous, naïve, respectful to name a few. I like designing in this way as I feel like learning in this way provides the pupils with opportunities to feel as I feel when I travel, to understand it is okay to make mistakes, to learn something new and important about other cultures and their way of life, that using a small amount of language can make massive strides in communication, all the while, they don't realize they are being assessed and they transfer skills without realizing they are doing it – it is not forced.

How does my AATT align with the SoWMs? The novice learner, in having the context from the inception of the transfer tasks, has their interest sparked. This way of backward learning, and providing them with what they 'can do' allows them to see how they will be able to transfer skills across a learning continuum with confidence, and the outcome is something that is achievable and visible but also purposeful; they have used language, recycled language, produced language and exhibited this in audience-specific deliverable – it has 'real world' meaning. Language is used for real-life functions where skills are transferred without the learner openly knowing they are processing language in this way, therefore, language is 'natural' and not forced. This aligns effortlessly with the SoWMs; Languages connect us, Understanding language is key to understanding the world around us, Expressing ourselves through language is key to communication, Literature fires the imagination. In terms of my chosen AATT, the two SoWMs it really showcases are (1) languages connect us; (2) understanding language is key to understanding the world around us.

The AATTs allow for the varying proficiencies of learner competence, there are three accessible learning points along the continuum that suit the needs of all learners in the classroom or cohort. I can see the more these AATTs are used in my planning, the more opportunity the learner will have to move along the continuum, building their linguistic competencies as they progress allowing them to ask and answer more complex questions, find information independently and use language effectively to express their own ideas. Eventually they will be able to adapt and manipulate language with confidence. The fact that there is a deliverable in each of the AATTs, provides learners to showcase their learning through effective communication for a target audience or range of different audiences.

Designing this way allows for review and consolidation as well as challenges to deal with new language. It offers a stretch in an unconventional manner in that learners have to think differently and transfer skills they have but may not realize they have, so that they are linking language with culture, opening up their ability to see the language outside of the classroom environment.

There is much work to do to change the attitudes of learners towards language learning. The problem goes beyond the classroom. But these AATTs are a step in the right direction in allowing language practitioners to open new possibilities to learners and broaden their horizons. It gives teachers a chance to really share what they are passionate about in terms of their love of languages; it's not just the language we love, it is everything around it, culture, heritage, travel, communities, food, drink and much more.

—Ms Lynette Sloan, Ysgol Grango, Wrexham, French

TABLE 5.5 Articulated Assessment Transfer Task – *La Baguette*

Enduring Understandings ✻ Food plays an important role in cultural heritage. ✻ Food differs around the world. ✻ Cultural history informs cuisine identity.
Essential Questions ? What makes food iconic? ? Why do we link foods to particular cultures? ? To what extent does culture and geography affect an individual's diet?
Context UNESCO has just awarded *La Baguette* world heritage status! Tasting national cuisine and food specialities are one of the most enjoyable ways to discover different cultures. You are thinking of traditional iconic foods from Wales and other countries and would like to promote them during your school's Wythnos Cymraeg (Welsh Week) which takes place at the beginning of March.
Articulation Spiral Points @ Create a poster of a shape poem to promote Welsh food. @ Design and write out a recipe card choosing the best ingredients. @ Write an article for the school newsletter outlining cultural importance of food.

HOW DO WE EXPRESS OURSELVES?

Intercultural Transfer Targets	Mediation for Transfer
• I can show understanding of why the baguette is part of daily life in France. • I can recognize ingredients used in traditional baguette making. • I can identify the similarities and differences in traditional foods. • I can show understanding that food plays an important role in cultural identity.	• Identify and explain key important factors that make a food/drink traditional and cultural. • Describe similarities and differences between iconic traditional foods to others unfamiliar with them. • Share via social media clip their experience of following a recipe and baking to others, using the language.

Year 8 Novice	Year 8 Novice +	Year 8 Novice ++
Authentic Videos		
Interpretive Task Descriptions **How do we understand the world around us and support others?**		
Watch the video about *La Baguette* in France and answer true or false/ vrai ou faux based on the information presented.	Watch the video about *La Baguette* in France including the baguette making process and identify the correct answers and order the method of making a traditional baguette.	Watch the videos outlining the recipe, method and way of eating traditional French baguette and Welsh Bara Brith. For each product, match the ingredients correctly and put the method for each product into the correct order.
I Can		
I can correctly identify the information I have heard.	I can identify and summarize the main points based on what I have seen and heard.	I can categorize ingredients from different recipes and organize information correctly based on what I have seen and heard.
Interpersonal Task Descriptions **How do we express ourselves and engage others?**		
With a partner, match the regional dishes (food/drink) with the correct country and give your opinion on the dish (food/drink).	With a partner, discuss and come to a consensus about what are the important considerations in making a product that is so integral to the culture and heritage of a country.	Create a Venn-diagram comparing the Baguette with Bara Brith with a partner.

	I Can	
I can decide with a partner the food/drink that belongs to which country and express my opinion on traditional food/drink.	I can discuss, identify and exchange correct and relevant information, with a partner, and come to a consensus on what makes a product traditional and true to its culture and heritage.	I can work with a partner to come to a consensus on the content of both regional dishes (ingredients, similarities, differences, etc.)
Presentational Task Descriptions **How do we create and share with others?**		
Create a poster or shape poem of a traditional Welsh food product that you would like to see on the UNESCO list, for example Bara Brith, providing key information such as ingredients and historical details.	Design and write out a recipe card, including precise measurements needed for a delicious traditional food from Wales or other cultures and create a video/flipgrid that shows you and a partner making the product following your written recipe instructions. to be shown at the Wythnos Cymraeg assembly.	Write an article for your school newsletter discussing a traditional regional dish of your choice and compare it to Welsh or French traditional food, including ingredients and cultural importance.
	I Can	
I can use language creatively to list/present the features and details of a typical Welsh food.	I can present information in the form of a recipe, in a clear set of instructions and use the language confidently to produce a product.	I can compare and contrast traditional regional foods, presenting information and expressing opinions.

Bridge to Design

Let's go deeper into Ms Sloan's design process and collaborate with colleagues for additional ideas and reflection on this exemplar before working on your own design.

Reflect to Reveal

1) What does cuisine identity mean? Why does it matter in the global context?
2) What else might UNESCO like to see as a deliverable on this concept?
3) What tasks might come next on iconic foods for the culture(s) you teach?

Questions for Colleagues

1) Why is it important for pupils to agree, plan and choose?
2) How do these tasks help prepare the presentational deliverables?
3) Can you explain cuisine in the collective identity to someone else? Do you have an example from your own culture?

Ask the Designer

What is your question for Ms Sloan? What else do you want to know about this exemplar and her design thinking?

Participate in the Practice

Which practices guided Ms Sloan in creating her exemplar? How did she design with these in mind? Explain below for each component.

1) Argument and consensus leading to transfer and problem-solving.
2) Learner autonomy and creating new products.
3) Risk taking with confidence on what you own right now.

Teacher to Leader on Design and Implementation

1. Don't be afraid to make mistakes! And let your learners make mistakes, that is how it is in the real world, acquiring and using language. Communication does not need to be perfect.
2. Don't overthink the authentic material, you could waste time trying to find the 'perfect' source that you will lose sight of what you want your learners to achieve. When you stumble across fantastic sources, save them down, they may inform your future planning the more confident with AATT planning you become.
3. If it doesn't work, it doesn't matter. Reflect, refine and improve. You have still provided your learners with authentic experiences. And listen to your learners, provide them opportunities to feedback. Pupil voice is a powerful and informative tool.

Since September 2023 the Curriculum for Wales is being delivered to all primary-aged learners and Years 7 and 8 secondary aged learners, and will be rolled out to Year 9 secondary aged pupils from September 2025. This has meant, for me, a complete overhaul of Schemes of Learning (SoL) and a shift in focus towards the four purposes of the Curriculum for Wales, with the learners at the heart of my planning.

I have taken risks to deliver content I wouldn't usually include at this level. For example, I have taught a whole unit to Year 8 on Le Monde Francophone, looking at the history of the Francophonie and how colonization changed and shaped nations, with a focus on the Caribbean and comparing it to Wales and loss of identity, developing the unit work to include complex discussions on reclaiming identity and language. These were some of the best lessons I have taught in terms of output. The pupil's reaction to the lessons was nothing short of inspiring. Their engagement to content which I thought was beyond their capacity in terms of age ability bowled me over. They were coming up with thoughts and ideas that I hadn't given them credit for and their thinking processes identified skills I didn't think they were able to develop at their level. Their language acquisition seemed better, because they were learning purposeful language (such as slavery, colonization, poverty, community) to a topic they were interested in. They wanted to use the language. As part of this unit of work, learners produced a piece of art work incorporating images of a Francophone country of their choice in a surreal setting, hiding key language in their drawings. This was judged by the art department in the school, making cross curricular links meaningful and easy to engage.

Whilst I may not have fully embraced the AATT model into ALL of my planning just yet, it has shifted my focus on how I plan. And it has given me the courage to make changes to my planning, but also delivery of lessons.

Ms Lynette Sloan, Ysgol Grango, Wrexham, French

From the Admin Desk

Just like in the interpretive, it is the nature of the task which will be the key to success for learners. Teachers can learn how to best support their pupils. The conversation prompts students to categorize what is essential, important and not so important for the issue they are discussing. Their focus is therefore to think hard on the actual concepts rather than having to do this and think hard about the language they need to express themselves in the TL.

Any language culture will be able to relate to such an AATT and the method. The key is to select the language judiciously ahead of the task so it is pertinent but also easy to use and remember for learners. This AATT was revised on several occasions to ensure the interpersonal tasks were complying with the intended outcomes of this mode. Colleagues can use this example to reflect on their own pair work activity, aims and objectives and impact on progress.

—Stephanie Ellis-Williams, International Languages, Global Futures GwE Lead

Design for Transfer

Using the interpretive tasks for consistency and follow-through, design at least one Interpersonal task across **three levels of learner engagement**. Try to incorporate different types: Ask and Answer, Arrange, Adopt, Assess, Argue, Agree. Use the AATT fillable template on the companion website, Chapter 1. (For a master list of task types, see Appendices D and E.)

Design for Transfer

Now that you have designed an interpersonal task at each level, compose the *'I can'* PASS statement for each. Keep in mind the function, skill, purpose, content and audience.

Design for Transfer

Check your tasks carefully. As a result of this task, could the learner bridge communication with someone unfamiliar with the language or culture? How does doing this task enable the learner to make language accessible and cultural perspectives visible for someone else? Find this evidence of Mediation for Transfer in your interpersonal tasks and include it on your AATT template.

Reflect and Revisit

1. In your tasks, do you see evidence that inter/transcultural perspectives are more visible and language more accessible? Give an example.
2. What are possible scenarios where learners can facilitate understanding with others through mediation and the task types in this chapter?
3. Why are tasks designed for improv more true-to-life than rehearsing or memorizing forms?
4. How can tasks free from habit or routine develop confidence and prepare the learner for transfer?
5. What are the ways that planning or co-creating the Presentational deliverable helps learners to mediate with others?

6 Why should learners ask and answer questions as soon as possible? What is the danger of the delay?

7 How can the novice learner arrange, plan, adopt or select, assess, judge, agree or come to a consensus? Give an example and explain why problem-solving should not wait until higher levels are achieved.

6

How Do We Create and Share with Others?

Enduring Understandings

- ∞ Optimal presentational tasks yield oral or written deliverables of value prepared for someone, an audience, or a community's needs beyond the classroom.
- ∞ Transfer depends on knowledge and skills repertoire applied differently to solve a problem or create a new product for someone else.
- ∞ The intentional act of transfer pushes mediation forward so others can see a concept, idea or information differently.
- ∞ Properly articulated curricula for progression contain a catalogue of novel, creative and complex deliverables.

Essential Questions

- **Q** How does transfer make our work relevant and applicable?
- **Q** Why is creativity a tool as well as a goal for mediation?
- **Q** Why does novelty matter?
- **Q** How does our creativity help others see things differently?

I can

- Determine how to create novel tasks that address the audience's needs in the Context.
- Describe Presentational tasks that solve challenges and create novel products for others.
- Design key performances for the catalogue of deliverables across different levels for articulation.
- Develop 'I can' statements specific to the task and intercultural transfer targets.

Let's Consider

In Chapter 5, we explored the question, 'How do we express ourselves and engage others?' Our tasks shifted from input to improv as we prepared learners to plan, choose, judge, discuss and agree with someone else in real-time. We do these improv tasks because those mirror how language works when authentic communication happens outside the classroom. We also create new texts, oral or written works for someone or other people, with time to revise and refine them. To prepare confident, enterprising learners for civic and global readiness, we must provide opportunities for learners to create these products of value, just as they have seen shared with them. They will need to solve problems or challenges and create deliverables that address someone else's needs beyond their own. These novel works allow others to notice and grasp concepts in a different light. Can we create something helpful to share, even as a beginner? How do I know if the task is novel enough for transfer? What does it look like when learners engage in creative transfer independently?

Create Something New with Others in Mind

Presentational (Glisan et al., 2003; National Standards in Foreign Language Education Project, 1996/2006; National Standards Collaborative Board, 2015) tasks for this curriculum design create oral and written works with intention for someone else or an audience in mind. The best ones are those which offer deliverables requested, expected or found to have value outside of the school setting or for an audience besides just for teachers and classmates. They require that the learner use their repertoire flexibly and to solve a need beyond themselves and create a tangible product. For that reason, these tasks allow learners time to consult their own resources and new ones, collaborate with others and revise their work, which happens in the world outside of school. These tasks prepare learners to be confident and enterprising individuals as they create new products for their communities, facilitating mediation with others unfamiliar with the language or unaware of the culture. These are the goals of the tasks you will see in this chapter by our designers.

In this framework, learners

1. Synthesize input from the previous two tasks either alone or in collaboration
2. Solve problems and create novel products that matter to others
3. Revisit, revise, rehearse, refine and respond with transactional, expressive and poetic deliverables

The teacher as designer has a few objectives when designing presentational tasks. The summative task must be novel enough so that the learner has not seen it before; it cannot be a repeat of a Stage Three task during one of the lessons. In Table 2.2, we examined the stages of transfer. The summative presentational task should be for far transfer which has few supports and cues are limited to none. In order to build confidence and adaptability, learners need to prepare for changing situations and contexts that demonstrate this flexibility of repertoire. The fewer directions, lists, supports, cues and word banks a task has, the more the task assesses for transfer (McTighe & Wiggins, 2005). These tasks ask pupils to create their own texts. It can be in the manner of the original, a renewal, or their own creation. The task should revisit information from the previous two modes and also provide opportunities for learners to find additional content or resources. When creating products for real-world applications, we rely on background knowledge and incorporate new material, with time to revise, rehearse and refine our work. Finally, our response is for someone else, a given audience. The product or deliverable should address the problem posed in the context and respond to that person or audience's needs. Your learners may introduce or suggest to the teacher their own complexity or variation, audience, or demographic on their own as an extension or elaboration to your task. When this happens, it is lovely; they have turned the corner to learner autonomy and transfer evidence when they provide their own complication to solve.

The presentational tasks you have seen thus far and in this chapter represent the three types of literary discourse: transactional, expressive and poetic (Britton et al., 1975). Did you notice the persuasive poster and the blog profile in Chapter 4, the infographic and poem in Chapter 5, the logo, video and poll in Chapter 3? Please include all of these task types and more varieties in your catalogue of key deliverables for your programme. This collection represents products that align with the context, the problem posed there and are for someone else other than the classroom teacher. They range from a variety of disciplines that we encounter outside school and throughout the lifespan. They also reveal skills and strategies for the learner to use when they act as mediators, where plurilingual and inter/transcultural communicative competence come into the fore (Beacco et al., 2016; Little & Kirwan, 2019). This curriculum design prepares learners for this, as a bridge from ownership to authorship, from comprehension to production, and to understand the other person and their awareness, reflecting on their cultural lens and providing clarifying language. These transfer tasks facilitate access between, through, within and among cultures as a transcultural learner and communicator. Mediation makes language and culture accessible to those unfamiliar, unacquainted or inexperienced within the new culture(s). Learners can provide that bridge and understand that the language they own is valuable and helpful to others, too. Table 6.1 shows the three task types (Britton et al., 1975) with a sample and strategies acquired and useful for mediation.

TABLE 6.1 Presentational task types and engaging others in mediation

Type	Sample Task	Strategy acquired for Mediation
Transactional	step-by-step instructions, information, public service announcements, letters, brochures, advertisements, videos, surveys, infographics, lectures and 'how to or what to do' talks.	Clarify information whole or in parts, indicating image aligned with word or phrase, and adapt language level to needs of individual or audience. Deconstructing complicated information. Summary in a different register: oral to written or vice versa.
Expressive	Blogs, vlogs, timelines, opinion essays, diaries and social media.	Relay feelings, opinions and personal connection. Facilitating and navigating inter/transcultural space between, through, among and within cultures.
Poetic	Songs, plays, poems, graphic novels, games, museum installations, films or stories.	Depict and reveal ideas and issues in a novel way using imagination, experiences and emotions shared through multimedia. Elaborate text. Change genre.

Put It to Practice: Collaborate to Articulate

Looking back at all of the AATT exemplars you have seen thus far, what types of presentational tasks do you see? How do they follow the previous two tasks? How can you include those in your catalogue of key deliverables? Would you add any others? For additional tasks, refer to Appendices D and E for the master lists. With colleagues in your department, take an inventory of tasks you currently implement with your pupils. Are the tasks designed to create a deliverable or product for someone else or with another audience in mind? Can you determine the strategy takeaway for mediation?

Meet Our Designers

As you have seen, all of our AATTs and Stage Three formative tasks have presentational mode deliverables. The ones chosen for this chapter by Ms Ellis-Williams look closely at the creativity in design, the use of literature and transfer of concepts and a personal, yet intercultural response. Ms Perkins welcomes multicultural newcomers into the Welsh community in School Life, Mr Conn moves past superficial hobbies when exploring extracurriculars, Ms Parry lets literature inspire a menu in Food Festivals, and architecture and identity become transcultural in *Les Maisons* by Ms Temple.

Helping Others Make a Fresh Start at a New School

Ms Perkins designs a wonderful exemplar for mediation with this AATT on school life. The problem of transitioning to a new school and possibly a new culture and country is daunting for anyone. These pupils solve the problem and create products to welcome year 6 to their new school. They read an excerpt from classic Welsh literature, Rhys Lewis' First day and designed new digital multimedia deliverables to mediate for children and parents. This articulated sequence of tasks provides an excellent model for children to welcome newcomers to their communities in our current times.

Teacher as Designer – School Life

Ysgol Friars is a very large secondary school in the heart of the University town of Bangor in North Wales. The Welsh language profile of the school is complex with a large proportion of students with good levels of Welsh and another proportion with varying levels from total beginners to near fluent. The school teaches Welsh within an English setting but a good proportion are taught Welsh as a first language too.

This AATT (see Table 6.2) is a good example for this Principle because the presentational task set enables pupils to be creative, independent and to use the language they have to create an effective product. The turnaround for this teacher was to ensure the task had a real purpose and responded to a real problem: how to ensure a better transition for pupils moving from the primary to the secondary school, alleviating their fears and preparing them for their life in their new school.

The audience is one that the learners can relate to as they were that particular audience only the year before. They understand the perspective of the pupils in their last year of primary and they have an insight into the new school. They are also exposed to a third person's experience of changing school settings through the literary piece in the interpretive mode which they will use to feed their discussions in the interpersonal. The presentational pieces address and start to answer the essential questions of the AATT.

The level of engagement of the pupils represents their place on the language continuum but all clearly express their reasoning about what a school should offer. As the audience becomes more specific, the response also becomes more refined and sophisticated.

Mrs Perkins has truly been inspired by the AATT process and has given a range of possible end tasks which the pupils could produce. It can be directed, left up to the students or limited to one. This may depend on the group it is given to or the individual pupil.

—Stephanie Ellis-Williams, International Languages,
Global Futures GwE Lead

HOW DO WE CREATE AND SHARE WITH OTHERS?

Voices from the Field

Ysgol Friars is a large school with over 1,400 children attending the school. Pupils arrive at the school from the catchment area schools and from other areas across Gwynedd and Anglesey. A number of pupils arrive in Bangor from foreign countries for year 7 and it is a completely unique community with over forty-nine different languages spoken here as the first language of our pupils. Due to the multicultural nature of our school, it was essential when planning our New Curriculum that the pupils understand and appreciate the values and culture of our school which led to the planning of this AATT and why I chose School as a context. A School context unites all pupils and within their experience. Everyone is a citizen of the school, and this context gives everyone the opportunity to realize that they are an essential part of the school and the unique culture here. School is part of their world and culture and a new Welsh community for them.

Other cultures should understand the importance of the school in a Welsh language community. Experience to understand the school's values and culture as part of their new community and to be principled and confident citizens at Ysgol Friars.

Planning in this way has given purpose to our tasks to ensure that our pupils succeed in realizing the four purposes. The essential question gives value to the planning and makes the pupils think more broadly. It is also an opportunity for us as a department to experiment by trying to plan for our second language and first language pupils using the same language continuum. The whole range uses the same skills.

As the subject is within their world it is suitable for all learners. The text is suitable for everyone with the obvious differentiation. There are challenges for everyone here and it is suitable for every SoWMs. Looking at different books, it was interesting to see which standard the pupils from a wide range of classes had reached. We noted a diversity of attainment. The comparison skills are suitable for a number of other day-to-day tasks and in different subjects.

Planning in this way is effective when there is a range of linguistic ability. It sorts out the difference between the learners and clearly shows how to transition from one stage of progress to another. It organizes planning to have the linguistic continuum across the ability range. It clearly shows what skills the learners need and gives purpose to the work in order to achieve the four purposes. Pupils and teachers can see progress in their work and where the pupils aim to improve their work.

Teachers, pupils and parents can see progress in the pupils' work rather than them working in a vacuum. I hope that the learners feel part of the community, part of Wales and Welshness. Work that is relevant gives purpose to assessment tasks. I really like the essential questions that make us think about how the work is suitable, relevant and purposeful for our learners.

—Ms Sioned Perkins, Ysgol Friars, Gwynedd, Welsh

TABLE 6.2 Articulated Assessment Transfer Task – School life

Enduring Understandings
✽ The culture and values of the school are an important part of their community.
Essential Questions
? What makes a good school?
? What experiences excite us?
? How can we improve the school?
? What is so special about our school community?
Context
The head of year 7 has asked you to create a resource to help them introduce the school. They will guide parents and new learners around the school on the open night to year 6, and will need resources to help and teach new pupils and their parents about the Ysgol Friars community.
Articulation Spiral Points
@ describe the concept of school community
@ compare schools
@ give information about the school
@ provide reasons and evidence to parents

Intercultural Transfer Targets	Mediation for Transfer
• I can identify good features about the school.	• Bridge and exchange ideas and concepts of
• I can justify why the school is good or not so good.	• Clarify typical visuals, signs, materials in schools.
• I can compare the secondary school with the primary school and recognize the difference between the two places.	• Explain features of school procedures to others.
• I can offer reasons and evidence for my opinion.	• Share expectations of school here and abroad.

Beginner	Intermediate	Advanced
Story: *Rhys Lewis* by Daniel Owen. 'First Day' Owen, D. (1885). *Rhys Lewis.* Hughes & Son. Wales.		
Interpretive Task Descriptions How do we understand the world around us and support others?		
Secondary / primary photos. Vocabulary topics. Categorize photos as they want. Categorizing the importance triangle of opinion topics Sorting good/bad adjectives.	Secondary / primary photos. Categorize as they want. Primary/ secondary comparison. Oral work, class discussion. Read the story 'Rhys Lewis' First Day'. The red chair game.	Secondary / primary photos. Categorize as they want. Primary/ secondary comparison. Oral work, class discussion. Read the story 'Rhys Lewis' First Day'. The red chair game.
I Can		
I can recognize adjectives and order them	I can ask Rhys questions about his first experience of school.	I can ask Rhys questions about his first experience of school.
Interpersonal Task Descriptions How do we express ourselves and engage others?		
Pair work to discuss like/ dislike topics, Ask why? Share details and personal experiences about the school/subjects. Create graphs about information gathered by members of the class. Worksheet expressing opinions using different structures to express opinions about topics.	Oral work to discuss the Venn diagram, and compare their day with Rhys. What would you change about your first day? What went well for you? How can the school prepare you better for your first day? Create a questionnaire to find suitable information about the class's impressions of the school. Draw a conclusion and analyse the information. Decide on the best advice to give to year 6 pupils. A lesson in using 'post it' and discussions in order to find opinions.	Deciding on the best advice to give to year 6 pupils. A lesson in using 'post it' and discussions in order to find opinions.

I Can		
I can express opinions using adjectives. I can question members of the class and receive information.	I can express opinions, reason and offer evidence by using analytical work.	I can analyse other reasons and come to a definite conclusion and opinion.
Presentational Task Descriptions **How do we create and share with others?**		
Write a letter/article expressing an opinion about a school giving clear reasons. Create a digital QR code.	Create a digital information brochure. Write a newspaper article to circle a letter to year 6 pupils giving your opinion about Friars school. Tell us about your favourite things, the things that need to be improved here and give them advice in advance of an open night in November.	Write an article for a letter circle to year 6! Express opinions, reasons and evidence. (different types of pupils, e.g. anxious pupils, pupils who like languages/sports/ technology etc.) Create a digital information pamphlet. Record using MP3 for the office. Give the oral work in the form of QR codes.
I Can		
I can express an opinion about a school, supporting my opinion with clear reasons.	I can offer advice and a definite opinion about the school.	I can offer advice to specific problems giving reasons and evidence and offer suitable advice to others.

Bridge to Design

Let's go deeper into Ms Perkins' design process and collaborate with colleagues for additional ideas and reflection on this exemplar before working on your own design.

Reflect to Reveal

1) Why is it important for learners to create their own texts?
2) How do the presentational products help parents and new learners' transition and adapt from primary to secondary?

3) What makes these tasks especially relevant and purposeful to this diverse community?

Questions for Colleagues

1) How might you see this exemplar adapted for your own school community?
2) What is the value of creating materials for someone else?
3) Why does the shared experience of the First Day help everyone to adapt to life changes?

Ask the Designer

What is your question for Ms Perkins? What else do you want to know about this exemplar and her design thinking?

Participate in the Practice

Which practices does Ms Perkins apply in creating her exemplar? How did she design with these in mind? Explain below for each component.

1) Transfer and the process of creating a product for a new audience.
2) Using classic literary texts to reveal contemporary issues.
3) A catalogue of deliverables as tools for mediation with increasing complexity.

Teacher to Leader on Design and Implementation

1. Collaboration with other teachers from the department.
2. Review different examples of existing AATT to fully understand the concept.
3. Don't overthink or overload your AATT. Keep it simple until you have become more confident in creating the AATT.

> **From the Admin Desk**
>
> This AATT can be useful to refine differentiation. Not just by outcome; the actual tasks frame the level of difficulty. It is also easy for the students to choose the level which best suits them at that time.
>
> The school is very cosmopolitan and many students arrive from different countries and need to adapt to a new system quickly. Helping students or other audiences to prepare for such changes can be relevant to any language and community.
>
> Colleagues can use this example to reflect on what issues are close to their students' heart and how their work could even influence the life of their community. In a time where well-being and mental health are at the forefront of our concerns and where the learner's voice should be taken seriously, the language classroom could become a vehicle for impactful debates with real outcomes. This would definitely raise the value and profile of languages.
>
> —Stephanie Ellis-Williams, International Languages, Global Futures GwE Lead

Well-being Advocates Become Capable Citizens

Mr Conn refreshes a typical and tired topic of hobbies and leisure time into a much deeper look at well-being and why it is important. The differentiation of presentational deliverables enable change for these pupils. To anyone new to wellness perspectives, this AATT and pupil products make the case for its inclusion and facilitates mediation for the uninitiated.

Teacher as Designer – Extracurricular Activities

The Alun school is a large secondary school where Welsh is taught within an English setting. The languages department is very dynamic and successful with many learners opting for both French and German at 14+. Including deeper cultural and conceptual aspects into the language classroom is what Mr Conn aimed to achieve with the AATT.

This AATT (see Table 6.3) is a good example for this Principle as it encourages students to think beyond the description of leisure activities. They need to consider and decide on the impact of a range of activities and the suitability for different ages, affinities and sensibilities. Health and well-being are other factors learners may consider in their choice of arguments in their presentational task. Mr Conn has managed to change a traditional languages topic 'free time' where students express their likes and dislikes about certain hobbies into a deeper topic of discussions: the importance of extracurricular activities for young people' health and well-being. The tasks enable all students to make valid contributions at their own level of engagement and with the language they own. They solve a problem and demonstrate they can transfer skills and knowledge in order to achieve this.

The authentic material is extremely simple but very effective. The range of activities is relevant to the learners, like stress management and yoga. Pottery, banking and robotics add variety and pique the learners' interest. The teacher expertly uses his craft to get his learners to express more sophisticated opinions and reasons from early stages in the learners' journey.

—Stephanie Ellis-Williams, International Languages,
Global Futures GwE Lead

Voices from the Field

Extracurricular activities (or AGs) play an important role in the wider school community within German schools. They offer a range of sporting and well-being activities and are popular amongst pupils, parents and supervisors. This is an important cultural difference enabling learners to deepen their cultural knowledge and understanding as well as developing their language skills. This AATT enables students to develop their intellectual curiosity addressing many elements of the Four Purposes. The endless possibilities pertaining to productive tasks also contribute heavily to the Digital Competence Framework opportunities within the curriculum.

Other cultures should understand the importance of extracurricular activities and how these provide students with a broad education. They should also appreciate the cultural importance and value placed on these clubs. These are not only coordinated by teachers but parents are heavily involved (and trusted) as supervisors.

Through designing these tasks, we are able to offer learners culturally rich experiences as the task is based on authentic materials from the country of study. The novice/intermediate/advanced approach automatically offers many creative opportunities for differentiation and the 'I can' statements link directly to CfW. Through a range of activities, a novice learner is able to use authentic materials to express themselves and communicate a range of likes and dislikes. As with intermediate and advanced learners, a novice is also able to extend cultural awareness and develop their creativity.

The AATT will be delivered during the next half-term but the task is designed to increase learners' effectiveness by asking their own questions and seeking information. Furthermore, they have opportunities to make connections between language and culture whilst also making progress in their language skills drawing upon prior learning and applying in new contexts.

Planning and designing in this way give practitioners much more freedom and place culture at the heart of learning. Differentiation is an inherent part of designing in this way and inspires creativity across all levels. Using authentic materials gives purpose to learning and enables learners to apply their language skills to real-life contexts and scenarios. A range of creative outputs will also be appealing to students as they can develop and utilise their own interests increasing learner autonomy.

—Mr Paul Conn, Alun School, Flintshire, German

TABLE 6.3 Articulated Assessment Transfer Task – Extracurricular activities

Enduring Understandings
✱ Extracurricular activities contribute to a broad and enriched education.
✱ Extracurricular activities help to shape ambitious and capable learners.
✱ Well-being and mindfulness clubs are just as important as sporting clubs.
Essential Questions
? Why do extracurricular activities matter in education?
? What makes an ambitious and capable learner?
? How do we determine the relevance of clubs and activities in school?
? To what extent are clubs and activities informed by culture and countries?
Context
Your school has asked the school council to devise the school's extracurricular timetable.
Articulation Spiral Points
@ Identify extracurricular clubs/sporting activities
@ Discuss popular clubs/activities in other countries
@ Justify opinions

HOW DO WE CREATE AND SHARE WITH OTHERS?

Intercultural Transfer Targets	Mediation for Transfer
• I can write and speak about extracurricular offerings in my own community and in another culture. • I can compare differences between clubs and activities in Wales and Germany. • I can create a multimedia presentation on extracurricular activities.	• Bridge and extend ideas and opinions on different activities. • Describe and compare popular clubs/activities of different countries for those unfamiliar with them. • Share opinions and appreciate the opinions of others. • Explain the cultural differences, meaning and importance of AGs in Germany.

Beginner	Intermediate	Advanced
\multicolumn{3}{Infographic showing a school's extracurricular offerings}
Interpretive Task Descriptions How do we understand the world around us and support others?		
Read the infographic and categorize the activities into sporting/well-being (personal development) areas.	Read a short description of the club and match with the activity.	Pick two clubs you like and two you don't and give reasons for your choices.
I Can		
I can recognize by pictures key vocabulary to identify the activity.	I can identify the activity from the written description.	I can express likes and dislikes and justify my choices.
Interpersonal Task Descriptions How do we express ourselves and engage others?		
In pairs, learners select different clubs from the timetable and express their opinions.	Interview with grid – Find someone who likes … – Wie findest du die_____ AG?	With a partner, learners come to consensus and choose with a partner which clubs should be included or discarded.
I Can		
I can share and talk about opinions on clubs/activities.	I can ask and seek information identifying the opinions of others.	I can exchange information, opinions and reasons with a partner and listen for key details about various clubs.

Presentational Task Descriptions How do we create and share with others?		
Create an extracurricular timetable for the school council to consider.	Create a video demonstrating the opinion polls of popular extracurricular activities to make a bid to the school council.	Deliver a presentation to the school council outlining what should be offered as part of the extracurricular programme.
I Can		
I can use my imagination and design a best-fit timetable of activities giving basic opinions.	I can present my findings using data to inform decision-makers.	I can persuade using a range of opinions and reasons.

Bridge to Design

Let's go deeper into Mr Conn's design process and collaborate with colleagues for additional ideas and reflection on this exemplar before working on your own design.

Reflect to Reveal

1) Why does creating a new product help learners understand their own and other cultures better?
2) Which cultural perspectives are uncovered in this exemplar?
3) Why are these concepts important across an articulated curriculum for all cultures?

Questions for Colleagues

1) How can one simple infographic yield tasks of increasing complexity?
2) Why is it important to reframe the typical unit on Leisure or Free time?
3) In what ways do the presentational deliverables enable a greater vested interest for learners?

Ask the Designer

What is your question for Mr Conn? What else do you want to know about this exemplar and his design thinking?

Participate in the Practice

Which practices guided in creating his exemplar? How did he design with these in mind? Explain below for each component.

1) Differentiation of task, well-being for different audiences and deliverables.
2) Novelty and decision-making for creating relevant products.
3) Essential questions transform the purpose of tasks and justify the 'why'.

Teacher to Leader on Design and Implementation

1. Find the authentic literature/material first and base your AATT around it. You don't want to come up with the perfect idea and then struggle to find authentic materials to match your plan.
2. Plan backwards in the AATT. Start with the advanced tasks and then move down to intermediate and novice.
3. Spend time thinking about and formulating the essential questions. Effective essential questions enable learners to think more broadly and add value to the planning and assessment tasks.

From the Admin Desk

Other language teachers can learn from this AATT that intercultural competence is not just about transmitting the culture but also to internalize it and use it to create a new product. The end product may not mention any of the German extracurricular activities or culture but learners use what they understand from studying it to refine their decision-making into what to include in their presentation.

This can be applied to any other languages and any other subject. The intercultural transfer is about the concepts of health and well-being, the rationale behind ensuring the necessity of a particular custom or system (i.e. extracurricular activities; national holidays etc …)

> An administrator could use this AATT to ask colleagues to reflect on the cross-curricular links which can be made through looking at practice in the target language country. Pupils are then tasked to compare, contrast and mediate the more suitable, effective or constructive new practice.
>
> —Stephanie Ellis-Williams, International Languages, Global Futures GwE Lead

A Story-inspired Menu Invites Normandy to the Local Festival

Ms Parry uses a short story set in Normandy as muse for a menu for the local festival, taking her year eight pupils beyond the classroom to prepare menus from different cultures. She uses the prominent festival in Wales to keep the context real and current for pupils while teaching them mediation strategies as they research and compare food and drink in Normandy and North Wales. This experience encourages uptake in language with good presentational deliverables.

Teacher as Designer – Food Festivals

Ysgol Glan y Môr is a medium-sized secondary school set in a rural and seaside town on the Llyn Peninsula of North Wales. The school is a Welsh-medium school. Most learners are from the area with strong roots in their Welsh heritage. Uptake for languages is low and often a challenge.

Still at the developing stage, we can already see the potential of this AATT (see Table 6.4). It is a good example for this Principle because it starts to engage learners in real-life, purposeful tasks of value to cultural communities beyond the classroom: presenting a food menu which is unique to their town's annual food festival. Ms Parry manages to shift the end of the unit task from what would normally be an assessment in cultural knowledge and understanding to a much more personal response. Even at the novice level, the product conveys a sense of identity linked with food. At the advanced level, the students can choose a much wider range of how their food choice relates to their identity and how they will convey this through their menu. Introducing feelings evoked by food is also interesting and opens a wide range of linguistic possibilities too.

—Stephanie Ellis-Williams, International Languages,
Global Futures GwE Lead

Voices from the Field

The school is located in the Llyn Peninsula. The cultural annual event of the National Eisteddfod, Eifionydd 2023, is taking place in the area in August 2023. There has been much emphasis locally and at school to highlighting this very important cultural event in the Welsh calendar. Eisteddfod is a festival celebrating the Welsh language and culture, including several competitions in music, drama, dance, poetry, art. Having this in mind the festival includes a food village and this is where the idea derives to include locally produced products to put on show at the event. As the National Eisteddfod moves its location annually, the other local annual food festival events take place in the nearby town of Caernarfon every May. This task could then be transferred and used to promote local and French products at any given food festival.

This task and unit of work is presented to year 8 learners. Authentic material used – short story *Le Pendentif* by Sylvie Lainé. There was a natural progression to explore the theme of food and drink with the main character ordering a drink at a café in Honfleur, Normandy. Food and drink vocabulary-based tasks were introduced to the pupils as a starting point. Developing their understanding and language structures to present sentences, asking and answering questions in the target language. Allowing the pupils to engage and interact, further developed pupils of higher abilities to communicate using different tenses. The pupils also practised comparing food and drink by looking at McDonald's menu in the UK and France, identifying further differences in food/drink items and culture represented through food and drink.

Throughout this unit of work, learners are expected to research local food and drink produce as well as further afield, in Normandy, a region of France. This enables to organically address the four purposes of the curriculum with aspects of what matters in the Languages, Literacy and communication Area of Learning and Experience.

The unit of work/tasks presented can be adapted for other languages and cultures. I wanted the pupils to express themselves and who they are by learning and researching local food/drink produce as well as broadening their horizon and looking at cultural differences through cuisine. The idea of food festivals and their concept over in France and in Wales are quite similar. However, to make it more relatable to the learners, access to information on *Gwyl Fwyd Caernarfon* (an annual local event) and furthermore *Y Pentref Fwyd* at *Eisteddfod Genedlaethol Llŷn & Eifionydd* 2023 made it realistic and current to the pupils.

Designing in this format allows more flexibility in the delivery of teaching and presenting tasks. I believe this keeps the interests of the learners, opens discussions and explores different avenues of teaching and learning. The use of current and authentic resources/materials are relatable to the learners which enables creative freedom in their final presentation.

Novice learners are able to engage fully in the unit, developing language skills that enables them to comfortably and confidently use the language and vocabulary learnt to prepare a deliverable. This AATT aligns with the statements of What Matters in the CfW as follows:

Languages connect us: Exploring culture through food and drink produced in the local area and Normandy, France.

Understanding languages is key to understanding the world around us: Learn and use language to a real purpose through literacy – Normandy, setting of the short story and exploring food and drink culture in Wales and France.

Expressing ourselves through languages is key to communication: Adapt language learning to complete a series of tasks that lead up to the deliverable. Learners making decisions on the correct register to express themselves to a given audience.

Literature fires imagination and inspires creativity: Authentic material, *Le Pendentif*, presenting the menu as the deliverable task.

Using the Principles of Progression with the AATT tasks guided the learners to make a choice on what tasks they were able to complete within the time frame. However, should individuals find a specific task not challenging enough they can easily opt for a more advanced task to suit their needs. I found this concept manageable especially in a mixed ability class.

Designing with the AATT is helpful because it's pupil lead and pupil-centred, enabling learners to fully engage in the concept of language learning and develop understanding of various cultures. It also gives the pupils responsibility for their development in language learning and decision-making when participating in tasks.

I believe the curriculum design may help in uptake of languages in Wales because the theme and authentic materials used can take learners to various avenues beyond what's introduced in the classroom. The main presentation task focuses on a local event that's realistic and relatable where language learnt can be adapted, and in the process, expand learners' knowledge of their local area and beyond. Whereby pupils can see and experience the use of language within different aspects of everyday life.

—Ms. Ceri Parry, Ysgol Glan y Mor, Gwynedd, French

HOW DO WE CREATE AND SHARE WITH OTHERS?

TABLE 6.4 Articulated Assessment Transfer Task – Food festivals

Enduring Understandings
✢ There are foods of interest all around the world.
✢ Knowledge of language allows me to access different cuisines.
✢ Food and drink can represent a region or area
Essential Questions
? What local produce reflects my place of interest or hobbies?
? What food specialties are in the Normandy region of France?
? What are the differences between food in Wales and France?
Context
Present a menu for the Food Village at the upcoming National *Eisteddfod* that represents who you are. Include suitable menus for the food festival in Wales that includes food and drink produce from both France and North Wales.
Articulation Spiral Points
@ I can identify food and drink items in the target language
@ I can justify my opinions
@ I can present my findings in a menu

Intercultural Transfer Targets	Mediation for Transfer
• I can identify food and drink which are specific to a region	• I can talk about food and drink
• I can research and find information on local produce	• I can compare local produce with food/drink produce from a region in France
• I can explain how certain foods/drinks are specific to a region	• I can research and identify food/drink produce in another country
• I can present a produce menu which represents identity	• I can create and present a menu/menus including different food/drinks.

Beginner	Intermediate	Advanced
Le Pendentif (Sylvie Laine) – Short story Websites on Normandy and Welsh Tourism		
Interpretive Task Descriptions How do we understand the world around us and support others?		
Following the passage from the short story of ordering a drink at a café in Honfleur, France, further explore food/drink products from Normandy. Using the articles from the websites, identify sweet and savoury food and drink items from the region that would be suitable at a food festival.	Following the passage from the short story of ordering a drink at a café in Honfleur, FranceExplore food and drink products from Normandy as well as product from North Wales and categorize into food/drink groups – *les produits latieres, les légumes et les fruits, les boissons, les protéines, les matieres grasses, les féculents, les sucreries.*	Following the passage from the short story of ordering a drink at a café in Honfleur, France Explore food and drink products from Normandy as well as products from North Wales to include in a food festival. Identify what products are currently eaten/drunk and those that were consumed more in the past.

I Can		
I can identify food and drink items in the target language and categorize sweet and savoury products from Normandy, France.	I can categorize food/drink products from North Wales and France that could be used as ideas to include as products to sell in a food festival.	I can summarize what I usually eat/drink and what I eat/drank in the past and what would be suitable for a local food festival.
Interpersonal Task Descriptions **How do we express ourselves and engage others?**		
Ask others what they normally eat/drink for breakfast, lunch, snack and dinner. Create a list of the most popular food and drink items mentioned as a guide of what to include in a food festival.	Ask others what they normally eat/drink for breakfast, lunch, snack and dinner as well as what they don't like to eat and drink. from the information collected of the opinions of your peers, Identify the most popular items that should be included in a food festival.	Using the food and drink vocabulary of products you would find in Normandy and North Wales. In pairs, ask others what they normally eat/drink for breakfast, lunch, snack and dinner as well as what they have eaten/drank the day before. Present your findings of the most popular food/drink items from your peers as suggestions to include in a food festival.
I Can		
I can ask and answer questions in the target language about what others normally eat and drink.	I can ask and answer questions in the target language of what is normally eaten in a day, as well as talking about food and drinks I don't like (je ne mange pas/ je ne bois pas) and ask opinion and reason.	I can ask and answer questions in the target language, answering what I normally eat and drink as well as what I ate/drank and add justifications (c'était …)
Presentational Task Descriptions **How do we create and share with others?**		
Present a menu suitable for young people at a food festival in North Wales that represents who I am and to showcase items of locally produced food and drink.	Present a menu suitable for young people at a food festival with local food and drink produced from Normandy, France that represents French culture.	Present two different menus suitable for young people, at a food festival in North Wales that represents who I am and to showcase items of locally produced food

HOW DO WE CREATE AND SHARE WITH OTHERS?

		and drink. Present local food and drink for a region in France (Normandy) that represents French culture.
I Can		
I can present items of food and drink in the target languages and express my opinion on the items.	I can present locally produced food and drink items as well as produce from Normandy, France in the target language including opinions and reasons.	I can present food and drink from different countries and compare them.

Bridge to Design

Let's go deeper into Ms Parry's design process and collaborate with colleagues for additional ideas and reflection on this exemplar before working on your own design.

Reflect to Reveal

1) Why is the local festival the perfect backdrop for intercultural perspectives on food?
2) How does the short story help learners shift from inference to performance in the deliverables for the festival?
3) How can this AATT enable transfer and mediation for people unaccustomed to foods past and present from two regions?

Questions for Colleagues

1) How is cultural knowledge transformed to transcultural communicative competence?
2) How do we elevate a common topic like food for a better spiral and meaningful reprise?
3) In what ways does Ms Parry allow her learners to grow with these tasks? What do the Principles of Progression look like in your school context?

> ### Ask the Designer
>
> What is your question for Ms Parry? What else do you want to know about this exemplar and her design thinking?
>
> ### Participate in the Practice
>
> Which practices guided Ms Parry in creating her exemplar? How did she design with these in mind? Explain below for each component.
>
> 1) Developing learner autonomy by creating products.
> 2) Local events and resources as a catalyst for novel tasks and deliverables.
> 3) Adapting the product to the audience's preferences or needs.

Teacher to Leader on Design

1. Think along the lines of local and worldwide culture and how they are connected to highlight the differences and similarities.
2. Trial and error, there is much flexibility in approaching the design of the AATT, if it does not work or you see the design taking another cultural awareness aspect, go with it.
3. Take ideas from the learners, cultural and language knowledge that they share, and implement into the design.

> ### From the Admin Desk
>
> As an administrator, I would ask my colleagues to explore ways to unlock the full potential of this AATT. What barriers need taking down? What extra steps and support do we provide the students so their end products communicate fully their messages?
>
> Food is an essential part of any culture and can be used to delve into many different issues such as identity, heritage, environment, health and well-being, families, work environment, religion, ethics, etc. Individual

colleagues could create an AATT around the theme of food but relate it to enduring understandings and essential questions which are most relevant to their programmes, languages and students. The result being a bouquet of AATTs on food which address different cross-curricular matters.

—Stephanie Ellis-Williams, International Languages, Global Futures GwE Lead

Homes Reveal the History of Our Culture and Ourselves

Ms Temple unfolds differentiation across year 7 with this AATT on *Les Maisons*. There are many opportunities to compare architectural styles of France, Wales and other countries. These novices did quite a bit of critical thinking for these tasks, which will serve them well as they continue exploring cultural history. Note the differentiation of deliverables in the presentational mode, all worthy of that key catalogue in an international language programme.

Teacher as Designer – *Les Maisons*

Ysgol Clywedog is a medium to large secondary school where Welsh is taught within an English setting with a high percentage of disadvantaged pupils. The French department is very creative and always aims to weave in as much culture as possible into their schemes, linking with their Welsh identity and culture whenever possible.

This AATT (see Table 6.5) is a good example for this Principle because it requires learners to show their understanding of the French regions and French houses layout, comparing with Welsh housing in order to explain possible differences and significant characteristics. This can be of interest for a specific group of people not necessarily familiar with French culture.

As language teachers, it is often easy to assume that our learners will know about such characteristics. Do teachers actually revisit what we know about French housing too? Has it changed since our time in France? What about the environmental new guidance and how is this relevant to our modern society? Can learners also delve into this more?

Ms Temple joined our group later than other teachers and embraced the process immediately. Looking at housing through the angle of architecture and its meaning in terms of cultural identity and heritage was exciting for the teacher as it gave a new purpose to her pupils' learning. This opened very different intercultural routes to explore, which she had not anticipated. She is now delving more into regional specificity and implications, overseas French territories and other French-speaking countries such as Quebec or African nations. The climate impact on housing, carbon footprint and effective solutions, house layouts, evolution and purpose could also be considered.

—Stephanie Ellis-Williams, International Languages, Global Futures GwE Lead

Voices from the Field

In designing this AATT, my aim was to develop an awareness of what houses look like in France and an ability to question what pupils see and make sensible comparisons across cultures. Some pupils have a very narrow view of the world and take for granted what they see around them every day. This will help them to understand that the architecture of an area or country is influenced by a range of factors, whether that is in their own area or in a different country. Pupils will develop an understanding of the concept of 'home'.

Just as France has its own domestic architectural styles that reflect particular aspects of their historical / cultural / geographical context, so too does Wales – and so too will other countries. The domestic architecture of an area can give clues about the cultural history of an area, and about the lives of people who have lived there.

I like the focus on not just what we teach, but why we teach it – an important question that is easily overlooked when we are too aware of being judged by exam results. I enjoy the focus on culture as an integral part of any language towards a more holistic approach that considers the development of the whole person and fosters a spirit of inquiry.

Planning the AATT made me question what other vocabulary would be useful for the pupils to be able to make sense of what they were doing, rather than teaching a unit of work, ticking it off and then wondering how to assess what they have learnt.

Where you live is part of your identity; novice learners generally find their way into a language through finding out how to talk about themselves and their own experiences. Even novice learners can access the vocabulary and structures for talking about what rooms there are in a house. It seems

HOW DO WE CREATE AND SHARE WITH OTHERS?

logical to extend this a bit further by considering how to talk about what the house is like on the outside.

This AATT asks learners to consider what they might find in a house, but it avoids the pressure that some learners may feel when asked to describe their own house. By exploring what houses are like in France, and comparing them with what they see in their own area, learners can focus on real facts, develop their cultural understanding and probe their assumptions about their own environment.

Using this approach helps learners to set the language they are learning in a clear, real-world context. They will be able to recognize key features of building styles in French culture and make comparison with their own culture. They will be encouraged to consider why different building styles evolve and will be asked to probe their own assumptions about the world. They will exchange opinions and reasons and they will consider how to present their ideas clearly.

Focusing on the relationship between culture, language and identity, with clear links to real-world context, is more engaging than just teaching topics for the sake of it.

Learners have more opportunity to explore their own ideas – this allows for greater independence of learning but also supports the notion of multiple possible answers. The focus is more on communication and less on accuracy, which will help to build confidence in learners who worry about 'getting it wrong'.

It supports a holistic approach to learning and aids the development of transferable skills – which will ultimately help to promote the message about the value of language learning for the sake of the skills it supports, as much as for the language itself.

—Ms Clare Temple, Ysgol Clywedog, Wrexham, French

TABLE 6.5 Articulated Assessment Transfer Task – *Les Maisons*

Enduring Understandings
✴ Housing structures vary in different countries.
✴ Many factors influence building style.
✴ The domestic architecture of a country reflects and informs cultural identity.
Essential Questions
? What is 'Home?'
? What does a 'typical' French house look like?
? What can we tell about the history of a house from its architecture?
? How does architecture reflect and define our cultures?

Context
You are working for an estate agent and need to advertise typical French houses available in different areas of France.

Articulation Spiral Points
@ Describe architectural features of homes in an advertisement.
@ Explain building materials and preferences.
@ Compare homes in France and Wales for a video.

Intercultural Transfer Targets	Mediation for Transfer
• I can recognize and compare different types of building styles. • I can match different types of houses to the region where they are found. • I can compare houses in France with houses in Wales / in my own area. • I can write and speak about houses in France. • I can create a presentation about houses in France.	• Bridge and exchange information on housing types. • Describe examples of typical houses by region. • Explain descriptions of each type of house shown on map to someone unfamiliar or unaccustomed to design and style.

Year 7 Novice	Year 7 Novice +	Year 7 Novice ++
\multicolumn{3}{c}{Fiches d'information 'Tour de France des Maisons Typiques map' 'Tour de France des maisons typiques text' *Trouver mon Architecte.com*}		
\multicolumn{3}{c}{**Interpretive Task Descriptions** How do we understand the world around us and support others?}		
Using a map of France with images of houses considered typical of certain areas, pupils identify features that are different from houses that they would see in their local area. Pupils annotate their map with comments on the features of 'typical' French houses.	Using images showing different types of houses in France, pupils describe what they look like and identify some differences between these houses and in their local area. Pupils choose one particular building style from the images and a short piece of written information about key features of that type of house.	Using texts, pupils organize written information on features from a variety of typical French houses, and how they might differ by region.
\multicolumn{3}{c}{**I Can**}		
I can identify key words relating to building style features and area in French and English.	I can compare and contrast variations in housing style features in France and Wales.	I can categorize housing styles and features by region.

Interpersonal Task Descriptions		
How do we express ourselves and engage others?		
With a partner, describe what a French house looks like, and how it differs from a house in my local area. Next, agree on what the key features are that distinguish houses in France from those in Wales.	With a partner, come to consensus on the key features that distinguish houses in France and Wales. Discuss with a partner my chosen building style, what area of France it represents and how it compares to what I see in Wrexham. I can listen to my partner's description and explanation of the building style that they have chosen.	With a partner, I can talk about different styles of housing throughout France – how they compare to each other and how they compare to my local area and also other areas of Wales.
I Can		
I can talk with a partner about possible reasons for why houses differ in various places. I can express my opinions about which styles of house I prefer and listen to my partner's opinions.	I can explain to my partner particular building styles of the houses we have chosen. I can speculate with my partner about other possible reasons for the specific building styles in my town and areas of France.	I can discuss with my partner factors that might also influence building styles in different countries, including France and Wales.
Presentational Task Descriptions		
How do we create and share with others?		
Pupils create a poster showing the key features of a French house: What the house will look like from the road (external features, building materials). What the house will be like inside (number of floors, floor plan, rooms).	Pupils create an advertisement to promote accommodation in a particular area of France or to that is linked to a particular aspect of French life, culture or history. (ski holiday, countryside holiday, stay in a former farm, vineyard, pirate's house).	Pupils create a PowerPoint or a short video to present options for accommodation in different areas of France with some information about the interior layout of my chosen house.

I Can		
I can explain the home and what area of France this house is most likely to be located by its features. I can list the architectural styles and features the home represents.	I can describe the interior as well as exterior features. I can provide information about what area of France this house is and the building style it represents.	I can explain some key features of different types of houses and where each house is located.

Bridge to Design

Let's go deeper into Ms Temple's design process and collaborate with colleagues for additional ideas and reflection on this exemplar before working on your own design.

Reflect to Reveal

1) How does this AATT explain cultural history for this concept?
2) In what ways are these deliverables valuable not only to learners but to others?
3) Why are these three products essential in your catalogue of key deliverables for your programme?

Questions for Colleagues

1) To what extent does designing with the 'why' in mind matter more than the 'what'?
2) Is there a cultural perspective related to home and lifestyle from your culture(s) that everyone knows that is a 'must have'? Has it changed over time? Please share it.
3) What is important for pupils to understand about the diversity of homes and lifestyles?

Ask the Designer

What is your question for Ms Temple? What else do you want to know about this exemplar and her design thinking?

HOW DO WE CREATE AND SHARE WITH OTHERS?

> ### Participate in the Practice
>
> Which practices guided Ms Temple in creating her exemplar? How did she design with these in mind? Explain below for each component.
>
> 1) Backward Design and what is essential to understand the intercultural perspectives.
> 2) Transdisciplinary interest for vertical progression and purposeful application in career and world.
> 3) Catalogue of key deliverables essential for any World/International Language programme.

Teacher to Leader on Design and Implementation

1. Always start the planning/designing by asking the question: why should we cover this? This helps to avoid artificial, unauthentic and exam-driven programmes of learning.
2. Authenticity is key: learners can focus on real facts, develop their cultural understanding and probe their assumptions about their own environment.
3. Focus more on communication and less on accuracy to raise confidence and enjoyment in pupils in using the language creatively.

Immigrant pupils tend to be quite polarised in our school: either they are very good at learning languages and fully embrace the opportunity, drawing on their mother tongue / heritage language knowledge as well as their experience of learning English to support their IL language learning, or they struggle with language overload and find trying to juggle learning English, Welsh and French all at the same time extremely challenging. With that in mind, I found that the more able EAL and immigrant pupils managed the tasks as well as, or even a bit better than, the non-immigrant pupils; the weaker immigrant pupils however were able to access the map task but did not manage to access the texts with the descriptions of the different houses.

Generally, in MFL lessons we have a department policy of trying to encourage pupils from different language backgrounds to share their knowledge and understanding – especially when it is clear that they are making links across languages. We also try to encourage them to think about how they would say things in their native language if they are finding something difficult. There are often some nice 'lightbulb moments'. We ask immigrant pupils to share cultural experiences and practices, partly to develop our own understanding and to model respect for other cultures to the rest of the class, partly to try to give immigrant pupils a voice – moments when they are the expert rather than the immigrant, and partly to arouse curiosity and develop empathy in the non-immigrant members of the class.

I am more aware of the importance of building in cultural references as an integral part of my teaching, not just saving it for special occasions as an 'end of term' extra. I have always enjoyed including cultural references, but I have always had some doubts as to how interested the pupils might be – and it is easy to worry about whether taking the scenic route of the culture-focused path is too much of a diversion from the 'proper' business of language learning – developing the grammar skills and vocabulary that pupils are required to demonstrate in exams, which set the standards that we are then judged on. In fact, this project showed me that the cultural element can contribute to pupils' language awareness and understanding, as well as the more obvious benefits of developing their ability to empathise, and to be open to other ideas / ways of seeing.

—Ms Clare Temple, Ysgol Clywedog, Wrexham

From the Admin Desk

This particular AATT can lead to many other AATTs on the subject. As an administrator, this could be used to ask colleagues to design the other AATTs around housing, regional characteristics due to culture, geography, climate and environmental concerns and policies. Each direction will have implications in terms of language skills and lexis, all valid and very rich in its nature and purpose.

Language teachers of other languages can use this model and create their own knowledge organizers for their own culture-specific lexis and language around housing: i.e. shutters, tile and slate roofs or geothermal heating in France can be avalanche and snow-related equipment in Scandinavia or mountainous regions etc.

HOW DO WE CREATE AND SHARE WITH OTHERS?

> Colleagues can reflect on some of the important concepts of housing in their language communities and start listing the essential questions their learners should address over the course of the programme.
>
> —Stephanie Ellis-Williams, International Languages, Global Futures GwE Lead

Design for Transfer

Design at least one Presentational task differentiated across three levels of learner engagement. Try to incorporate three types: Expressive, Poetic and Transactional. Please make sure these tasks address the problem posed and the audience you indicated in the Context. Use the AATT fillable template on the companion website, Chapter 1. (For a master list of task types, see Appendices D and E.)

Design for Transfer

Now that you have designed a presentational task at each level, compose the 'I can' PASS statement for each. Keep in mind the function, skill, purpose, content and audience.

Design for Transfer

Check your tasks carefully. As a result of this task, could the learner bridge communication with someone unfamiliar with the language or culture? Find this evidence of Mediation for Transfer in your presentational tasks and include it on your AATT template.

Design for Transfer

Between the summative tasks in the AATT and the formative AfL tasks in Stage Three, you will build the catalogue of key deliverables, the anthology of performance evidence, if you will. Are there ones that for your programme are must-haves? What do you want all pupils to be able to create, share and contribute to demonstrate evidence of transcultural communicative competence by the time they have completed your programme? Which ones demonstrate evidence of transfer for community, career and global readiness?

Reflect and Revisit

1. Why is it important to focus on needs, problems or action issues within a particular career, organization, group, individual or community setting?
2. How do these presentational tasks differ from fill-in exercises or memorized skits?
3. What is the difference between near and far transfer tasks? When would you use them in your unit design?
4. How might someone use a presentational task deliverable to make language more accessible or a perspective more visible to someone else?
5. How do you start developing your programme's anthology or catalogue of key deliverables? How can this list show proper evidence of what the learner can 'do' for themselves and to help someone else?
6. Why should we have fewer concepts and themes in a curriculum, but more frequent and novel performances that demonstrate flexibility with those concepts?
7. You are faced with textbook tasks that merely satisfy classroom exercise or focus solely on pupil preferences. With a colleague, turnaround one of these tasks to address different needs of groups and solve a problem with a creative deliverable.

7

Design with No End in Mind

Enduring Understandings

- ∞ Transcultural concepts resonate across texts and time. They matter to many or all cultures; the practices derived from them differ.
- ∞ Communication and language expect creativity and demand improvisation.
- ∞ Transfer shifts what we know and can do, into contexts beyond the known and have done.
- ∞ Topic or text does not determine the level; the task you design with it does.
- ∞ Mediation channels and extends understanding between, across, within and among cultures.
- ∞ Novel tasks are wise short- and long-term investments; do more differently with what you own.
- ∞ Language validates and rewards imperfection; communication still moves forward.

Essential Questions

- **Q** How are transcultural concepts and perspectives made visible over time?
- **Q** What do creativity and surprise teach us?
- **Q** How can a novel task show what I can do?

Q To what extent can I help someone else?

Q How do I know I have learned?

Q What can I do with the language I've got?

Backward Design (Wiggins & McTighe, 2005) tells us we should design curriculum and assessment with the end in mind. Indeed, it is important to design the summative assessment first and work backward from there for the formative tasks throughout that unit. Every teacher in this project did so. Where is the end, then? Is it the end of the unit or module? The end of a scheme of work? Or the end of the programme? Starting with the end moves us away from our familiar key stage, target, module or single year we are accustomed to teaching. Designing in collaboration with colleagues lets everyone know what happens before and after the level you teach and makes vertical articulation happen. It also lets you know what every pupil can create with the language when they finish your programme. Enter our *catalogue of deliverables*. If we took at least all the presentational task deliverables these teachers created, and some of the others, we would have the start of that catalogue, an anthology of transfer evidence for your programme. Some departments compile all of these after they have designed them. Fair enough, however, I suggest you start the discussion right at the onset of curriculum (re) design or reform. Discuss and suss out the deliverables you want every pupil to have in their evidence catalogue before they leave. They can be universal for your programme, the same list regardless of what language a pupil chooses to take up at your school.

Conversely, some languages may wish to include other products that are outside the catalogue for another language. Your department may not have the specifics fleshed out yet; that happens with the AATTs. These litmus test questions are helpful. If the answers to the following litmus test are yes, then you have ideal items for your catalogue of deliverables and evidence along the Articulation Spiral Points as well.

- Is this a novel task, product, deliverable or 'ask' that they have not done previously?

- Is it valued, found, required or expected outside of school? Might people be asked to make, do or create this for a given career or community project?

- Could skills acquired from making this product help someone else who is unfamiliar, unaware or unaccustomed to the language and culture? Could even a beginner help someone else with single words and images?

- Could the task provide an opportunity for learners to reflect on their own cultural practices, navigate participation or engagement within and among other cultural spaces without leaving behind their cultural, ethnic or national identities?

If so, then you have a great task for transfer, mediation and transcultural communicative competence.

Your anthology of evidence makes the case for **design with no end in mind**. In the preface, I stated, *Design for what matters when students are with us, so that they can thrive in all cultures without us.* This is why your AATTs and ICANADAPT curriculum design are framed with EQs and EQs. They stand the test of time and are meant to carry the concept and the learner forward long after they have left you. When the last third person, irregular verb ending is forgotten and gone, they will remember what matters for inter/transcultural communicative competence as they navigate with poise between, within and across cultures. The tasks you design with the deliverables they yield are transferable. They support and encourage uptake when pupils are with you, and when they are finished with school, living and working among cultures. They are learning languages for life, so your curriculum and deliverables must enable them to see its relevance and applicability.

To guide you in developing your programme catalogue of deliverables, I developed and revised AATT criteria (Eddy, 2022b) (see Appendix G). Adapted from Jay McTighe's Cornerstone Tasks (2014, 2018), these criteria will serve as a good check to fine-tune both the AATT and your programme catalogue. The Teacher as Designer Evidence Collab tool (see Appendix II) will help departments see where they will start on this design journey. It places past practice and the tenets we speak of here, side by side. You can see if you are 'already there', 'on your way' or 'not just yet'.

To design with no end in mind, I conclude with a new look at the guiding principles for design (Eddy, 2022b) aligned with the EUs above, each of which closes with a quote from a teacher designer in this book.

Transcultural Concepts Resonate across Texts and Time. They Matter to Many or All Cultures; the Practices Derived from Them Differ

1 Intercultural perspectives unfold articulated curriculum and scaffold key tasks of meaningful performance. Choose concepts that reprise across different genres of texts. Sure, you will find those that are specific to a culture that you wish to unpack over time. But when you

find one that many or all cultures share and which matter so much, we see it resonate in fiction, arts and informational texts over time. These are the ones where the most connections, reflections and tasks can happen. Cultural practices descended from these concepts will be different across cultures, but that is where excellent comparisons can happen and opportunities for mediation with someone who needs that supportive bridge and mediation skills which are transcultural. Your learners will be able to recognize them from the texts and the tasks you designed from them. You will have trained them to carry that forward when they encounter the concept again later and have the opportunity to clarify for someone else.

What has had the biggest impact on me is ensuring that there is a 'hook' at the beginning of the unit to maintain interest. Also, it is important to set a 'problem/context' that needs to be solved as part of the unit and therefore, the pupils get to solve the problem and have the opportunity to do tasks relevant to everyday life.

– Ms Nicola Hughes

It ensures that cultural perspective is an integral part of the learning. The Enduring understanding and questions help ensure that the 4 purposes of CfW are covered. The format of the AATT ensures differentiation across the levels of ability.

– Ms Emma Green

I hope that the learners feel part of the community, part of Wales and Welshness. Work that is relevant assigns purpose to assessment tasks. I really like the essential questions that make us think about how the work is suitable, relevant and purposeful for our learners.

– Ms Sioned Perkins

This process allows the teacher to approach a commonly taught topic from a different, often overlooked, angle. The concept promotes independence and creativity of thought, whilst also being intrinsically challenging in nature.

– Mr Mark Cameron

The AATT inspires further cultural curiosity. Through lessons delivered inspired by the AATT, students also see context and meaning to their work. This helps to engage their interest and make them intrigued to know more.

– Ms Emma Adams

Communication and Language Expect Creativity and Demand Improvisation

2. We own language through creativity and unpredictable interactions. They might be small at first, but important. Language not only expects these, it demands them. We really do not know what someone is going to say to us. Spontaneity and improvisation are quite different although both are unrehearsed. Spontaneity is often unprompted. This can happen to be sure, but most of our interactions with someone else are improvisation, our reaction to someone or something. Life in the language world is constant improv, thus, proper design with no end in mind means going off script. By design, we are fidelitous to a script, thereby the resulting pressure for perfection and no mistakes. Likewise, exercises with only one correct answer are misleading and a poor use of class time. Language does not work this way or no one would get anything accomplished. Theatre and film have scripts. There is a big difference between theatre, film and improv. What we are looking for in communication is improvisation.

As our learners understand that making mistakes and expressing simple messages is what is expected at this stage, they will embrace taking more risks and aspiring to higher levels.

– Ms Stephanie Ellis-Williams

Transfer Shifts What We Know and Can Do, into Contexts beyond the Known and Have Done

3. It is not enough to practise what was taught multiple times and expect that sameness means pupils have learned or own anything. Transfer tasks involve flexible use of repertoire, exactly what is expected when outside of school. Transfer will not happen one day solely as a result of repetitive drills. A person must voluntarily place themselves in situations or, they suddenly realize they are waist deep, and their verb charts, translations and memorized skits have been for naught. Unpredictability teaches flexibility. When designing with no end in mind, create those transfer tasks so that learners can handle ambiguity, incomplete information, new situations and audiences with aplomb.

The fact that there is a deliverable in each of the AATT's, provides learners to showcase their learning through effective communication for a target audience or range of different audiences.

– Ms Lynette Sloan

Creating and designing this way has really helped enrich my understanding of the CfW framework so much that culture is now the driving force behind my planning. It has challenged me to think about how we can make language learning more real, more authentic and more relevant to our learners. My planning of assessment tasks now focuses on learners creating something for an audience beyond the classroom.

– Ms Jamie McAllister

Topic or Text Does Not Determine the Level; the Task You Design from It Does

4 As teachers have stated in their *Voices*, do avoid the practice of retrofitting or jawboning sequential textbook exercises or *pret a porter* worksheet packets to design an AATT. If there is a great piece of cultural community text to use, then by all means do but think differently about what the learner will do with it and how you can design for many levels of complexity with it. Please do not wait to unpack a topic for some later time in the curriculum because of its apparent difficulty. That time will not come if they do not stay and continue with the language. You are not asking for paragraph-length output from them right away even though the text looks like that. The learner can build that concept and vocabulary base early and know they can do something with the language they have at each level of engagement, even if it is just at the word level with images to start. Your task will always reveal the complexity and target desired. Let learners grow with the text. Some of the best AATTs and implementations have used the same texts across all levels, used differently each time.

In this AATT, even a novice is able to explore and work with keywords and key phrases relevant to the topic. These can very easily be used to create a poster raising awareness amongst peers of the issues and solutions linked to the topic and hence create a valuable deliverable.

– Ms Nicole Piesch

Through planning the tasks in this way, differentiation is an integral part of the task and allows learners from novice to intermediate to access the lessons. It also allows creative skills to be developed at every opportunity and every level within the task.

– Ms Emma Adams

Differentiation is an inherent part of designing in this way and inspires creativity across all levels. Using authentic materials gives purpose to learning and enables learners to apply their language skills to real-life contexts and scenarios. A range of creative outputs will also be appealing to students as they can develop and utilise their own interests increasing learner autonomy.

– Mr Paul Conn

Mediation Channels and Extends Understanding between, across, within and among Cultures

5. Learners mediate at any level; visuals and single words facilitate understanding for countless opportunities rarely planned or scripted. It is not wise to keep language fixed and static with an illusion of sameness present in manipulative tasks that do not lend themselves to be shared or negotiated. In order to design with no end in mind for ongoing engagement, the takeaway from each task should answer this question: What skill set or takeaway from this task helps the learner clarify information and exchange meaning with someone else who may be less familiar than I? That mediation opportunity can happen with someone in another country or right in town. Transfer tasks for mediation enable agency because they offer access, an invaluable asset for transcultural communicative competence within, across and among cultures.

I believe the curriculum design may help in uptake of languages in Wales because the theme and authentic materials used can take learners to various avenues beyond what's introduced in the classroom. The main presentation task focuses on a local event that's realistic and relatable where language learnt can be adapted, and in the process, expand learners' knowledge of their local area and beyond.

– Ms Ceri Parry

Within the AATT, learners will explore and analyse how the Welsh language impacts upon identity and culture and how the association between the language and culture in Wales is preparing the learner for Welsh and global citizenship.

– Ms Jeni Morris

Traditionally we have taught topics required for the curriculum, and maybe slightly losing sight of the 'bigger picture' and of what the learners will take away with them long-term, further than the end assignment. They take away some deeper understanding of culture and how languages connect us around the world. The use of authentic materials and practical tasks are very engaging. The learners take ownership of their learning.

– Ms Viviane Vick

Language Validates and Rewards Imperfection; Communication Still Moves Forward

6   The goal is to communicate between, among and within cultures with self-reliance and agility, but not perfection. We are preparing a flexible, self-directed communicator. Autonomy happens through tasks that emphasize novelty, creative transfer and improv and less on rehashing everything learned before, yet again. This is the moment when we must ask ourselves: does the design of the task itself make perfection the default? If there is only one possible answer, yes. If it is a script to memorize, yes again. Is that what we are looking for in a flexible communicator? Is that what it looks like? If we are honest and the answer is no, then we must look at the task design and shift accordingly. Language creativity still happens when flawed and mottled; we move forward with partial and fractured control and even that mediation can help ourselves and someone else.

Students from a rather small town are able to see what else is out there and there is a sense of excitement about that. The interest levels mean that fear of making grammar mistakes has fallen far behind the joy of being able to talk about something the students have discovered. As a teacher, I feel that I am able to show much more of something that inspires me. I love languages because of what I can see and do as a result of knowing them. Now my students are doing the same.

– Dr Jane Byrne

Learners have more opportunity to explore their own ideas – this allows for greater independence of learning but also supports the notion of multiple possible answers.

– Ms Clare Temple

I feel brave, nervous, curious, adventurous, naïve, respectful to name a few. I like designing in this way as I feel like learning in this way provides the pupils with opportunities to feel as I feel when I travel, to understand it is okay to make mistakes, to learn something new and important about other cultures and their way of life, that using a small amount of language can make massive strides in communication, all the while, they don't realise they are being assessed and they transfer skills without realising they are doing it – it is not forced.

– Ms Lynette Sloan

Novel Tasks Are Wise Short- and Long-term Investments; Do More Differently with What You Own

7   Novelty is one of the best gifts we can give learners when designing with no end in mind. Keep it new every day. Not only are novel tasks the best evidence of transfer while students are with you, but these tasks are the best investments for the future. They will come to expect and be able to handle novelty, change and flux after they have finished school, all the happenstance we discussed within this VUCA world. This tenet also speaks to quantity: an extensive vocabulary is great and I hope pupils acquire a lot with cultural community texts and the tasks you design. However, rather than front loading huge lists of vocabulary and verbs which will end up on the proverbial cutting-room floor and adding more, it is better that they do more and differently with what they have. They should create something new with fewer cues to no supports from you and consider someone else's needs beyond their own: *by themselves and beyond themselves.* The wonderful thing is once the learner experiences tasks you have designed this way, they will come up with the contexts, diverse audiences and novel situations. As we said earlier, that is how you know they are self-selecting transfer opportunities and building autonomy. Novelty is not saved for Fridays or only for certain pupils or exemplary schools. Novelty for transfer is an essential skill we

use daily and don't even realize it. Keeping it new every day moves learners to transfer, a skill they need for every context when they leave you.

When learners feel that they are making progress and are able to use language in a purposeful way, pupils will be more likely to continue the journey at GCSE.

– Ms Sian Bennett

These dedicated language educators let us see that language curriculum design resides with you and your learners. No matter what curriculum, syllabus or scheme of work you have, I hope the tenets within the CfW, ICANADAPT, AATT design and the creativity from these teachers inspires you towards revision of curriculum design for transcultural communicative competence.

Keep it new every day with creative transfer. Prepare learners for the inevitable unexpected.

Jenny

Appendix A

Transcultural Mediation For Transfer

Theme	Language Accessible	Perspectives Visible	Transcultural Mediation for Transfer	Transcultural Mediation for Transfer	Transcultural Mediation for Transfer
	Enduring Understanding	Essential Question	Beginner	Intermediate	Advanced
Cuisine	Food is charged with personal, familial and cultural symbolism.	To what extent does our lifestyle influence our diet? Why does eating together matter?	Identify foods and eating habits between cultures through gestures, images and phrases to someone else unfamiliar with them.	Compare dishes served in schools across the world to others and clarify menu details and practices that may be new for someone else.	Clarify cultural dietary rules, concerns or preferences to make them accessible to someone uninformed of them.
Health	Health depends on many factors, including our habits, culture, diet and lifestyle. Health is a combination of mind, body and spirit.	What is good health? How do culture, media and lifestyle affect health?	Identify common remedies across cultures to someone unacquainted with these products or practices.	Compare health practices or health systems across cultures for people unaccustomed to them.	Explain to someone unaware of remedios caseros why a culture chooses some remedies and practices over others.

Adapted from Eddy, J. (2022b) *Designing World Language Curriculum for Intercultural Communicative Competence*, with permission from Bloomsbury Academic, an imprint of Bloomsbury Publishing, Plc.

Appendix B

Unit Plan Guide

Liberté, égalité, fraternité

Enduring Understandings

- Democracy enables a nation to give its citizens the right to decide who should govern their country.
- Democracy needs to be protected.
- Everyone has the right and duty to be involved in political decisions.

Essential Questions

- What is democracy?
- What is the role of government?
- What is the right to vote and is it a duty?
- Can anyone become a political leader?
- What qualities and traits make a good leader?
- What impact can the individual play and at what level?

Context or Scenario

In January 2024, the French president decided to appoint a new prime minister. Gabriel Attal, at thirty-four, is the youngest and first openly homosexual prime minister in France. A national youth web magazine is asking young people to give their views on politics, leadership and the individual's role in shaping the future of their country.

PASS Can-Do Statements

- I can understand and label key concepts and facts about the role of the French prime minister and government.
- I can organize the main facts about the current voting system in France and the challenges it faces.
- I can answer questions about the importance of voting.
- I can compare, contrast and relay current political practices in France and their historical origins.
- I can identify and agree with my partners on the most important personal traits required to be a political leader.
- I can ask and answer questions on why young people should vote.
- I can listen to my peers' opinions to develop mine further.
- I can come to a consensus on political choices to include in a political manifesto.
- I can choose relevant issues to address.
- I can ask and answer questions on such choices.
- I can explain simply what makes a great leader and show that anyone could become one.
- I can explain and justify important facts about voting rights for democracy.
- I can convince others of my choices.
- I can explain how my choices will affect their lives for the better.
- I can persuade people to play a more active role in political decisions in future.

Intercultural Transfer Targets

- I can identify, compare and write about some of the attributes valued and required to play a part in my community.
- I can understand and explain the implications and impact of the act of voting or not on different communities.
- I can identify and explain reasons behind political choices in different cultures.

Appendix C
Stage One and Stage Three at a Glance

Stage One and Stage Three at a glance

Stage One	Stage Three
Enduring Understandings Essential Questions	Objective Statements Focus Questions
Concepts and Themes Recursive Use cultural perspectives to design them Last a lifetime	Skills and Facts Recall Use lesson content to design them Answerable end of class
Good health combines mind, body, spirit. *What is a healthy lifestyle?*	*Students will be able to identify healthy food choices.* *What are common breakfast foods in Mexico?*

Adapted from Eddy, J. (2022b) *Designing World Language Curriculum for Intercultural Communicative Competence*, with permission from Bloomsbury Academic, an imprint of Bloomsbury Publishing, Plc. (Wiggins & McTighe, 2005).

Appendix D
Task Types and Strategies for Mediation

**Supporting other people in mediation:
Identify, Index, Inquire, Interpret, Infer,
Illustrate, Improve**

Type	Sample Task	Strategy acquired for Mediation
Identify	Select or match image to word. Check off on a list as you listen. Draw what you hear.	Indicate unfamiliar items or action with image, word or gesture.
Index	Categorize items on a chart. Sequence events in order.	Group similar items, places and objects for others. Retell the story.
Inquire	Develop questions from facts found in one or multiple places in text.	Bridge understanding for others by posing questions, sorting relationships and combining information.
Interpret	Listen for the gist or main idea. Compose title or headline.	Summarize and paraphrase for someone else.
Infer	Uncover not only what is directly in the text, but also what is not and only implied.	Offer examples to make language more accessible for someone else. Resolve ambiguity.
Illustrate	Draw a picture of what is described or implied. Find covert information that is hidden, muted or 'between the lines' in the text.	Draw a picture or scene that extracts and points out tacit or implied examples. Clarify intended message for someone unaware of cultural cues.

Type	Sample Task	Strategy acquired for Mediation
Improve	Form questions based on prior knowledge interpretation. Elaborate when information is not found in the text.	Elaborate to bridge and improve on text to help others using their own interpretation and collaborative background knowledge.

Engaging Other People in Mediation: Ask/Answer, Arrange, Adopt, Assess, Argue, Agree

Type	Sample Task	Strategy acquired for Mediation
Ask and Answer	Ask questions composed in the Interpretive mode; ask and answer questions on items from previous tasks, lists, charts and images.	Relating new information to previous knowledge. Breaking down complicated information. Identifying questions and giving feedback.
Arrange	Plan with someone else, schedule or organize in steps.	Simplifying, clarifying or organizing with someone unfamiliar with culture or content
Adopt	Choose or decide on items or ideas.	Link to previous knowledge. Distinguish or separate information or concepts for someone.
Assess	Judge, appraise or give opinion or feelings on an issue or concept.	Facilitate communication in pluricultural space. Describe emotions and clarify facts. Change style, register or words depending on the audience.
Argue	Debate, discuss or dispute an issue.	Understand different points of view. Assist and ease sensitive situations or relay difficult information.
Agree	Negotiate and come to consensus.	Accept alternative ideas and methods. Manage interaction and collaboration.

Sharing with Other People in Mediation: Transactional, Expressive and Poetic

Type	Sample Task	Strategy acquired for Mediation
Transactional	step-by-step instructions, information, public service announcements, letters, brochures, advertisements, videos and survey infographics, lectures, 'how to or what to do' talks.	Clarify information whole or in parts, adapt language level to needs of individual or audience. Deconstructing complicated information. Summary in a different register: oral to written or vice versa.
Expressive	blogs, vlogs, timelines, diaries, social media.	Relay feelings, opinions, personal connection. Facilitating intercultural space.
Poetic	Songs, plays, poems, graphic novels, museum installations, films or stories.	Depict and reveal ideas and issues in a novel way using Imagination, experiences and emotions shared through multimedia. Elaborate text.

Adapted from Eddy, J. (2022b) *Designing World Language Curriculum for Intercultural Communicative Competence*, with permission from Bloomsbury Academic, an imprint of Bloomsbury Publishing, Plc. (Britton et al., 1975; Glisan et al., 2003; COE, 2020).

Appendix E
Master List of Tasks

How do we understand and support others?	How do we understand and support others?
<ul><li>Match image to listening</li><li>Drag and drop the picture that matches what is being described</li><li>Match gesture to text</li><li>Use physical objects or props</li><li>Identify, List or Sequence events in order</li><li>Listen to recorded media for comprehension</li><li>Categorize with graphic organizer</li><li>Listen, read, watch and write questions</li><li>Fill in a table, chart or graph</li><li>Listen to the song melody without the lyrics</li><li>Can take notes in a list</li><li>Listening and completing graphic organizers</li><li>Note-taking from a listening passage or video</li><li>Brainstorming with mind maps</li><li>Comparing between visuals</li><li>Written responses after listening for information</li><li>Listening and checking off items you hear from a list</li><li>Interpret and draw conclusions from a recorded source</li><li>View video and take notes on organizer</li><li>Label stages of a procedure</li><li>Reconstructing texts for collaborative jigsaw readings</li></ul>	<ul><li>Reading and completing graphic organizers</li><li>Note-taking from texts</li><li>Sort information into paragraphs</li><li>Read headline and summarize by choosing correct picture or word</li><li>Match image to informational or literary text</li><li>Read song lyrics without music</li><li>View film without sound</li><li>Assign words/phrases</li><li>Interpret proverbs and quotations</li><li>Drawing and labelling maps, diagrams etc.;</li><li>Identify and summarize main points and significant details</li><li>Interpret idioms and idiomatic expressions</li><li>Recognize literary genres</li><li>Form questions after reading</li><li>Infer the purpose and intention of the speaker/writer</li><li>Read and respond to literature</li><li>Identify literary elements and techniques (e.g., tone, characterization, point of view, conflict, poetic structures)</li><li>Use of visual stimuli to make inferences</li><li>Classify information after reading</li><li>Graphic organizers</li><li>Completion of online or paper forms</li></ul>

How do we understand and support others?	How do we understand and support others?
<ul><li>Summarize and synthesize information from a recorded sample</li><li>Make a simple choice or two categories</li><li>Form questions after listening</li><li>Interpret oral and written dialectical/regional registers</li><li>Listen, draw maps and graphs</li><li>Make inferences and predictions from spoken, written and auditory sources using authentic materials</li><li>Classify/categorize information after listening</li><li>List events, dates, cost, information</li><li>Draw what you hear</li><li>Circle the correct picture</li><li>Circle the correct word or phrase</li><li>Label or identify as you listen or watch</li><li>Make a list while listening or watching a video</li><li>Listen to pre-recorded author's interview</li><li>Listen for the gist – identify main idea</li><li>Guess meaning from context</li><li>Compose a title or headline</li><li>Paraphrase in native language</li></ul>	<ul><li>Put sentences or comic strip sections in logical order</li><li>Sequence within paragraphs</li><li>Summarize short fiction and non-fiction texts</li><li>Read and respond to Time-related exercises with schedules, agendas and timelines</li><li>Summarize text</li><li>Identify the topic from an article using Poll Everywhere or Mentimeter</li><li>Word Wall for sorting</li><li>Wordle or Taxedo for word clouds with a text</li><li>Manipulate text in correct order with Vocaroo and Flippity</li><li>Take notes from text with Evernote</li><li>Summarizing and paraphrasing texts</li><li>Say step by step instructions out loud after you watch</li><li>Hear instruction, mediate with word/phrase, other person does activity</li></ul>

Adapted from Eddy, J. (2022) *Designing World Language Curriculum for Intercultural Communicative Competence*, with permission from Bloomsbury Academic, an imprint of Bloomsbury Publishing, Plc.

How do we express ourselves and engage others?

- Paired discussions
- Guided small-group discussions
- Organize and define the task for collaboration and contributions
- Maintain focus of planning and discussion
- Information Gap tasks
- Negotiate who does what
- Come to consensus on what, where, when, how, with whom, how much, how often, etc.
- Give limitations, come to compromise/consensus Respond to interpretive mode questions.
- Improvised, unscripted role play
- Group discussions in response to a variety of stimuli
- Word Wall for choosing and deciding and sorting together
- Organize plans
- Controversial topic debates

How do we express ourselves and engage others?

- Ask and/or respond to spontaneous, unscripted oral questions
- Propose solutions with a classmate on issues presented in work of art
- Change the time frame of the scene and improvise seconds, minutes, days or years before or after the key event occurs
- Come to consensus, plan and choose with a partner
- Create an on-air talk show that is spontaneous and unscripted
- Find the differences in two pictures.
- Share details of a personal experience
- Interviews with grid
- Explain important event from a cultural community's past
- Brainstorming lists with peers
- Retell a sequence of events, real or imagined
- Circumlocution tasks
- Make suggestions on what to see and do
- Accept or reject choices

How do we create and share with others?

Oral products

- Innovate a familiar text.
- Write a new episode of the story
- Write new verse to song
- New stanza to poem.
- Opinion polls
- Commercials
- Create a new character who responds,
- Animate a previously inanimate feature.
- Theatre production
- Public Service Announcement
- Recite poetry
- Oral histories
- Poetry reading

How do we create and share with others?

Written products

- Flipgrid video
- Cultural comparison
- Brochure or Itinerary
- Letter
- Commentary or brief
- Social media sites
- Video or Podcasts
- Advertisement
- Agenda or Schedule
- New beginning or ending of story, song
- Change genre: story/art/ poem/ screenplay
- Design a survey and present findings
- Essays, Plays

How do we create and share with others?	How do we create and share with others?
- Broadcasts - Oral multimedia/video presentations - Defend ideas and points of view - Demonstration - TV or Radio spot - Infomercial - Respond to critical commentary - Marketing campaigns - Radio shows - Oral presentation using Graphic organizers - Rehearsed role play or skit	- Cause and effect essays - Written response to an oral or written prompt - Narratives or descriptive writing - Storytelling - Magazine article - Clip art - Written response to an oral presentation - Fable, myth, and/or legend writing - Research paper - Titles for a play, story, or article - Headlines in newspaper style - Literary journal - Informational list development - Curate museum exhibit - Written material for online magazine, TV series - Written material for public service organization - Pear Deck interactive presentation

Adapted from Eddy, J. (2022) *Designing World Language Curriculum for Intercultural Communicative Competence,* with permission from Bloomsbury Academic, an imprint of Bloomsbury Publishing, Plc.

Appendix F
Cultural Community Authentic Texts

Audio	Printed	Visual
Commercials	Websites	Sculpture
News	Newspapers and magazines	Street signs
Voicemail	Blogs, tweets, texts	Cartoons and emojis
Radio	Brochures and menus	Picture books and graphic novels
TV	Infographics	Drawing and painting
Film	Fiction/non-fiction literature	Film and theatre
Music videos	Advertisements	Posters
PSAs	Promotional materials	Public Information Films
Songs and all music	Lyrics, scripts and scores	Dance
Interviews	Surveys	Charts, graphs, symbols, images
Talk shows	Food labels	Signing
Announcements	Maps	Photographs

Adapted from Eddy, J. (2022b) *Designing World Language Curriculum for Intercultural Communicative Competence*, with permission from Bloomsbury Academic, an imprint of Bloomsbury Publishing, Plc.

Appendix G
AATT Review Criteria

Articulated Assessment Transfer Task Deliverable Review Criteria

KEY TO RATINGS: 3 = *extensively* 2 = *somewhat* 1 = *not yet*

CRITERIA

1. The task assesses recurring performances at targets across levels of learner engagement for vertical articulation with increased complexity. 3 2 1

2. The task calls for transfer; applying learning flexibly, beyond knowledge to real-world, novel situations or contexts. The task is designed to solve problems and/or create products, not to simply recall or provide formulaic response. 3 2 1

3. The task requires interdisciplinary content with twenty-first century skills: critical thinking, creativity, collaboration – not just a fact-based or rote answer. 3 2 1

4. The task is framed within an 'authentic' context: realistic purpose, a target audience, and relevance beyond the classroom, applicable to community, career, civic or world readiness. 3 2 1

5. The task addresses or assesses inter/transcultural perspectives, practices and products relevant to the cultural communities and does not simply focus on surface features of a product or performance. 3 2 1

6. The task integrates cultural community texts from various media across content areas. 3 2 1

7. The task generates specific I Can statements indicating transferable skills beyond knowledge acquisition. 3 2 1

© 2020 Jennifer Eddy. Adapted with permission from ©2013/2018 Jay McTighe **Cornerstone Tasks**

Adapted from Eddy, J. (2022) *Designing World Language Curriculum for Intercultural Communicative Competence*, with permission from Bloomsbury Academic, an imprint of Bloomsbury Publishing, Plc.

Appendix H
Teacher as Designer Evidence Collab

Traditional grammar or topic coverage model	Articulated Intercultural transfer design	Evidence in our Practice
Learner as passive, dependent, and reliant.	Learner as active, independent and autonomous.	
The textbook as curriculum.	Teacher designed curriculum as a cohort of practice.	
Curriculum uses pedagogically prepared, classroom-ready or adapted materials graded by level.	Curriculum uses cultural community texts for intercultural transfer goals.	
Units and schemes of work focus on drill, mechanical practice, or memorized dialogues.	Relevant and applicable contexts and catalogue of deliverables frame curriculum, schemes of work and units.	
Assessment is most often paper-pencil; grammar in isolation.	Transfer tasks and formative assessments prevail within a variety of assessment evidence.	
Learning about the language as four skills is the goal.	Learners use language to appraise, evaluate, critique and create cultural products of value discovered, expected or required outside the classroom.	

Traditional grammar or topic coverage model	Articulated Intercultural transfer design	Evidence in our Practice
Topics, themes or subjects are distributed or allocated by proficiency or performance target level.	Concepts of value in cultures inform all disciplines across all texts. These concepts and tasks appear at all levels for participation at any level of learner engagement.	
Grammar is the topic of units or schemes of work and chosen before unit and lesson is designed.	The task is designed first. Grammar to do the task is chosen after it is designed. It is not the topic of the unit, lesson or scheme of work.	
Learner receives isolated cultural facts that are fixed and static.	Learners engage in mediation strategies to bridge, exchange and clarify language between inter/transcultural perspectives with the practices and products they reveal and inform.	
Teacher is a passive transmitter of information	Teacher is an active co-creator for novel transfer	

Adapted from Eddy, J. (2022b) *Designing World Language Curriculum for Intercultural Communicative Competence*, with permission from Bloomsbury Academic, an imprint of Bloomsbury Publishing, Plc.

Glossary

AATTs Articulated Assessment Transfer Tasks are designed across at least three performance target levels of differentiation but with a common context for deliverable product or problem-solving.

Authorship for Interpretive tasks indicates texts in which intercultural perspectives and transdisciplinary concepts begin, reside and become accessible to any learner.

Autonomy is a teacher as designer for transfer which enables learner autonomy and flexible, novel language use: by themselves and beyond themselves.

Articulation in this book is intentional, collaborative curriculum and assessment design between levels via intercultural concepts and transdisciplinary performance transfer tasks or AATTs.

Articulation Spiral Points are tasks for tangible evidence of concepts, integrated perspectives, novel performances and products.

Catalogue of Deliverables is a set of transfer tasks yielding products that all learners in your programme will complete by the time they finish your school or programme. These are designed across languages and levels by teaching faculty.

Complexity is a feature of AATTs; a shift from self to others, problem-solving or different variables for transfer. It is not a consequence of the text but the task set designed with it.

Conception is our first contact with anything we listen to, watch, view, read and need to understand. It indicates authorship, ownership, interaction and mediation.

Consensus is a strategy between learners when they plan, choose, decide and agree together within a task, in order to plan and organize the final product or deliverable within an AATT.

Context within the AATT presents a possible audience, problem to solve and deliverable. Contexts typically have value beyond the classroom or school and are relevant and applicable to community, work and world.

Creation for this book is when the language user designs or delivers something new for someone else with their needs in mind, allowing that person to see differently and move mediation forward.

Cultural Community Authentic Texts are spoken, written, signed, created, or viewed media designed by cultural communities for the public to consume, use or experience.

Enduring Understandings in this design framework are overarching, curricular and programme level concepts recursive through cultural perspectives, cultural history and transdisciplinary content.

Essential Questions in this design are overarching and recurring questions on concepts and themes derived through intercultural

GLOSSARY

perspectives which are not answerable in a unit or lesson.

Far Transfer is indicated by a completely novel task not done previously in class. These tasks carry no cues or support information from the teacher on how to solve the problem or create the product.

Formative Assessment in this book are lesson level performance tasks that represent some novelty but also offer scaffolds or support strategies.

ICANADAPT Intercultural Curriculum Aligns Novel Assessment Design Articulated Performance and Transfer is the unit and curriculum framework for this book. The AATTs represent Stage Two of the unit; develop one level panel backward into Stage Three lessons.

Intercultural Communicative Competence is effective and appropriate interaction with others to understand, contribute and mediate between languages and cultures. Acquisition of attitudes, knowledge and skills result in greater empathy and adaptability between cultures.

Intercultural Transfer Targets are perspectives, practices, comparisons, transdisciplinary connections and community engagement, designed for utility beyond the classroom. They enable mediation, making culture accessible to others new to the culture and need a bridge to understand these elements.

Improvisation for this book is spoken or signed response to input from a partner, group or text. Every interaction is co-created improvisation, a more accurate characteristic of communication than spontaneous, which has no external input.

Mediation for Transfer are tools within AATTs to clarify, compare, elaborate, facilitate, revise, reconstruct and collaborate with others to move both plurilingual and pluricultural space forward and place new language and cultural contexts within reach for someone unfamiliar with them.

Near Transfer are formative performance tasks during lessons that are new but provide cues and supportive suggestions on how to do the task.

Novelty for this design is essential for transfer; learners should experience novel tasks every day, using what they learned in a different way as not to expect predictability in language use.

Ownership for interpretive tasks is when learners develop an intercultural mindset from texts which uncover enduring understandings and essential questions over time.

Performance is defined as language learned and demonstrated within a controlled environment such as a classroom, using familiar contexts.

Performance for Transfer provides evidence that one can resolve and create something within a prepared, yet novel and unanticipated situation with someone else's needs in mind and provides a bridge to proficiency.

Proficiency refers to how well someone uses the language in an unplanned manner at any given time wherever they are, regardless of when, how, or where language is acquired.

Review, Spiral, New is stage three on the ICANADAPT template; grammar and vocabulary reviewed from the same year, spiralled from a previous year or new to the unit.

Summative Assessment in this book is the final performance assessment for the unit that indicates far transfer, problem-solving and deliverables that are novel from previous tasks.

Transdisciplinary for this design emphasizes unifying concepts between subjects and facilitates new meaning-making within real-world themes, contexts and issues.

Transfer evidence for language education is when we can use our knowledge and skills repertoire independently to solve novel intercultural challenges or create a product of value with no cues or instructional supports.

Transcultural Communicative Competence is to learn, participate, adapt, contribute and mediate through, across, within and among various cultural spaces, fully interacting in daily contexts with identities intact for community inclusion and expanded worldview as flexible global citizens.

Turnarounds for Transfer is a professional learning activity within this design where teachers revise drill/mastery tasks to become transfer performance assessments with complexity, autonomy and novelty.

References

Adair-Hauck, B., Glisan, E., Koda, K., Swender, E., & Sandrock, P. (2006). The Integrated Performance Assessment (IPA): Connecting assessment to instruction and learning. *Foreign Language Annals*, 39(3), 359–82.

American Council on the Teaching of Foreign Languages (ACTFL) (2012). *Performance descriptors for language learners*. Alexandria, VA: Author.

American Councils for International Education (2017). *The national K-12 foreign language enrollment survey report*. Retrieved from https://www.americancouncils.org/sites/default/files/FLE-report-June17.pdf.

Anderson, L.W., Krathwohl, D.R., Airasian, P.W., Cruikshank, K.A., Mayer, R.E., Pintrich, P.R., Raths, J., & Wittrock, M.C. (Ed.) (2001). *A taxonomy for learning, teaching, and assessing: A revision of Bloom's taxonomy of educational objectives*. Complete edition. New York, NY: Longman.

Baker, W. & Sangiamchit, C. (2019). Transcultural communication: Language, communication and culture through English as a lingua franca in a social network community. *Language and Intercultural Communication*, 19(6), 471–87.

Beacco, J., Byram, M., Cavalli, M., Coste, D., Cuenat, M.E., Goullier, F., & Panthier, J. (Eds.) (2016). *Guide for the development and implementation of curricula for plurilingual and intercultural education*. Strasbourg: Council of Europe.

Bianconi, C. (2022). Capoeira: The symbol of resistance. In J. Eddy (Ed.), *Designing world language curriculum for intercultural communicative competence* (pp. 63–6). London: Bloomsbury Academic.

Bloom, B.S. (1956). *Taxonomy of educational objectives, handbook I: The cognitive domain*. New York, NY: David McKay.

Bower, K., Coyle, D., Cross, R., & Chambers, G.N. (Eds.) (2020). *Curriculum integrated language teaching: CLIL in practice*. London: Cambridge University Press.

Britton, J., Burgess, T., Martin, N., McLeod, A., & Rosen, H. (1975). *The development of writing abilities* (pp. 11–18). London: Macmillan.

Bruner, J.S. (1962). The conditions of creativity. In H.E. Gruber, G. Terrell, & M. Wertheimer (Eds.), *Contemporary approaches to creative thinking* (pp. 1–30). New York, NY: Atherton Press.

Bruner, J. (1996). *The culture of education* (pp. 241–55). Cambridge, MA: Harvard University Press.

Byram, M. (1997). *Teaching and assessing intercultural communicative competence*. Clevedon: Multilingual Matters.

Byram, M. (2009). Intercultural competence in foreign languages – the intercultural speaker and the pedagogy of foreign language education. In D.K. Deardorff (Ed.), *The SAGE handbook of intercultural competence* (pp. 321–32). Thousand Oaks, CA: Sage.

Byram, M. (2011). Using the concept of perspective to integrate cultural, communicative, and form focused language instruction. *Foreign Language Annals*, 44(3), 525–43.

Byram, M. & Fleming, M. (Eds.) (1998). *Language learning in intercultural perspective: Approaches through drama and ethnography.* Cambridge: Cambridge University Press.

Byram, M. & Wagner, M. (2018). Making a difference: Language teaching for intercultural and international dialogue. *Foreign Language Annals*, 51(1), 140–51.

Byram, M., Gribkova, B., & Starkey, H. (2002). *Developing the intercultural dimension in language teaching: A practical introduction for teachers.* Strasbourg: Council of Europe.

Byrnes, H. (1990). Addressing curriculum articulation in the nineties: A proposal. *Foreign Language Annals*, 23(4), 281–92.

Byrnes, H. (2008). Articulating a foreign language sequence through content: A look at the culture standards. *Language Teaching*, 41(1), 103–18.

Byrnes, H. (Ed.) (2010). Perspectives: Revisiting the role of culture in the foreign language curriculum. *Modern Language Journal*, 94(2), 315–36.

Clarke, S. (2023). Formative assessment [Conference Presentation]. Llandudno Professional Learning Day. Llandudno, Wales.

Collen, I. (2023). *Language trends 2023: Language teaching in primary and secondary schools in England.* Survey Report. British Council.

Corbett, J. (2003). *An intercultural approach to English language teaching.* Clevedon and New York, NY: Multilingual Matters.

Couet, R., Duncan, G., Eddy, J., Met, M., Smith, M., Still, M., & Tollefson, A. (2008). *Starting with the end in mind: Planning and evaluating highly successful foreign language programs.* Boston, MA: Pearson Education.

Council of Europe (1998). *Modern languages: Learning, teaching, assessment: A common European framework of reference.* Strasbourg: Council of Europe, Council for Cultural Cooperation, Education committee, CC-LANG (95) 5 rev. V.

Council of Europe (2001). *Common European framework of reference for languages: Learning, teaching, assessment.* Cambridge: Cambridge University Press. www.coe.int/t/dg4/linguistic/Source/Framework_EN.pdf.

Council of Europe (2020). *Common European framework of reference for languages: Learning, teaching, assessment – Companion volume [First published 2018].* Strasbourg: Council of Europe.

Coyle, D. (2007). Content and language integrated learning: Towards a connected research agenda for CLIL pedagogies. *International Journal of Bilingual Education and Bilingualism*, 10(5), 543–62.

Coyle, D., Bower, K., Foley, Y., & Hancock, J. (2021). Teachers as designers of learning in diverse, bilingual classrooms in England: An ADiBE case study. *International Journal of Bilingual Education and Bilingualism*, 26(9), 1031–49. DOI: 10.1080/13670050.2021.1989373.

Cruickshank, K., Black, S., Chen, H., Tsung, L., & Wright, J. (2020). *Language education in the school curriculum: Issues of access and equality.* London: Bloomsbury Academic.

Curriculum for Wales (2019). Digital ISBN 978 1 80038 057 8 © Crown copyright January 2020 WG39993.

Dann, R. (2014). Assessment as learning: Blurring the boundaries of assessment and learning for theory, policy and practice. *Assessment in Education: Principles, Policy & Practice*, 21(20), 149–66.

Deardorff, D.K. (2006). Identification and assessment of intercultural competence as a student outcome of internationalization. *Journal Studies in International Education*, 10(3), 241–66.

Deardorff, D.K. (2008). Intercultural competence: A definition, model and implications for education abroad. In V. Savicki (Ed.), *Developing intercultural competence and transformation: Theory, research, and application in international education* (pp. 32–52). Sterling, VA: Stylus.

Deardorff, D.K. (2009). Implementing intercultural competence assessment. In D.K. Deardorff (Ed.), *The SAGE handbook of intercultural competence* (pp. 477–91). Thousand Oaks, CA: Sage.

Deardorff, D.K. (2011). Intercultural competence in foreign language classrooms: A framework and implications for educators. In *Witten Harden's intercultural competence: Concepts, challenges, evaluations, ISFLL Vol. 10*. Lausanne: Peter Lang International Academic Publishers.

Deng, Z. (2022). Powerful knowledge, educational potential and knowledge-rich curriculum: Pushing the boundaries. *Journal of Curriculum Studies*, 54(5), 599–617.

Donaldson, G. (2015). *Successful futures: Independent review of curriculum and assessment arrangements in Wales*. Welsh Government, © Crown copyright 2015.

Drew, V. & Priestley, M. (2016). *Successful futures, successful curriculum development: Developing the new curriculum in your school*. Paper commissioned by EAS, p. 2.

Durand, G. (2022). Child labour. In J. Eddy (Ed.), *Designing world language curriculum for intercultural communicative competence* (pp. 152–4; Chapter 4, Appendix JJ. Companion Website). London: Bloomsbury Academic.

Earl, L.M. (2003). *Assessment as learning using classroom assessment to maximise student learning*. Thousand Oaks, CA: Corwin Press.

Eddy, J. (Writer) & Couet, R. (Director) (2006a). What is performance assessment? [Television series episode]. In *South Carolina Department of Education (Producer), teaching and language learning collaborative*. Columbia, SC: ETV.

Eddy, J. (2006b). *Sonidos, sabores, y palabras*. Boston, MA: ThomsonHeinle.

Eddy, J. (2007a). Children and art: Uncovering cultural practices and perspectives through works of art in world language performance assessment. *Learning Languages*, 12(2), 19–23.

Eddy, J. (2007b). Uncovering content, designing for performance. *Academic Exchange Quarterly*, Spring, 233–7.

Eddy, J. (2007c). Discover languages through song: Designing performance assessment. *Hispania*, Spring, 142–6.

Eddy, J. (2007d). Coverage without pity: World Language Assessment exposed in the light of backward design. In R. Fry (Ed.), *Languages: Connecting students with the world. Annual Series, No. 23*. New York State Association of Foreign Languages. Buffalo, NY: NYSAFLT.

Eddy, J. (2007e). Unpacking the standards: Informing instruction through performance assessment. In *The NCLRC Language Resource*. 11(5). Washington, DC: National Capital Language Resource Center.

Eddy, J. (2007f). Unpacking the standards with backward design: World language assessment uncovered. Honolulu, HI: Hawaii International Conference on Education.

Eddy, J. (2009a). Developing teacher expertise in backward design and performance assessment [Conference Presentation]. Sixth International Conference on Language Teacher Education. Washington, DC: Georgetown University, George Washington University and the Center for Applied Linguistics.

Eddy, J. (2009b). Unpacking the standards with backward design [Conference Presentation]. San Diego, CA: American Council on the Teaching of Foreign Languages (ACTFL).

Eddy, J. (2010a). Becoming designers: Paradigm shifts for performance and transfer. In Davis (Ed.), *World language teacher education: Transitions and challenges in the twenty-first century* (pp. 97–102). Charlotte, NC: Information Age.

Eddy, J. (2010b). Backward design and standards-based instruction: Making the essentials come alive. National Capital Language Resource Center [Conference Presentation]. Washington, DC: Georgetown University and George Washington University.

Eddy, J. (2014). Turnarounds to transfer: Design beyond the modes. *Learning Languages, Spring/Summer*, XIX(2), 16–18.

Eddy, J. (2015). Uncovering curriculum: Language performance through culture by design. *Journal of the National Council of Less Commonly Taught Languages*, 17(1), 1–22.

Eddy, J. (2016a). (Re) imagining learning: Releasing creativity for transfer. [Conference Keynote Address]. Annual Conference. Foreign Language Educators of New Jersey.

Eddy, J. (2016b). Uncovering curriculum: Designing for intercultural competence and transfer. American Council on the Teaching of Foreign Languages [Conference Presentation]. Boston, MA.

Eddy, J. (2016c). Intercultural competence and transfer by design. New York State Association of Foreign Language Teaching [Conference Presentation]. Syracuse, NY.

Eddy, J. (2016d). Uncovering curriculum: Intercultural competence by design. Northeast Conference on the Teaching of Foreign Languages [Conference Presentation]. New York, NY.

Eddy, J. (2017). Unpacking the standards for transfer: Intercultural competence by design. In Rebecca Fox (Ed.), Special Volume on Intercultural Competence for Northeast Conference on the Teaching of Foreign Languages. *NECTFL Review*, 79(1), 53–72.

Eddy, J. (2019a). Preparing teachers of critical languages for articulated performance assessment task design. *Journal of the National Council on Less Commonly Taught Languages*, 25(1), 1–19.

Eddy, J. (2019b). Literature and drama for transfer. In F. Diamantidaki (Ed.), *Teaching literature in modern foreign languages* (pp. 45–62). London: Bloomsbury Academic.

Eddy, J. (2022a). Collaborate to differentiate: Become designers of authentic tasks for social justice and language learning beyond the classroom. Association for Language Learning [Conference Presentation]. Sheffield, England.

Eddy, J. (2022b). *Designing world languages for intercultural communicative competence*. London: Bloomsbury Academic.

Eddy, J. & Bustamante, C. (2020). Closing the pre and in-service gap: Perceptions and implementation of the IPA during student teaching. *Foreign Language Annals*, 53, 634–56.

Ein Llais Ni (2023). GwE, Bangor University. https://www.einllaisni.cymru.

Evans, G. (2022). Back to the future? Reflections on three phases of education policy reform in Wales and their implications for teachers. *Journal of Educational Change*, 23, 371–96.

Freire, P. (2018). *Pedagogy of the oppressed: 50th anniversary edition*. London: Bloomsbury.

Garcia, P. & McCloskey, M. (2022). Familienstrukturen in der deutschsprachigen Welt. In J. Eddy (Ed.), *Designing world language curriculum for intercultural communicative competence* (pp. 152–4; Chapter 4, Appendix JJ. Companion Website). London: Bloomsbury Academic.

Garcia, P., Moser, K., & Davis-Wiley, P. (2019). Facing reality: A survey of methods instructors' perspectives on world language teacher development. *Foreign Language Annals*, 52(1), 165–83.

Gee, J.P. (2012). *Situated language and learning: A critique of traditional schooling*. London: Routledge.

Glisan, E.W., Adair-Hauck, B., Koda, K., Sandrock, S.P., & Swender, E. (2003). *ACTFL integrated performance assessment*. Yonkers, NY: ACTFL.

Gorrara, C., Jenkins, L., Jepson, E., & Machin, T. (2020). Multilingual perspectives: Preparing for language learning in the new curriculum for Wales. *Curriculum Journal*, 31(2), 244–57.

Grundy, S. & Robinson, J. (2004). Teacher professional development: Themes and trends in the recent Australian experience. In C. Day & J. Sachs (Eds.), *International handbook on the continuing professional development of teachers* (pp. 146–66). Maidenhead: Open University Press.

Hagger-Vaughn, L. (2016). Towards 'languages for all' in England: The state of the debate. *The Language Learning Journal*, 44(3), 358–75.

Hattie, J. (2012). *Visible learning for teachers*. Abingdon: Routledge.

Hawkes, R., Marsden, E., Avery, N., Kasprowicz, R., & Woore, R. (2019). Making language learning make sense at the National Centre for Excellence for Language Pedagogy. *Languages, Society & Policy*, May. DOI: 10.17863/CAM.40160.

Hazell, C. (2020). *MFL: How to make modern foreign language teaching exciting, inclusive and relevant*. Carmarthen, Wales: Independent Thinking Press.

Holec, H. (1988). *Autonomy and self-directed learning: Present fields of application*. Strasbourg: The Council of Europe.

Hull, R. (2023). What does Oracy mean to you. Ein Llais Ni Conference. October. LLandudno:Wales.

Ilieva, G. (2022). The paper boy. In J. Eddy (Ed.), *Designing world language curriculum for intercultural communicative competence* (pp. 152–4; Chapter 4, Appendix JJ Companion Website). London: Bloomsbury Academic.

Johansen, B. (2012). *Leaders make the future: Ten new leadership skills for an uncertain world*. 2nd ed. Oakland, CA: Berrett-Koehler Publishers.

Jurkova, S. (2021). Transcultural competence model: An inclusive path for communication and interaction. *Journal of Transcultural Communication*, 1(1), 102–19.

Kalmanson, E. (2022). Axe Porridge. In J. Eddy (Ed.), *Designing world language curriculum for intercultural communicative competence* (pp. 49–53). London: Bloomsbury Academic.

Kramsch, C. (2006). From communicative competence to symbolic competence. *The Modern Language Journal*, 90(2), 249–52.

Kramsch, C. (2013). *Teaching culture and intercultural competence*. Hoboken, NJ: Blackwell Publishing.

Kunschak, C. (2021). Translingual transcultural competence: Student agency, teacher guidance, and program support. *Language Learning in Higher Education.* Berlin, 11(2), 343–58.

Kuo-Flynn, S. (2022). Inside-outside spaces. In J. Eddy (Ed.), *Designing world language curriculum for intercultural communicative competence* (pp. 56–9). London: Bloomsbury Academic.

Lamb, T.E. (2000). Finding a voice: Learner autonomy and teacher education in an urban context. In B. Sinclair, I. McGrath, & T. Lamb (Eds.), *Learner autonomy, teacher autonomy: Future directions* (pp. 118–27). London: Addison Wesley Longman.

Lamb, T.E. (2001). Language policy in multilingual UK. *Language Learning Journal*, Summer, (23), 4–12.

Lamb, T.E. (2008). Learner and teacher autonomy: Synthesizing an agenda. In T.E. Lamb & H. Reinders (Eds.), *Learner and teacher autonomy: Concepts, realities and responses* (pp. 269–84). Amsterdam: John Benjamins.

Lamb, T.E. (2017). Knowledge about language and learner autonomy. In J. Cenoz & D. Gorter (Eds.), *Language awareness and multilingualism* (pp. 173–86). Switzerland: Springer International Publishing.

Lamb, T. & Reinders, H. (2005). Learner independence in language teaching: A concept of change. In D. Cunningham & A. Hatoss (Eds.), *An international perspective on language policies, practices and proficiencies*. Belgrave: FIPLV.

Lange, D. (1982). The problem of articulation. In Theodore V. Higgs (Ed.), *Curriculum, competence, and the foreign language teacher* (pp. 113–37). Lincolnwood, IL: ACTFL Foreign Language Education series, vol. 13. National Textbook Company.

Lange, D. (1988). Articulation: A resolvable problem. In John F. Lalande II (Ed.), *Shaping the future of language education: FLES, articulation, and proficiency* (pp. 11–31). Lincolnwood, IL: Report of Central States Conference on the Teaching of Foreign Language.

Lantolf, J. & Appel, G. (1994). *Vygotskian approaches to second language research*. New Jersey: Ablex Publishing.

Lee, M. (2022). Chuseok, Korean Thanksgiving. *DesignSpace.* https://queenscollege.classroad.org/ICANADAPT/2334.

Lewis, J. (2002). From culturalism to transculturalism. *The Iowa Journal of Cultural Studies*, 1(1), 14–32.

Liddicoat, A.J. & Scarino, A. (2013). *Intercultural language teaching and learning*. Malden, MA: Wiley-Blackwell.

Liddicoat, A.J., Papademetre, L., Scarino, A., & Kohler, M. (2003). *Report on intercultural language learning*. DEST, Canberra: Commonwealth of Australia.

Little, D. (1995). Learning as dialogue: The dependence of learner autonomy on teacher autonomy. *System*, 23(2), 175–82.

Little, D. (Ed.) (2003). *The European language portfolio in use: Nine examples*. Strasbourg, France: Council of Europe. Available from www.coe.int/portfolio.

Little, D. (2007). Language learning autonomy: Some fundamental considerations Revisited. *Innovation in Language Learning and Teaching*, 1(1), 14–29. https://doi.org/10.2167/illt040.0.

Little, D. (2009a). *The European language portfolio: Where pedagogy and assessment meet*. Strasbourg: Council of Europe.

Little, D. (2009b). Language learner autonomy and the European language portfolio: Two L2 English examples. *Language Teaching*, 42(2), 222–33.

Little, D. (2011). The common European framework of reference for languages, the European language portfolio, and language learning in higher education. *Language Learning in Higher Education*, 1(1), 1–21.

Little, D. (2012). The common European framework of reference for languages and the European language portfolio: Some history, a view of language learner autonomy, and some implications for language learning in higher education. *Language Learning in Higher Education*, 2(1), 1–16.

Little, D. (2020). Language learner autonomy: Rethinking language teaching. *Language Teaching*, 55(1), 64–73.

Little, D. & Kirwan, D. (2019). *Engaging with linguistic diversity: A study of educational inclusion in an Irish primary school*. London: Bloomsbury Academic.

Little, D. & Perclová, R. (2001). *The European language portfolio. Guide for teachers and teacher trainers*. Strasbourg: Council of Europe.

Little, D., Dam, L., & Legenhausen, L. (2017). *Language learner autonomy*. Bristol: Multilingual Matters.

Looney, D. & Lusin, N. (2018). *Enrollments in languages other than English in United States institutions of higher education, Summer 2016 and Fall 2016: Preliminary Report*. Modern Language Association of America. Retrieved from https://www.mla.org/Resources/Research/Surveys-Reports-and-Other-Documents/Teaching-Enrollments-and-Programs/Enrollments-in-Languages-Other-Than-English-in-United-States-Institutions-of-Higher-Education.

Lusin, N., Peterson, T., Sulewski, C., & Zafer, R. (2023). *Enrollments in languages other than English in US institutions of higher education*. Modern Language Association of America. [Report]. Fall 2021.

Malihah, N. (2010). The effectiveness of speaking instruction through task-based language teaching. *Register Journal*, 3(1), 85–101.

McTighe, J. (2018). Transfer goals. Retrieved from http://jaymctighe.com/wordpress/wpcontent/uploads/2013/04/Long-term-Transfer-Goals.pdf.

McTighe, J. & Wiggins, G. (2004). *Understanding by design professional development workbook*. Alexandria, VA: ASCD.

Mishan, F. (2005). *Designing authenticity into language learning materials*. Fishponds, Bristol: Intellect.

Moeller, A. & Nugent, K. (2014). Building intercultural competence in the language classroom. *Unlock the gateway to communication*. In S. Dhonau (Ed.), *Central States Conference Report* (pp. 1–18). Eau Claire, WI: Crown Prints.

National Council of State Supervisors of Foreign Language (2017). *NCSSFL-ACTFL can-do statements*. Alexandria, VA: author.

National Curriculum (2008). *Modern foreign languages in the national curriculum for Wales: Key stages 2–3*. Cathays Park, Cardiff: Welsh Assembly Government.

National Standards Collaborative Board (2015). *World-readiness standards for learning languages*. 4th ed. Alexandria, VA: Author.

National Standards in Foreign Language Education Project (2006). *Standards for foreign language learning in the 21st century*. Lawrence, KS: Allen Press (Original work published 1999).

North, B. (1992). European language portfolio: Some options for a working approach to design scales for proficiency. In R. Schärer & B. North (Eds.), *Towards a common European framework for reporting language competency* (pp. 158–72). Washington, DC: NFLC Occasional Paper, National Foreign Language Center.

North, B. (2000). *The development of a common framework scale of language proficiency*. New York, NY: Peter Lang.

North, B. & Piccardo, E. (2016). Developing illustrative descriptors of aspects of mediation for the Common European Framework of Reference (CEFR). *Research report*. Strasbourg: Council of Europe, Language Policy Unit.

OECD (2020). *Achieving the new curriculum for Wales: OECD education policy perspectives*. Paris: Organization for Economic Cooperation and Development.

Opai, K. (2022). Takiwatanga. In J. Eddy (Ed.), *Designing world language curriculum for intercultural communicative competence* (pp. 152–4; Chapter 4, Appendix JJ. Companion Website). London: Bloomsbury Academic.

Panthalookaran, V. (2021). Beyond Bloom's taxonomy: Emergence of entrepreneurial education. *Higher Education for the Future*, 9(1), 45–61.

Panthalookaran, V. (2022). Education in a VUCA-driven world: Salient features of an entrepreneurial pedagogy. *Higher Education for the Future*, 9(2), 234–49.

Pearson, P.D. & Gallagher, M.C. (1983). The instruction of reading comprehension. *Contemporary Educational Psychology*, 8, 317–44. DOI: 10.1016/0361-476X(83)90019-X.

Perkins, D.N. & Salomon, G. (1988). Teaching for transfer. *Educational Leadership*, 46(1), 22–32.

Perkins, D.N. & Salomon, G. (1992). *Transfer of learning*. International Encyclopedia of Education. 2nd ed. Oxford, England and New York: Pergamon Press.

Perkins, D.N. & Salomon, G. (2012). Knowledge to go: A motivational and dispositional view of transfer. *Educational Psychologist*, 47(3), 248–58.

Piccardo, E. (2013). Plurilingualism and curriculum design: Towards a synergic vision. *TESOL Quarterly*, 47(3), 600–14.

Piccardo, E. & North, B. (2019). *The action-oriented approach: A dynamic vision of language education*. Bristol: Multilingual Matters.

Raphael, T.E. & Au, K.H. (2005). QAR: Enhancing comprehension and test taking across grades and content areas. *Reading Teacher*, 59, 206–21.

Sanchez, I. (2022). In xochitl, In cuicatl. In J. Eddy (Ed.), *Designing world language curriculum for intercultural communicative competence* (pp. 152–4; Chapter 4, Appendix JJ. Companion Website). London: Bloomsbury Academic.

Scarino, A. (2010). Assessing intercultural capability in learning languages: A renewed understanding of language, culture, learning, and the nature of assessment. *The Modern Language Journal*, 94(2), 324–9.

Scarino, A. (2014). Learning as reciprocal, interpretive meaning-making: A view from collaborative research into the professional learning of teachers of languages. *The Modern Language Journal*, 98(1), 386–401.

Scarino, A. & Liddicoat, A. (2016). Reconceptualising learning in transdisciplinary languages education. *L2 Journal*, 8(4), 20–35.

Sercu, L. (2006). The foreign language and intercultural competence teacher: The acquisition of a new professional identity. *Intercultural Education*, 17(1), 55–72. DOI: 10.1080/14675980500502321.

Shrum, J.L. & Glisan, E.W. (2016). *Teacher's handbook: Contextualized language instruction*. 5th ed. Boston, MA: Heinle.

Slimbach, R. (2005). The transcultural journey. *Frontiers: The Interdisciplinary Journal of Study Abroad*, 11(1), 205–30.

Stoller, F. (1994). The diffusion of innovations in intensive ESL programs. *Applied Linguistics*, 15(3), 300–27.

Stoller, F. (2006). Establishing a theoretical foundation for project-based learning in second and foreign language contexts. In G.H. Beckett & P.C. Miller (Eds.), *Project-based second and foreign language education: Past, present, and future* (pp. 19–40). Greenwich, CT: Information Age.

Stoller, F. (2009). Innovation as the hallmark of effective leadership. In M. Christison & D. Murray (Eds.), *Leadership in English language education: Theoretical foundations and practical skills for changing times* (pp. 73–84). New York, NY: Routledge.

Taylor, F. & Mardsen, E. (2014). Perceptions, attitudes, and choosing to study foreign languages in England: An experimental intervention. *The Modern Language Journal*, 98(4), 902–20.

Thomas, E.M. & Caulfield, G. (2022) *O Enau Plant*. From the mouths of children. Welsh Government.

Trinter, C.P. & Hughes, H.E. (2021). Teachers as curriculum designers: Inviting teachers into the productive struggle. *RMLE Online*, 44(3), 1–16.

Tschirner, E. & Bärenfänger, O. (2012). Bridging frameworks for assessment and learning: The ACTFL guidelines and the CEFR. *Paper presented at the 34th Language Testing Research Colloquium (LTRC)*, Princeton, NJ, 3–5 April 2012.

VanPatten, B. (2003). *From input to output: A teacher's guide to second language acquisition*. New York, NY: McGraw-Hill.

VanPatten, B. (2004). Input processing in SLA. In B. VanPatten (Ed.), *Processing instruction: Theory, research, and commentary* (pp. 5–31). Mahwah, NJ: Lawrence Erlbaum Associates.

VanPatten, B. (2010). The two faces of SLA: Mental representation and skill. *International Journal of English Studies*, 10(1), 1–18.

VanPatten (2017). *While we're on the topic*. Alexandria, VA: ACTFL.

VanPatten, B. & Rothman, J. (2015). Against 'rules'. In A. Benati, C. Lavale, & M. Arche (Eds.), *The grammar dimension in instructed second language acquisition* (pp. 15–35). London: Bloomsbury Publishing.

Verhoeven, L. & Perfetti, C. (2008). Advances in text comprehension: Model, process and development. *Applied Cognitive Psychology*, 22(3), 293–301.

Vygotsky, L.S. (1978). *Mind in society: The development of higher psychological processes*. Cambridge, MA: Harvard University Press.

Wagner, M., Perugini, D., & Byram, M. (Eds.) (2018). *Teaching intercultural competence across the age range: From theory to practice*. Bristol: Multilingual Matters.

Welsch, W. (1999). Transculturality – the puzzling form of cultures today. In Mike Feathersone & Scott Lash (Eds.), *Spaces of culture: City, nation, world* (pp. 194–213). London: Sage.

Welsh Government (2016). *Global futures: A year into our plan.* https://gov.wales/sites/default/files/publications/2018-02/global-futures-a-year-into-our-plan-annual-report-december-2016.pdf.

Welsh Government (2017). *Cymraeg 2050: A million Welsh Speakers.* https://gov.wales/sites/default/files/publications/2018-12/cymraeg-2050-welsh-language-strategy.pdf.

Welsh Government (2019). National approach to professional learning. *Welsh Government*, April 30. https://hwb.gov.wales/professional-development/national-approach-to-professional-learning.

Welsh Government (2020a). Education is changing. *Welsh Government*, October 16. https://gov.wales/education-changing.

Welsh Government (2020b). *Area of learning and experience: Languages, literacy and communication.* Retrieved from https://hwb.gov.wales/curriculum-for-wales/languages-literacy-and-communication/.

Wiggins, G. & McTighe, J. (2005). *Understanding by design.* 2nd ed. Alexandria, VA: Association for Supervision and Curriculum Development.

Wiggins, G. & McTighe, J. (2007). *Schooling by design: Mission, action, and achievement.* Alexandria, VA: Association for Supervision and Curriculum Development.

Wiggins, G. & McTighe, J. (2011). *The understanding by design guide to creating high-quality units.* Alexandria, VA: Association for Supervision and Curriculum Development.

Xie, L. (2022). School and education. In J. Eddy (Ed.), *Designing world language curriculum for intercultural communicative competence* (pp. 293–302). Appendix DD. London: Bloomsbury Academic.

Zhu, H., Conlon, C., Smith, C., Diamantidaki, F., & McAllister, A. (2022). Language teaching and learning beyond vocabulary and grammar: Our success stories, available at https://blogs.ucl.ac.uk/ioe/2022/03/15/languageteaching-and-learning-beyond-vocabulary-and-grammar-our-success-stories

Index

ACTFL Performance Descriptors (2012) 15
Adair-Hauck B. 39, 42, 47
Adams, E. (St Brigid's school) 32, 111, 118–21, 124, 216, 219
Alun school 31, 183, 190–4, 219
Areas of Learning Experiences (AoLE) 7, 19, 28
Articulated Assessment Transfer Tasks (AATTs) 2–5, 16, 29–33, 42–7, 56–63, 72, 79–80, 85–6, 240
  alignment to CfW 14–15, 37
  with annotations guide 74–5
  child labour in Mexico 57–8
  Chuseok/Thanksgiving festival in Korea 56–7
  environment 73, 111, 118–24
  extracurricular activities 190–5
  Ffair Borth Menai Bridge Fair 111–17
  food poverty 103
  France 160–5
  heroes 126–30
  International *Eisteddfod* 31, 46, 48–9, 60, 72
  key priorities for 24–5
  Les Maisons 183, 203–9
  Liberté, égalité, fraternité 60, 63–5, 67, 69, 72, 225–7
  ourselves and others 78–83
  protest 86–92
  review criteria 237
  for school contexts 20–1
  school life 184–9
  school uniforms 145–51
  Solidarité 93–100
  types of talk 28
  Who Am I? 131–6
articulation 22–3, 32, 38, 42, 240. *See also* vertical articulation
Articulation Spiral Points 52, 72, 214–15, 240

assessment for learning (AfL) task 56–8, 63, 101, 212
assessment system contrast and alignment 14–15
Attal, G. 62–3, 226
authorship 182, 240
autonomy, learner 5, 29, 36, 44, 108, 145, 181, 192, 219–21, 240

Bennett, S. 78–9, 83–5, 222
Byram, M. 16
Byrne, J. (Ysgol Uwchradd Tywyn) 145, 160–6, 220

Cameron, M. (Ysgol Emrys ap Iwan) 145–8, 151, 216
catalogue of deliverables 22, 52, 214–15, 240
Clarke, S. 61
Common European Framework of Reference (CEFR) for Languages 15, 51
community language 18–19
Companion Volume (COE) 16
complexity (feature of AATTs) 14, 28, 39, 44, 73, 101, 108, 181, 218, 240
conception 106, 240
Concept Map 67–70
Conn, P. (Alun school) 20, 31, 183, 190–4, 219
consensus 50, 143, 145, 153, 160, 167, 240
context (AATT) 47, 240
Council of Europe 15
creation 13, 19, 44, 52, 94, 181, 240
cultural community authentic texts 38, 73, 107–8, 111, 218, 221, 236, 240
Curriculum for Wales (CfW) 2–3, 5–9, 11–16, 19, 23–5, 28, 30–3, 37,

INDEX

43–4, 59, 62, 78–80, 87–8, 113, 127, 132, 148, 159, 168, 174, 192, 198, 218
Cymraeg (the Welsh language) 87
'Cymraeg 2050 – Miliwn o siaradwyr' campaign 87
cynefin 78

Descriptions of Learning (DoL) 23
Designing World Language Curriculum (DWLC) 106–7
Donaldson, G., *Successful Futures* 13, 18, 28–9
Dyffryn Ogwen school 20, 31, 111, 126–7, 129–30, 216

Eddy, J. 2–4, 13–14, 22, 29, 36–9, 42–3, 45, 47, 50, 52, 68–9, 73, 75, 78, 99–101, 106, 108–9, 142–3, 169, 215
Ein Llais Ni project 26–8, 113, 117
Eisteddfod festival 31, 46, 48–9, 60, 72, 197, 199
Ellis-Williams, S. (International Languages, Global Futures GwE lead) 5–6, 18–19, 33, 36, 60–1, 63–6, 78–9, 85, 87, 93–4, 103, 111–12, 118, 120, 125–6, 130–1, 137, 145–6, 152–3, 159–60, 167–8, 175, 183–4, 190–1, 196, 202–4, 210–11, 217
enduring understandings (EUs) 46–7, 51–2, 73–4, 76–8, 86, 127, 154, 240
environment 73, 111, 118–24
essential questions (EQs) 29, 46–7, 52, 54, 73–4, 76–8, 85–6, 94, 103, 112, 119, 126, 184–6, 215, 240–1
exploratory task 27–8
'Expressing Ourselves is Key to Communication' 80, 133
expressive type 181–2
extracurricular activities 190–5

far transfer task 50, 54, 181, 241
Ffair Borth Menai Bridge Fair 111–17
flipgrid 84
focus questions 54, 74, 76–7

food festivals 196–203
food insecurity 93
food poverty 78, 93–4, 103
formative assessment 47, 54, 241
formative tasks 53–8, 131, 183, 214
Four Purposes 19, 28, 43, 59, 62, 80, 87, 120, 127, 132, 153, 161, 168, 174, 185–6, 191
France 160–5
Freire, P., *Pedagogy of the oppressed* 17

Garcia, P. 17, 78
Glisan, E. W. 26, 29, 39, 42, 47, 106, 142, 180
Gorrara, C. 11, 17
Green, E. (Dyffryn Ogwen school) 20, 31, 111, 126–7, 129–30, 216

Hattie, J. 54, 61
heads of departments (HoDs) 19
heroes 126–30
Hopwood, M. 113
Hughes, N. (Ysgol Morgan Llwyd school) 17, 21–2, 32, 111–13, 116–18, 216
Hull, R. 27–8

I'm a Celebrity, Get Me out of Here (TV programme) 79
improvisation 36, 142–3, 145, 167, 217, 241
infographics 57, 131, 147, 193
integrated performance assessments (IPAs) 47
intercultural communicative competence (ICC) 5, 16, 36, 38, 43–4, 47, 52, 73–4, 78, 101, 215, 241
intercultural competence (IC) 4, 14, 16, 28, 32, 55, 195
Intercultural Curriculum Aligns Novel Assessment Design Articulated Performance and Transfer (ICANADAPT) 2, 4–5, 15–17, 26–30, 33, 36, 40–1, 53–5, 58–61, 99–101, 241
intercultural transferable goals 38–9, 46, 51–2

INDEX

intercultural transfer targets (ITTs) 51, 76–7, 132, 227, 241
international languages (IL) 11, 17–19, 23–7, 33, 94, 133, 152, 203, 209
interpersonal/interactive tasks 50, 84, 88, 109–10, 142–5, 152–3, 160, 166–8, 175
interpretive/receptive tasks 50, 88, 106, 108–11, 119–20, 143, 160, 166–7, 175, 184

Jenkins, L. 11

La Baguette 167–73
language assessment transfer 50–1
Language Connect Us statement 94
language curriculum design (seven guiding principles for) 14, 22, 39
language learning journey 6, 59, 67, 87–8, 94, 112, 134
'Languages Connect us' 58, 71–104, 133, 147, 154, 161, 169, 198
Languages, Literacy and Communication (LLC) 19, 22, 58
Languages, Literacy and Communication Area of Learning Experience (LLC AoLE) 9–10, 24–5, 36
Lee, M., Chuseok, Korean Thanksgiving 55–6
Le Pendentif (Lainé) 197–9
Les Maisons 183, 203–9
Llangollen International Musical Eisteddfod festival 46

Macron, E. 62
master list of tasks 232–5
McAllister, J. (Ysgol Aberconwy) 111, 131, 134, 136–7, 218
McCloskey, M. 78
McTighe, J. 16–17, 42, 46–7, 50, 54, 73–4, 181, 214–15
Mediation for Transfer 43–4, 132, 224, 241
mediation strategies 43–4, 196, 229–31
Menai Bridge Fair. *See Ffair Borth* Menai Bridge Fair

modern foreign languages (MFLs) 7, 9, 11–13, 19, 30, 32, 81, 96, 209
Morris, J. (Ysgol Tryfan school) 21, 31–2, 78, 86, 88, 91–2, 220
multiculturalism 9, 11, 58
multilingualism 9, 11, 23, 132, 155

National Curriculum (2008) 11–13
National Standards Collaborative Board 15, 39, 46, 47, 106, 142, 180
National Standards in Foreign Language Education Project 15, 106, 142, 180
NCSSFL-ACTFL Can Do Statements 15, 51
near transfer task 50, 54, 101, 241
North, B. 16, 43, 51
North Wales 26, 32, 79, 86, 93, 126, 184, 196
novelty 17, 42–4, 119, 142, 220–2, 241

O Enau Plant guide 27
ownership 17, 50, 106, 111, 142, 154–5, 241

Parry, C. (Ysgol Glan y Môr) 183, 196–202, 219
Performance Assessment Specific Statements (PASS) 108–9, 176, 211, 226
performance, defined 241
performance for transfer 241
Perkins, S. (Ysgol Friars) 42, 183–4, 186, 188–9, 216
photographs (living memory texts) 126
Piccardo, E. 16, 43, 108
Piesch, N. (Ysgol Friars) 78, 93–6, 101–2, 184–6, 218
plurilingualism 9, 23
poetic type 181–2
presentational task 27–8, 50, 52–3, 88, 154, 180–4, 188, 191, 194, 200, 211, 214
Prestatyn High School 20, 30, 145, 152–9, 220
Principles of Progression 14–15, 23, 36, 43, 88, 119, 127, 133, 154, 198
proficiency 19, 27, 50, 108, 112, 241

recursive curriculum 73
regional desserts 152–8
retrieval task 27–8
review, spiral, new (stage three on ICANADAPT) 56, 241

Schemes of Learning (SoL) 31, 174
school life 184–9
school uniforms 145–51
Sloan, L. (Ysgol Y Grango school) 21, 31, 145, 167, 170–5, 218, 221
Solidarité 93–100
spontaneity 217
Stage One plans 47, 74, 228
Stage Two plans 47, 50, 54, 74, 101
Stage Three plans 54–8, 62–3, 67, 74, 101, 131, 153, 181, 183, 212, 228
Standards for Foreign Language Learning 15
Statements of What Matters (SoWMs) 9–11, 22–3, 36, 38–43, 47, 58, 72, 95–6, 147, 169, 185
St Brigid's school 32, 111, 118–21, 124, 216, 219
Successful Futures 13, 28–34
summative assessment 7, 46–7, 50, 53–4, 56, 101, 214, 242

talk types (retrieval, exploratory and presentational) 27–8
Teacher as Designer Evidence Collab tool 215, 238–9
teacher-leader-designers 20–1
Temple, C. (Ysgol Clywedog) 183, 203–10, 221
transactional type 181–2
transcultural communicative competence (TCC) 15–18, 42–4, 54, 86, 182, 215, 219, 222, 242

transcultural mediation for transfer 224
transdisciplinary content 14, 22, 39, 46, 51, 73, 242
transfer concept 42–4, 242
turnarounds for transfer 242

UNESCO 153–4, 159, 168–9

vertical articulation 22–3, 38, 44, 46, 109, 118, 214
Vick, V. (Prestatyn High school) 20, 30, 145, 152–9, 220

Welsh and English curriculum 18–19
Welsh government 13, 18–19, 23, 26, 87
Wiggins, G. 16–17, 42, 46–7, 50, 54, 73–4, 181, 214
world languages (WL) 5–6, 17, 73
World-Readiness Standards for Learning Languages 15

Ysgol Aberconwy school 111, 131, 134, 136–7, 218
Ysgol Clywedog school 203–10
Ysgol Emrys ap Iwan school 145–8, 151, 216
Ysgol Friars school 78, 93–6, 101–2, 184–6, 218
Ysgol Glan y Môr school 196–202
Ysgol Morgan Llwyd school 32, 111, 113, 116–18
Ysgol Tryfan school 21, 31–2, 78, 86, 91–2, 220
Ysgol Uwchradd Tywyn school 145, 160–6
Ysgol Y Grango school 31, 145, 167, 170–5, 218, 221

zone of innovation (phenomenon of) 13